# Iraq

# WORLD BIBLIOGRAPHICAL SERIES

General Editors:
Robert G. Neville (Executive Editor)
John J. Horton

Robert A. Myers                     Hans H. Wellisch
Ian Wallace                         Ralph Lee Woodward, Jr.


**John J. Horton** is Deputy Librarian of the University of Bradford and currently Chairman of its Academic Board of Studies in Social Sciences. He has maintained a longstanding interest in the discipline of area studies and its associated bibliographical problems, with special reference to European Studies. In particular he has published in the field of Icelandic and of Yugoslav studies, including the two relevant volumes in the World Bibliographical Series.

**Robert A. Myers** is Associate Professor of Anthropology in the Division of Social Sciences and Director of Study Abroad Programs at Alfred University, Alfred, New York. He has studied post-colonial island nations of the Caribbean and has spent two years in Nigeria on a Fulbright Lectureship. His interests include international public health, historical anthropology and developing societies. In addition to *Amerindians of the Lesser Antilles: a bibliography* (1981), *A Resource Guide to Dominica, 1493-1986* (1987) and numerous articles, he has compiled the World Bibliographical Series volumes on *Dominica* (1987), *Nigeria* (1989) and *Ghana* (1991).

**Ian Wallace** is Professor of German at the University of Bath. A graduate of Oxford in French and German, he also studied in Tübingen, Heidelberg and Lausanne before taking teaching posts at universities in the USA, Scotland and England. He specializes in contemporary German affairs, especially literature and culture, on which he has published numerous articles and books. In 1979 he founded the journal *GDR Monitor*, which he continues to edit under its new title *German Monitor*.

**Hans H. Wellisch** is Professor emeritus at the College of Library and Information Services, University of Maryland. He was President of the American Society of Indexers and was a member of the International Federation for Documentation. He is the author of numerous articles and several books on indexing and abstracting, and has published *The Conversion of Scripts and Indexing and Abstracting: an International Bibliography*, and *Indexing from A to Z*. He also contributes frequently to *Journal of the American Society for Information Science*, *The Indexer* and other professional journals.

**Ralph Lee Woodward, Jr**. is Professor of History at Tulane University, New Orleans. He is the author of *Central America, a Nation Divided*, 2nd ed. (1985), as well as several monographs and more than seventy scholarly articles on modern Latin America. He has also compiled volumes in the World Bibliographical Series on *Belize* (1980), *El Salvador* (1988), *Guatemala* (Rev. Ed.) (1992) and *Nicaragua* (Rev. Ed.) (1994). Dr. Woodward edited the Central American section of the *Research Guide to Central America and the Caribbean* (1985) and is currently associate editor of Scribner's *Encyclopedia of Latin American History*.

VOLUME 42

# Iraq

## Second Edition

### C. H. Bleaney

*Compiler*

CLIO PRESS

OXFORD, ENGLAND · SANTA BARBARA, CALIFORNIA
DENVER, COLORADO

British Library Cataloguing in Publication Data

Iraq. – 2nd ed. – (World
Bibliographical series; vol. 42)
I. Bleaney, C. H.   II. Series
016.9567

ISBN 1–85109–229–3


ABC-CLIO Ltd.,
Old Clarendon Ironworks,
35A Great Clarendon Street,
Oxford OX2 6AT, England.

————

ABC-CLIO Inc.,
130 Cremona Drive,
Santa Barbara,
CA 93116 USA

Designed by Bernard Crossland
Typeset by Columns Design and Production Services Ltd, Reading, England.
Printed and bound in Great Britain by Bookcraft (Bath) Ltd., Midsomer Norton

# THE WORLD BIBLIOGRAPHICAL SERIES

This series, which is principally designed for the English speaker, will eventually cover every country (and many of the world's principal regions), each in a separate volume comprising annotated entries on works dealing with its history, geography, economy and politics; and with its people, their culture, customs, religion and social organization. Attention will also be paid to current living conditions – housing, education, newspapers, clothing, etc.– that are all too often ignored in standard bibliographies; and to those particular aspects relevant to individual countries. Each volume seeks to achieve, by use of careful selectivity and critical assessment of the literature, an expression of the country and an appreciation of its nature and national aspirations, to guide the reader towards an understanding of its importance. The keynote of the series is to provide, in a uniform format, an interpretation of each country that will express its culture, its place in the world, and the qualities and background that make it unique. The views expressed in individual volumes, however, are not necessarily those of the publisher.

## VOLUMES IN THE SERIES

1 *Yugoslavia*, Rev. Ed., John J. Horton
2 *Lebanon*, Rev. Ed., C. H. Bleaney
3 *Lesotho*, Shelagh M. Willet and David Ambrose
4 *Zimbabwe*, Rev. Ed., Deborah Potts
5 *Saudi Arabia*, Rev. Ed., Frank A. Clements
6 *Russia/USSR*, Second Ed., Lesley Pitman
7 *South Africa*, Rev. Ed., Geoffrey V. Davis
8 *Malawi*, Robert B. Boeder
9 *Guatemala*, Rev. Ed., Ralph Lee Woodward, Jr.
10 *Pakistan*, David Taylor
11 *Uganda*, Robert L. Collison
12 *Malaysia*, Ian Brown and Rajeswary Ampalavanar
13 *France*, Rev. Ed., Frances Chambers
14 *Panama*, Eleanor DeSelms Langstaff
15 *Hungary*, Thomas Kabdebo
16 *USA*, Sheila R. Herstein and Naomi Robbins
17 *Greece*, Richard Clogg and Mary Jo Clogg
18 *New Zealand*, R. F. Grover

19 *Algeria*, Richard I. Lawless
20 *Sri Lanka*, Vijaya Samaraweera
21 *Belize*, Second Ed., Peggy Wright and Brian E. Coutts
23 *Luxembourg*, Carlo Hury and Jul Christophory
24 *Swaziland*, Rev. Ed., Balam Nyeko
25 *Kenya*, Robert L. Collison
26 *India*, Brijen K. Gupta and Datta S. Kharbas
27 *Turkey*, Merel Güçlü
28 *Cyprus*, P. M. Kitromilides and M. L. Evriviades
29 *Oman*, Rev. Ed., Frank A. Clements
31 *Finland*, J. E. O. Screen
32 *Poland*, Rev. Ed., George Sanford and Adriana Gozdecka-Sanford
33 *Tunisia*, Allan M. Findlay, Anne M. Findlay and Richard I. Lawless
34 *Scotland*, Eric G. Grant
35 *China*, Peter Cheng
36 *Qatar*, P. T. H. Unwin
37 *Iceland*, John J. Horton
38 *Nepal*, John Whelpton
39 *Haiti*, Rev. Ed., Frances Chambers
40 *Sudan*, Rev. Ed., M. W. Daly
41 *Vatican City State*, Michael J. Walsh

# Contents

# Contents

# Preface and Acknowledgements

This revised edition of the bibliography brings the coverage of Iraq up to date. However, it is not merely a supplement to the first edition, but an entirely new selection of work. It includes a wide range of important material in French, German and some other European languages and much periodical literature lacking in the first edition. Preference has been given to English-language items, but there was comparatively little Western interest in modern Iraq until recently. The Gulf War of 1991, however, stimulated a huge output of books and articles, many of which were concerned with the agenda and tactics of the Western governments during the crisis. A selection of some of the more important of these works is included here. There is a substantial bibliography of material on Iraq's ancient history and archaeology, and some introductory matter on these subjects is incorporated in this book, but the focus is on the country's modern history and character.

The last decade has seen an expanded interest in women's studies among academics, and also in translations of Arabic literature into European languages, and relevant material in these fields has been included. Other sections of the bibliography are devoted to Iraq's complex social, ethnic and religious make-up, and to its recent political history, all of which have contributed to the sequence of events which has brought the country to its current unhappy state of affairs.

*Acknowledgements*

I should like to express my gratitude to Dr G. J. Roper, Editor of *Index Islamicus*, for making available to me the resources of the Islamic Bibliography Unit at Cambridge University Library, without which I would not have been able to carry out this project. I should also like to thank Dr Harriet Crawford of the Institute of Archaeology, University College London, for helpful advice and suggestions concerning the literature on Iraq's ancient history and archaeology.

*C. H. Bleaney*

# Introduction

The Republic of Iraq lies at the eastern edge of the Arab world. Its northern border is shared by Turkey, and its eastern one by Iran. The southern and western boundaries in the steppe and desert areas join Iraq with other Arab states: Syria to the northwest, a short stretch with Jordan in the west, a long border with Saudi Arabia to the southwest, and a short one with the small state of Kuwait leading to the Persian (or Arabian) Gulf. The small patch of oil-bearing territory just to the west of Kuwait is known as the Iraq–Saudi Arabia neutral zone, and the revenues from its oil wells are shared by agreement between the two countries. The boundaries with Iran and Kuwait have been the subject of dispute. Iraq's principal grievance is that the border with Iran runs along its only large waterway to the sea, and that it has only a very short stretch of coastline on the Gulf. The adjustment of the border with Kuwait by the United Nations team after the 1991 war in Kuwait's favour will not be agreeable to any government of Iraq.

Iraq's territory covers some 433,970 square kilometres (not including the neutral zone shared with Saudi Arabia). There are four principal geographical regions: highlands in the north and northeast; rolling upland between the upper Euphrates and Tigris rivers; alluvial plain in the central and southeast areas; and desert in the west and southwest. The two important rivers (both rising in Anatolia) provide ample water for agriculture in much of Iraq, in contrast with the desert areas of Syria and Arabia. The ancient Greek name for the country was Mesopotamia.

The population was given in the 1987 census as 16,278,000 persons (preliminary figures). The people are ethnically mixed, mainly Arabs in the south, with a large admixture of Iranians, and Kurds in the north. Approximately 75 per cent of the population are Arabs, some 19 per cent are Kurds (who are almost all Sunni Muslims), and the remainder is made up of small populations as follows: Turkmens (mostly Sunni Muslims), Assyrians (mainly Christians), Armenians (Christians), Yazidis (of Kurdish origin, but with their own syncretistic faith), and a few Jews (the vast majority of the large and ancient Jewish community left for Israel in 1950-51). Religious divisions are deeply embedded in Iraqi society. About 95 per cent of the population are Muslims, of which between 55 and 65 per cent are Shiʿis (mainly Arabs). Shiʿi Muslims nowadays outnumber Sunni Muslims in Iraq, and large sections of the Sunni population are not Arab. Shiʿi Muslims comprise the largest single community in the country, but modern Iraqi governments have tended to be monopolized by the relatively small group of Sunni Arabs.

Mesopotamia was the home of one of the earliest urban civilizations – that of the Sumerians. They developed sophisticated irrigation systems to control the flooding of the rivers and created possibly the first cereal agriculture. They also invented what is probably the oldest writing system and later developed it into the cuneiform script. Their civilization flourished around 3000 BCE, and Mesopotamia was subsequently ruled by various other ancient powers – the Akkadians, the Babylonians, and the Assyrians. The Persian ruler, Cyrus the Great, conquered Mesopotamia in 539 BCE. The Persians used Aramaic as the language of imperial rule, and it became widespread in Iraq.

Alexander the Great of Macedon defeated the Persian forces in Babylonia in 331 BCE and died in Babylon on his return from the Indus expedition in 323 BCE. Under the Seleucids and other successor regimes, Hellenistic influence penetrated the whole Near East including Mesopotamia. The Romans gained control over Iraq briefly under Trajan (98-117 CE) and again in 195-199 CE, but another period of Persian rule began with the conquest of Mesopotamia in 227 CE by the Sasanians. The continuing struggle with the Roman Empire left the northern part of the country devastated by battles. Lengthy periods of frontier warfare over the territory of Iraq characterize the country's history. The Sasanians carried on their wars with the Byzantines in the following centuries and Mesopotamia's irrigation and agriculture was neglected.

In 636-640 CE, the country fell to the Muslim invaders from Arabia. The Byzantine and Sasanian empires, mutually exhausted, could not defend their Arab provinces, and the local inhabitants had little to lose by co-operating with the invaders.

Iraq was largely Christian at the time of the Islamic conquest. The Muslim Caliphs founded two new garrison cities, Kufah and Basra, to maintain their control over Iraq. The principal elements of the Persian administrative system were retained and adopted by the Islamic empire, but Arabic replaced Persian as the official language. Efforts were made to rebuild the flood control and irrigation systems and improve agricultural production. Over the succeeding centuries, Iraq became a predominantly Muslim, Arabic-speaking country.

In 750, the Abbasid dynasty took control of the Islamic Empire and established the seat of the Caliphate at Baghdad. In the late eighth and ninth centuries CE, Iraq became the centre of the Islamic golden age of philosophical, scientific and literary effort, and a centre of prosperity. Baghdad became known to the West as the setting of the Thousand and one Nights (Arabian Nights) constructed around the figure of the Caliph Harun al-Rashid (who actually ruled from 786 to 806 CE). The elements of ancient Mesopotamian culture and knowledge (mathematical and scientific), transmitted and enlarged by the Greeks during the Hellenistic period, were extended by the literature and science brought from Persia and India after the Islamic conquests and the opening up of trade with South Asia and the Indian Ocean.

In 945 CE, an Iranian dynasty (the Buwayhids or Buyids) took control of Baghdad and ruled the Empire from behind the throne, inaugurating a long period of slow decline of central power and loss of the provinces to local rulers. The Buwayhids were followed by Seljuk Turks and other powerful military chiefs. The Abbasid Caliphs were maintained as nominal rulers until the sack of Baghdad by the Mongols in 1258 when the dynasty was brought to an end. The Mongols destroyed the cultural and artistic production of centuries as well as much of the irrigation system. Iraq became a provincial backwater neglected by the Mongol capital in Tabriz (Iran). In 1401 Timur Lang (Tamerlane) sacked Baghdad again and once more huge numbers of the inhabitants were slaughtered. The Mongol invasions left the country in political chaos, suffering from severe economic depression and social disruption. With the deterioration of settled agriculture, tribally based pastoral nomadism became more widespread, and the cities declined.

The Ottoman Turkish Empire began to expand into Iraq in 1534, and, from the 16th to the 20th centuries, Iraq was the scene of a continuing struggle between the Turks and the Persians. The Ottomans were Sunni Muslims, as the Abbasid Caliphs had been, but the Safavids who ruled Iran from Isfahan declared Shiʿi Islam the official religion of their domain. Two of the most holy Shiʿi shrines are in Najaf and Karbala in southern Iraq. The Safavids were anxious to gain control of these cities and to capture Baghdad because of its associations with the great Islamic Empire of the Abbasids. The Ottomans were similarly keen to prevent the Safavids from expanding westwards. Baghdad was conquered by the Persians in 1509, and after a long-running campaign, the Ottomans drove them out in 1535. The Safavids reconquered it in 1623, but lost it to the Ottomans again decisively in 1638.

The struggle between the competing empires deepened the rift in Iraq between Sunni and Shiʿi Muslims. The Safavids oppressed the local Sunni population during their brief rule in 1623-38, while the Iraqi Shiʿis were excluded from power altogether by the Ottomans during their extended period of supremacy from 1638 to 1916. Access to power and influence enabled Iraqi Sunnis to benefit from modernizing efforts in education and economic and political reform in the 19th century, and they still retained their dominance in the late 20th century. Shiʿi resentment at political impotence and lack of economic advancement was a continuing and important fact of Iraqi political life throughout the period of British and independent rule.

Ottoman control over the further provinces of its huge empire had weakened by the 17th century, and tribal authority predominated in Iraq. Kurdish resistance ensured that the Ottomans could not maintain even nominal sovereignty over the mountainous areas of northern Iraq which form part of Kurdistan, and elsewhere tribal warfare and insecurity were general. In the early 18th century, a local dynasty of Mamluks succeeded in asserting their own authority over Iraq, extending their rule from Basra to the foothills of Kurdistan. They imposed some order and stability and their rule was marked by considerable economic revival. In 1831, the Ottomans once more established control over Iraq, but stability was not achieved until the able and progressive Midhat Pasha was appointed governor of Baghdad.

The Ottoman Empire was embarking on efforts to modernize and reform the administration of the Empire, to create codes of criminal and commercial law, to reorganize the army, and to secularize the education system. The most lasting impact of the Ottoman reforms in Iraq was caused by Midhat Pasha's attempts to carry out the Ottoman land reform there in 1869. The old tribal system of landholdings and tax-farms was to be replaced by registered and legally held rights to property. In practice, the tribal shaykhs managed to establish themselves as large-scale landowners of the previously communally-held tribal lands. Tribesmen were reduced to impoverished sharecroppers and the old shaykh–tribesman relationships were transformed into landlord–peasant relations.

After 1920, the British maintained their rule over Iraq by alliance with the tribal chiefs, and the peasantry were excluded from political life and expectation of economic improvement. Land reform was a priority for the new government after the Revolution in 1958.

The First World War and the defeat of the Ottoman Empire in 1918 enabled the Western powers to take over the Ottoman provinces themselves. Great Britain was granted the Mandate over Iraq in 1920, and established an Arab king, Faysal (son of the Sharif of Mecca) as monarch in order to defuse Arab nationalist resentment at foreign rule. While the King of Iraq tried to foster some kind of national unity in his new country, Britain cultivated the support of the traditional tribal shaykhs to counter the King's position and ensure his dependence on

Britain. Iraqi nationalist resentment continued to grow in the following decades. Iraq was granted independence under the Anglo-Iraqi Treaty of 1930, but British influence in the government remained pervasive and Britain retained the use of military bases in Iraq. The dispute with the Republic of Turkey over the fate of the oil-bearing regions of Mosul and Kurdistan was finally settled by treaty in 1926 in favour of Iraq. The state of Iraq eventually benefited enormously from oil revenues (oil was first struck in 1927), but the large Kurdish population has proved a thorn in the flesh of all Iraqi governments.

The Kurds (mainly Sunni Muslims, but speaking their own language) have struggled for special recognition of their distinct culture and for autonomy in their own area, and have mounted long and partially successful rebellions for much of the 20th century. However, in their land-locked region, Kurdish rebels have only been able to maintain resistance to central Iraqi control when they have received outside support. This has come principally from Iran, which has so often had poor relations with the Iraqi government, and at one time also from the United States Central Intelligence Agency (when the Iraqi government was perceived as an ally of the Soviet Union). Their rebellion collapsed when such support was suddenly withdrawn in 1975 after the Iraqi government of the day came to an agreement with the Shah of Iran. Later, in the early 1990s, outside support for the Kurds once again proved to be critical to their ability to sustain independence from central control.

British rule in Iraq was largely maintained in its latter years through the influence of Nuri al-Said, who was influential behind the scenes in the relatively few years when he was not actually prime minister after 1939.

In 1958 the autocratic pro-British regime was overthrown in a bloody revolution carried out by military officers under 'Abd al-Karim Qasim. He was himself overthrown in 1963 in a coup orchestrated by the Ba'th Party which advocated a blend of socialist, Arab nationalist and secularist ideas. It had been founded in Syria in the early 1940s and had spread quite widely in Syria, Lebanon and Iraq, particularly among the military. The Ba'th Party held power for less than a year, but regained control in 1968. One of its key leaders behind the scenes was Saddam Husayn, who slowly emerged as the strong man of the Iraqi government over the succeeding years. He was not from a military background, but a Party man, and under his direction the Ba'th Party became the supreme instrument of government control of all the political institutions of the country. Saddam Husayn eventually became the President of the Republic in 1979, Secretary-General of the Ba'th Party Regional (i.e. Iraqi) Command, Chairman of the Revolutionary Command Council and Commander in Chief of the armed forces.

He was now openly in control of power and ran a totalitarian state that tolerated no political opposition or criticism and dealt ruthlessly with its enemies. At the same time, after the nationalization of the Iraq (formerly Anglo-Persian) Oil Company in 1972, and the rise in oil prices after 1973, the Iraqi government benefited from plentiful oil revenues and used them to pursue social and economic programmes that increased prosperity and social mobility. A successful adult literacy campaign was launched and education and welfare provision increased. After the end of the Kurdish rebellion in 1975, the government once again promised the Kurds a measure of local autonomy (earlier promises made in 1970 had not been kept) and began to promote some economic development in the area. For a short time, and for the first time in modern Iraqi history, a government achieved some success in forging a national community out of the disparate social elements which made up the country, albeit at the cost of authoritarian single-party rule. With some domestic success behind him Saddam Husayn began to seek a leading role for Iraq, as one of the more populous Arab countries, in the foreign affairs of the Arab world.

In 1979, the Islamic Revolution in Iran brought to power a government led by Ayatollah Khomeyni which was openly hostile to secularization and committed to exporting its religious revolution abroad. Moreover, Saddam had expelled Ayatollah Khomeyni from his 13-year exile in Iraq in 1978, reportedly at the request of the Shah of Iran, and Khomeyni had not forgiven him. After a series of skirmishes along their common border, Iraq invaded Iran in force in September 1980. Saddam had evidently hoped that the depleted and demoralized Iranian army would put up little fight, and that the large Arab population of Khuzistan would rise in his support. His calculations, however, proved to be false, and national solidarity in the face of invasion swung popular support behind Khomeyni's government.

The war dragged on for eight long years, costing over one million lives in all, and entailing the devastation of cities, land and oil installations. Economic development in Iraq slowly ground to a halt, and the country fell into debt, in spite of oil revenues and enormous loans from the Arab Gulf countries who feared Iran's revolutionary aims and felt obliged to support Iraq.

Iraq was first accused of using chemical weapons in its efforts to contain the massive Iranian offensive in the southern marshes of Iraq in 1984. The Kurds in the north were aggrieved by the Iraqi government's reneging on the promise of autonomy and the Kurdish separatist movement revived during the war years. As the immediate Iranian military threat to Iraq began to fade after 1987, the Iraqi government moved forces north to deal with the Kurds. At this period, the Kurds claimed to control a considerable 'liberated zone', but in areas regained by the Iraqi army Kurdish villages were razed to the ground and whole areas were systematically depopulated. The Kurds were resettled further south, or were driven into more remote districts. Large numbers took refuge in Iran. In early 1988, Kurdish fighters supported an Iranian offensive which established a bridgehead in Iraqi Kurdistan, and themselves made further inroads into areas controlled by the Iraqi government. In a retaliatory attack on the captured town of Halabjah in March 1988, Iraq was accused of using chemical weapons and of killing 4,000 Kurdish civilians. A United Nations report concluded that chemical weapons had been used by both sides. The initial success of the Iranian/Kurdish offensive soon gave way to a series of Iraqi victories. The Iraqi army recaptured all territory previously lost to the Iranians along the length of their common border, and crossed into Iranian territory for the first time since 1986. A cease-fire with Iran was agreed in August 1988, and Iraqi troops moved in force against Iraqi Kurdistan in an attempt to crush the separatist movement, allegedly using chemical weapons once again. By mid-September 1988, over 100,000 Kurdish refugees had fled across the border to Turkey, and others had joined the approximately 100,000 refugees already in Iran. Once its army was effectively again in control of all Iraqi territory, Iraq announced an amnesty for the Kurds, and later claimed that more than 60,000 had returned to Iraq. The government began a huge evacuation programme clearing all the inhabitants from a wide 'security zone' along Iraq's border with Turkey and Iran. Kurdish leaders denounced the programme as forcible deportation of the Kurdish population to areas more susceptible to government control.

Iraq's attack on Halabjah had attracted international condemnation and focused attention on the regime. In late 1989 increased concern was expressed in Western countries about the military expansion programme apparently under way in Iraq, now that the war with Iran was over. The involvement of Western countries in the development of advanced military technology was highlighted, and anxieties expressed about nuclear, chemical and missile technology programmes in Iraq. At the end of March 1990, the British government claimed to have thwarted attempts by Iraq to import British-made components for a long-range 'super-gun'. Relations with the West deteriorated badly, although Western governments had generally supported Iraq during the war against Iran and supplied weaponry and military material.

When the war finally came to an end in 1988, Saddam was desperately short of money and his people expected the troops to be demobilized and prosperity to return. He regarded the campaign by the Arab Gulf states to keep down the price of oil as a threat, given that he needed to gain the maximum possible revenue to rebuild Iraq.

In August 1990, he sent his troops to occupy the neighbouring oil shaykhdom of Kuwait, and reasserted Iraq's previous claim to it. The world was taken by surprise, but the United Nations called on Iraq to withdraw and on 29 November 1990 Resolution 678 was passed by the UN which called on governments to use 'all necessary means' to ensure that Iraq withdrew completely from occupied Kuwait. Western leaders responded to this resolution and the threat to both Western oil supplies and the existing regional order by putting together a coalition of 29 states. This coalition included Gulf Arab states, the United Kingdom, France, Syria and Egypt, and was led by the United States. In a brief but devastating campaign in January-March 1991, the allies drove the Iraqi armed forces out of Kuwait and well back into Iraq. Simmering discontent in Iraq exploded into separate uprisings in the south and the north but Saddam's forces soon crushed the Shiʿi rebellion in the south. While the Iraqi army was occupied in the south, the Kurds in the north drove Iraqi government troops out of Kurdistan, and established their own autonomous government there. As Iraqi forces threatened reconquest and people fled over the mountains, emergency Western air cover and aid was brought in and the Iraqi army was banned from the area. The future of Kurdistan remains in the balance, as any Iraqi government which feels itself strong enough will attempt to reassert its control over the region, and Kurdish leaders would perhaps be unwise to rely on Western help.

By late 1991, Saddam Husayn's regime no longer appeared to be in imminent danger of falling. He had crushed the unorganized southern uprising and a negotiated settlement with the Kurds was under discussion. Moreover, the government had strengthened its control of the army after a number of reported *coups d'état*. It became ever more clear that the United States did not wish to see the break-up of the state. However, it did wish to see the fall of Saddam himself. This became evident by the end of 1994, when, in spite of eventual reluctant compliance by Iraq with the United Nations' demands for the disclosure and destruction of Iraq's advanced weapons programmes, the United States was unwilling to permit the lifting of sanctions. Saddam attempted to force the issue in October 1994 by sending several divisions of troops up to the buffer zone with Kuwait and by demanding that sanctions be lifted at the end of the review period on 10 October on the grounds that Iraq had cooperated with the United Nations. This manoeuvre prompted a costly but immediate response by the United States and its allies who deployed troops to defend Kuwait but did not obtain any easing of the sanctions on Iraq, in spite of a favourable report from the United Nations inspectors.

In April 1992, Saddam ordered the evacuation of the southern marshlands, where so many army deserters and rebels had taken refuge, and the resettlement of their inhabitants elsewhere. A huge canalization scheme was undertaken which would drain approximately 70 per cent of the southern marshlands, destroying for ever the ancient way of life of their inhabitants. The environmental consequences are as yet unknown. By late 1994, the drainage project was well under way and enormous number of Iraqis were seeking refuge in Iran.

Economic sanctions imposed on Iraq after the invasion of Kuwait in 1990 remain in force at the beginning of 1995. Iraq had made efforts to repair the extensive damage to the electricity-generating system, sewage and water systems, and industrial plant ruined in the 1991 war, but supplies and spare parts could not be imported. Hunger and malnutrition, and lack of medicines have affected the health of the Iraqi population as the effects of raging inflation and economic depression take their toll on people's incomes. Saddam Husayn retains his grip on power, although it is becoming more difficult for the regime to keep its supporters and maintain its comfortable lifestyle. Nevertheless, the political opposition outside Iraq is fragmented and no opposition has ever been allowed to survive inside the country. Popular discontent in Iraq is widespread. The government has introduced savage punishments for relatively minor crimes, indicating a breakdown of law and order and the crumbling of society, but little obvious alternative to the continuance of the present government is in prospect.

# The Country and Its People

1 **Iraq's people and resources.**
Doris Goodrich Adams.   Berkeley: University of California Press,
1958. (University of California Publications in Economics, XVIII).
Reprinted Westport: Greenwood Press, 1980. 150p. map. bibliog.
Based on a doctoral thesis entitled 'Population trends in relation to the economic
development of Iraq' (1955), this study provides a portrait of Iraq in the mid-1950s
covering the geographical, cultural and ethnic setting; population structure; vital rates;
income and consumption; and economic development: potentialities and obstacles.

2 **The Middle East.**
Edited by Michael Adams.   New York: Facts on File Publications,
1988. 839 p. maps. ᵢ(Handbooks to the Modern World).
This handbook covering the Middle East is divided into six sections. 'Basic
information' provides statistics and brief notes on agriculture, history, politics and
government of each country in turn (Iraq, p. 32-40). Part One 'General background'
contains an outline of Islamic history, and articles on the region's religion and
culture. Part Two 'The countries of the Middle East' has an essay on Iraq by Marion
Farouk-Sluglett and Peter Sluglett (p. 376-94) which gives a concise history of Iraq
together with a short bibliography. Parts Three, Four, and Five 'Political affairs',
'Economic affairs' and 'Social affairs' respectively, each contain several essays on
general aspects of these subjects affecting the whole region. All the essays have short
lists of further reading appended.

3 **A Middle East studies handbook.**
Jere Bacharach.   Seattle: University of Washington Press; Cambridge:
Cambridge University Press, 1984. rev. ed. 147p. maps.
A revised edition of *A Near East studies handbook* published in 1974. This is a basic
reference book giving the Islamic calendar and conversion tables to the Gregorian
calendar; lists of dynasties which ruled the Islamic world from AD 570 to 1983

1

including the Abbasid Empire based in Baghdad; acronyms of 20th-century organizations; and a historical atlas which includes maps of Iraq together with a gazetteer.

## 4 Iraq: its people, its society, its culture.

George Lawrence Harris, Moukhtar Ani (et al.). New Haven, CT: HRAF Press, 1958. 328p. maps. bibliog. (Survey of World Cultures, 3).

A portrait of Iraq and its social, economic, religious, and political organization as it was shortly before the Revolution of 1958. For a personal account of Iraq at this time by two Englishmen employed as teachers, see *New Babylon: a portrait of Iraq* by Desmond Stewart and John Haylock (London: Collins, 1956).

## 5 Middle East contemporary survey.

Edited by Colin Legum. New York: Holmes & Meier. Vol. 1 1976-77- . 1978- . annual.

Every volume of this annual survey contains a section on Iraq, covering the political developments during the period in question. Articles also cover regional developments. A reliable source, but with particular interest in the Arab–Israeli conflict.

## 6 Iraq: a country study.

Edited by Helen Chapin Metz. Washington, DC: U.S. Department of the Army, 1990. 4th ed. 267p. maps. bibliog.

Metz notes on the title-page that the research was completed in May 1988. A general introduction to the history, and current social, economic and political situation of the country. The chapters are: 'Historical setting' by Mark Lewis; 'The society and its environment' by Stephen Pelletiere; 'The economy' by Robert Scott Mason; 'Government and politics' by Eric Hooglund; 'National security' by Joseph A. Kechichian. The bibliography is extensive.

## 7 The Cambridge encyclopedia of the Middle East and North Africa.

Edited by Trevor Mostyn, Albert Hourani. Cambridge: Cambridge University Press, 1988. 497p. maps.

Not an encyclopaedia in the standard sense, but a major reference-work covering the geography, history and culture of the Middle East and North Africa. The sections of the book describe in turn the lands and peoples, history of the region (from the earliest times to 1939), societies and economies, culture and religion. The recent history and political events of individual countries are then described: Iraq is covered on p. 340-49.

## 8 Iraq: the land and the people.

Nazim Ramzi. London: Artscan, 1989. 159p.

Good black-and-white photographs showing the varied landscape and population of Iraq.

9  **L'Irak.** (Iraq.)
Philippe Rondot.  Paris: PUF, 1979. 126p. map. bibliog. (Que Sais-je?, 1771).

A general introduction to modern Iraq, its land and people, history, institutions and political life, economy and foreign affairs, with a chapter devoted to the Kurdish problem.

10  **Iraq: the land of the new river.**
Pierre Rossi, photographed by André LePage.  Paris: Les Editions, 1980. 286p. map.

The work consists predominantly of photographs of modern Iraq, its land, buildings and people, accompanied by an essay enthusiastically describing the changes brought about under Baʿth Party rule.

11  **Iraq: land of two rivers.**
Gavin Young, photographs by Nick Wheeler.  London: Collins, 1980. 272p. maps. bibliog.

A general history of Iraq and description of its modern lifestyle, together with the author's account of his travels around the country. Many colour photographs are included.

12  **The Middle East and North Africa.**
London: Europa Publications, 1948- . annual.

The section on Iraq briefly describes the country's physical and social geography, traces its history and is a good source for information on recent political and economic developments. It also includes a statistical summary and basic information on the government, diplomatic representation, judicial system, press, radio and television, banking, trade and industry, transport and education. A short bibliography is appended.

13  **Quarterly Economic Review Annual Supplement: Iraq.**
London: Economist Intelligence Unit, 1970- . annual.

An annual supplement to the *Quarterly Economic Review: Iraq* containing news items and analyses of the Iraqi economy and the country's political life.

# Geography and Geology

## Geography

14  **Soil groups of Iraq: their classification and characterization.**
Flayeh H. Altaie, C. Sys, G. Stoops. *Pedologie*, no. 19(1969), p. 65-148.
A detailed systematic description and fundamental study of the most representative soils of Iraq, with 27 figures, two photographs and three tables.

15  **The Middle East: a geographical study.**
Peter Beaumont, Gerald H. Blake, J. Malcolm Wagstaff.  London: Fulton, 1988. 2nd ed. 550p. maps. bibliog.
A standard text on the Middle East. The first 10 chapters treat the area as a whole and describe: 1: Relief, geology, geomorphology and soils; 2: Climate and water resources; 3: Landscape evolution; 4: Rural land use; 5: Population; 6: Towns and cities; 7: Problems of economic development; 8: Industry, trade and finance; 9: Petroleum; 10: The political map. See Chapter 12 'Iraq – a study of man, land and water in an alluvial environment' on p. 349-69.

16  **The Middle East: a physical, social and regional geography.**
W. B. Fisher.  London: Methuen, 1978. 7th ed. completely revised. 590p. bibliog. maps.
Originally published in 1950 and now brought up to date, this is a standard text. Part 1 covers physical geography (structure and land-forms, climate, soils and vegetation); Part 2 deals with social geography (human society, historical geography, economic life, oil resources, demographic trends); Part 3 treats regional geography: chapter 13 'The Tigris–Euphrates lowlands' on p. 363-97 is a study of part of Iraq. This section deals with regional structural features, geographical sub-regions, climate, minerals, industry, communications and trade.

17  **Land of the Arabs.**
M. Abdel-Kader Hatem.  London: Longman, 1977. 132p. maps.
Discusses in turn the general geography of the Arab League states, and the utilization of land and water in each. Iraq is described on p. 248-69. A short bibliography is appended to each chapter.

18  **A bibliography of the Iran–Iraq borderland.**
Keith McLachlan, Richard N. Schofield.  London: Middle East & North African Studies Press, 1987. 365p.
This unannotated bibliography of 3381 items is arranged under the following headings: Geography, geology and geomorphology; Maps; Modern history and international relations; Treaties, reports and bibliographies; Appendix 1: Public Record Office; Appendix 2: India Office Records; Appendix 3: Addendum (recent publications). The entries are mainly, but not exclusively, in English.

19  **Physiographic regions of Iraq.**
Raoul C. Mitchell.  *Bulletin de la Société de Géographie d'Egypte,* vol. 30 (1959), p. 75-96.
Mitchell identifies eleven distinct physiographic regions in Iraq and outlines their characteristics.

20  **Forests and forestry in Iraq: prospects and limitations.**
M. H. Nasser.  *Commonwealth Forestry Review,* vol. 63, no. 4 /no. 197 (December 1984), p. 299-304.
Describes Iraq's forest resources, the consequences of past over-exploitation and abuse, and the need for skilled management and education of the population regarding the forests.

21  **Land and water resources in Iraq: an updated assessment.**
M. H. Nasser.  *Journal of Arid Environments,* vol. 12, no. 3 (1987), p. 191-98.
Nasser describes the major agro-climatic regions in Iraq, its water resources, land resources and the pattern of land use.

22  **Euphrates and Tigris, Mesopotamian ecology and destiny.**
Julian Rzóska, with contributions by J. F. Talling, K. E. Banister.  The Hague: Junk, 1980. 119p. map. bibliog. (Monographiae Biologicae, 38).
Sets out to present the natural history of the land which is largely created and dominated by the two great rivers. Part one describes the geology, morphology, climate and vegetation and the emergence of humankind as the dominating agent. Part two describes the waters, their biological life and the ecological panorama. The chapters on 'Water characteristics' and 'Phytoplankton' are by J. F. Talling, and the chapter on 'The fishes of the Euphrates and Tigris' is by K. E. Banister.

23 **Gazetteer of Arabia: a geographical and tribal history of the Arabian Peninsula.**
Sheila A. Scoville. Rev. ed. rp. Graz, Austria: Akademische Druck, 1979. 4 vols. (First published 1917).

A reference work listing in alphabetical order the geographical features, cities, towns, and tribes of the Arabian Peninsula, based on a 1917 British gazetteer produced during the First World War. It included the Ottoman Wilaya of Basra and Baghdad, so much material on southern Iraq is to be found in it, with quite detailed descriptions of conditions in Baghdad and Basra (listed as Bosra).

24 **Texts and studies on the historical geography and topography of Iraq.**
Collected and reprinted by Fuat Sezgin in collaboration with Mazen Amawi. Frankfurt am Main, Germany: Institute for the History of Arabic–Islamic Science at the Johann Wolfgang Goethe Univ., 1993. 423p. (Publications of the Institute for the History of Arabic–Islamic Science: Islamic Geography, 83).

A collection of texts on the historical geography of Iraq in French, English, German and Arabic.

25 **Turkey, Syria, Iraq: the Euphrates.**
Randa M. Slim. In: *Culture and negotiation: the resolution of water disputes*, edited by Guy Olivier Faure, Jeffrey Z. Rubin. Newbury Park, CA: Sage, 1993, p. 135-55.

Slim focuses on the dispute between Turkey, Syria and Iraq over the distribution of Euphrates water. Ambitious dam projects on the upper reaches of the river by Turkey and Syria threaten to lower the water quality of the Euphrates in Iraq, especially in terms of increased salinity and pollution. This article reviews the history of the dispute and negotiations over water distribution, and discusses the political and cultural considerations which bedevil them, not least the political feud between the Syrian and Iraqi regimes during the 1970s and 1980s.

26 **The evolution of Middle Eastern landscapes: an outline to A.D. 1840.**
J. M. Wagstaff. London: Croom Helm, 1985. 268p. bibliog.

Describes the history of cultivation, trade and modes of living in the Middle East from earliest times to the present day, and the impact of the rise and fall of empires, political, military and economic developments, the emergence of capitalism and the industrial revolution in the West. In particular, the harshness of the climate in large parts of the Middle East and the relative scarcity of natural resources have always been major constraints on human activity. Iraq itself is the home of one of the earliest centres of human civilization.

**Lower Tigris basin: mismanagement of surface water resources.**
*See* item no. 662.

# Geology

27 **Sedimentological and geomorphological study of sand dunes in the Western Desert of Iraq.**
A. Jawad Ali, R. A. al-Ani. *Journal of Arid Environments*, vol. 6 (March 1983), p. 13-32.
Presents the results of a study of the sand dune belts in southern and southwestern parts of Iraq's Western Desert.

28 **Geology of Iraq: bibliography.**
V. Arad, A. Ehrlich, Y. Bartov. Jerusalem: Geological Survey of Israel, 1991. 153p. map.
An unannotated bibliography of 225 items describing itself as a 'comprehensive bibliography on the geological research of Iraq from its beginning until the present'. The great majority of the items are in English, with a few in other European languages. It is arranged alphabetically, with author and subject indexes.

29 **The Middle East: regional geology and petroleum resources.**
Z. R. Beydoun. Beaconsfield, England: Scientific Press, 1988. 263p. maps. bibliog.
Iraq is included in both parts. Part 1: 'Regional geology' describes the Pre-Cambrian, Infra-Cambrian, Palaeozoic, Mesozoic, and Cenozoic geology of the region; Iraqi oil deposits are dealt with on p. 174-82 of the Petroleum resources section of Part 2 'Resources', and mentioned in the brief section on 'Mineral resources' at the end.

30 **The regional geology of Iraq. Vol. 1: Stratigraphy and palaeogeography.**
Tibor Buday (et al.), edited by Ismail I. M. Kassab, Saad Z. Jassim. Baghdad: State Organization for Minerals, 1980. 420p. maps. bibliog.
The work describes itself as an up-to-date textbook on the stratigraphy and mineral wealth of Iraq. Part 1 deals with stratigraphy, part 2 with palaeogeography.

31 **Seismology in Iraq.**
Khalid J. Fahmi. *Earthquake Information Bulletin*, vol. 14 (May-June 1982), p. 108-14.
Describes the activities and capabilities of the Iraqi Seismological Network which was established in 1977, and the areas of current research in which it is active.

32 **Journal of the Geological Society of Iraq.**
Baghdad: Union of Iraqi Geologists, vol. 1- , 1968- . annual.
Contains articles in both English and Arabic on all aspects of the geology of Iraq.

33 **Lower Paleozoic rocks of the Middle East.**
Reinhard Wohlfart. In: *Lower Palaeozoic of the Middle East, eastern and southern Africa, and Antarctica: with essays on Lower Palaeozoic trace fossils of Africa and Lower Palaeozoic palaeoclimatology*, edited by C. H. Holland. Chichester, England: Wiley, 1981, p. 5-130. (Lower Palaeozoic Rocks of the World, 3).
A general survey of the whole Middle East region for this geological period, with numerous maps and illustrations. An extensive bibliography is appended to the article.

# Maps and atlases

34 **The Cambridge atlas of the Middle East and North Africa.**
Gerald Blake, John Dewdney, Jonathan Mitchell. Cambridge: Cambridge University Press, 1987. 121p. maps. bibliog.
Not a traditional atlas, but a series of outline maps, each with accompanying explanatory text. The 58 maps illustrate the following: the physical environment; cultural history (including the Islamic conquests, and present-day religious and linguistic distributions); demography; economic subjects (including natural resources, oilfields, agricultural exploitation and trade patterns); communications (including railways, roads, etc). Map 48 'The upper Gulf region' describes Iraq, western Iran and Kuwait. Bibliographical references and a gazetteer are included.

35 **Atlas of the Middle East.**
Edited by Moshe Brawer. New York, London: Macmillan, 1988. 140p. maps. bibliog.
This atlas was originally prepared by Carta of Jerusalem. It is a 'current affairs' atlas rather than a traditional book of maps. The first part describes the climate, fauna, flora and political history of the whole region. In the second part, each country of the Middle East, including Iraq, is covered in turn with a map showing natural features and towns, etc. and a second map of 'agriculture, industry and minerals'. The accompanying text gives a concise description of the geographical features, population, economic and social characteristics, and recent political history of the country.

36 **Climatic atlas of Iraq 1941-1970.**
Baghdad: Iraqi Meteorological Organization, 1979. 131 maps.
Contains no text, just maps with legends in Arabic and English which show rainfall, sunshine, temperature, windspeed, etc.

37 **Iraq, official standard names gazetteer.**
United States Board on Geographic Names.    Washington, DC:
Department of the Interior, 1957. 175p. map.

This gazetteer contains some 13,200 entries for places and features in Iraq. The entries include standard names approved by the Board and unapproved variant names, the latter cross-referenced to the standard names. The scale of map coverage is generally about 1:500,000.

38 **Atlas of Iraq showing administrative boundaries, areas and population.**
Ahmed Sousa.    Baghdad: Surveys Press, 1953. 34p. maps.

A general atlas showing administrative and political divisions, tables of area and population for each of the 14 provinces and extra maps of Baghdad city and environs. Translated from the original version published in Arabic.

# Travel

## Travel guides

39 **The Middle East: Lebanon – Syria – Jordan – Iraq – Iran.**
Writtten by Robert Boulanger, translated by J. S. Hardman. Paris: Hachette, 1966. 1046p. maps. (Hachette world guides).
The introduction includes an essay on ancient Near Eastern civilization by André Parrot, and general practical information. The section covering Iraq is on p. 653-763. This standard travel guide with suggested itineraries and descriptions about sites of interest is somewhat dated in practical information.

40 **Middle East on a shoestring.**
Tom Brosnahan (et al.). Hawthorn, Australia: Lonely Planet, 1994. 763p.
One of a series of travel guides for the independent but enterprising traveller. This volume includes Iraq in its coverage.

## Travellers' accounts

41 **Baghdad in bygone days, from the journals and correspondence of Claudius Rich, traveller, artist, linguist, antiquary and British Resident at Baghdad 1808-21.**
Constance M. Alexander. London: Murray, 1928. 326p. map.
Written by his great-great-niece, this book tells in colourful style the story of Claudius Rich's visits to Iraq where he spent the years 1816-21 travelling the country and collecting Oriental manuscripts and antiquities.

42 **The Nestorians and their rituals: with the narrative of a mission to Mesopotamia and Coordistan in 1842-1844, and of a late visit to those countries in 1850; also researches into the present condition of the Syrian Jacobites, Papal Syrians, and Chaldeans, and an inquiry into the religious tenets of the Yezeedees.**
George Percy Badger. [London], 1852, rp. London: Darf, 1987. 2 vols. map.

An account by a Catholic missionary of his work in the Mosul area in the mid-19th century, and description of the local Christians. Volume 2 consists of the texts and liturgy of the Assyrians/Chaldeans/Nestorians.

43 **A year in Baghdad.**
Joan Baez, Albert V. Baez. Santa Barbara, CA: Daniel & Company, 1988. 205p.

A personal account of a recent extended visit to Baghdad by an American physicist and his wife, with illustrations by the authoress.

44 **Bedouin tribes of the Euphrates.**
Lady Anne Blunt, edited, with a preface and some account of the Arabs and their horses by W. S. Blunt. London: Cass, 1968. 2 vols.

First published in 1879, this is a famous travel account, notable for the authors' interest in the horses of the Bedouin as much as in the people they travelled among.

45 **The desert route to India, being the journals of four travellers by the great desert caravan route between Aleppo and Basra, 1745-1751.**
Edited by D. Carruthers. London: Hakluyt Society, 1929. 179p. map. (Hakluyt Society Publications, 2nd Series, 63). Reprinted, Nendeln (Liechtenstein): Kraus Reprint, 1967. 179p. map. bibliog.

The 1967 edition contains a bibliography in addition to the reprinted text. The great desert route functioned as a short cut overland from Aleppo to Basra for travellers from England to India or vice versa. The four journeys recounted in this volume were undertaken by Englishmen en route to or from India in the eighteenth century. They are: A journey from Aleppo to Basra in 1745, by William Beawes; A journey from Basra to Aleppo in 1748, by Gaylard Roberts; A similar journey in 1750, by Bartholomew Plaisted; A journey from Aleppo to Basra in 1751, by John Carmichael.

46 **A voyage up the Persian Gulf, and a journey overland from India to England, in 1817. Containing notices of Arabia Felix, Arabia Deserta, Persia, Mesopotamia, the garden of Eden, Babylon, Bagdad, Koordistan, Armenia, Asia Minor, etc. etc.**
William Heude. Reading, England: Garnet, 1993. new ed. 252p. map.

This edition contains a photographic reprint of the London edition of 1819, together with a new introduction by Robin Bidwell, and provides an account of the overland route from India to England in the early 19th century.

### 47 Foreign travellers in Baghdad.
Margaret Makiya. *Bulletin of the College of Arts* (Baghdad), no. 10 (1967), p. 63-120.
Reviews and contrasts descriptions of Baghdad culled from Western travellers' accounts of the 16th to the early 20th centuries.

### 48 A reed shaken by the wind: a journey through the unexplored marshlands of Iraq.
Gavin Maxwell. Harmondsworth, England: Penguin, 1983. new ed. 224p. map; Oxford: ISIS (large print), 1989. 265p.
First published in 1957, this is an account of his travels in the Marshlands of southern Iraq undertaken with Wilfred Thesiger in 1957.

### 49 The Middle Euphrates: a topographical itinerary.
Alois Musil. New York: Crane, 1927, rp. 1978. (American Geographical Society Oriental Explorations & Studies, 3). Reprinted, Frankfurt am Main, Germany: Institute for the History of Arabic–Islamic Science, 1993. 426p. (Publications of the Institute for the History of Arabic–Islamic Science: Islamic Geography, 87).
An account of several of the author's journeys around Iraq and northern Arabia, with extensive descriptions of the history of the area in the appendices. Part one covers the expedition of 1912, and part two the expedition of 1915.

### 50 Narrative of a residence in Koordistan and on the site of ancient Nineveh.
Claudius James Rich. London, 1836. 2 vols.
Travel account by an Englishman who spent the years 1816-1821 in Iraq, collecting manuscripts and antiquities.

### 51 To Mesopotamia and Kurdistan in disguise: with historical notices of the Kurdish tribes and the Chaldeans of Kurdistan.
Ely Bannister Soane. London: 2nd ed. 1926, rp. Amsterdam: Armorica/APA-Philo Press, 1979. 407p. map. bibliog.
A travel account of a visit to Iraqi Kurdistan and southern Iraq in 1909, with extensive descriptions of the land and its peoples.

### 52 Beyond Euphrates: an autobiography 1928-1933.
Freya Stark. London: Century, new ed. 1983, rp. 1989. 330p. map.
First published in London in 1951, this is Freya Stark's account of her travels, including many of the letters written on her journeys, between 1928 and 1933. The chapters are headed: 'The first journey, 1928'; 'Canada, 1928-29'; 'To Baghdad, 1929'; 'Into Persia, 1929-30'; 'The Persian summer, 1931'; 'Journalism in Baghdad, 1932'; 'The last of Baghdad, 1933'. For a short biography of Freya Stark, see *Freya Stark* by Caroline Moorehead (Harmondsworth, England: Penguin Books, 1985).

53   **The travels of Pedro Teixeira, with his "Kings of Harmuz", and
     extracts from his "Kings of Persia".**
     [Pedro Teixeira], translated by W. F. Sinclair.   London: Hakluyt
     Society, 1902. 269p. (Hakluyt Society Publications, 2nd Series, 9).

Pedro Teixeira was born in Lisbon around 1587 and travelled extensively in India and
eastern Asia. In 1604 he set sail for Basra, travelled to Baghdad, and proceeded via
Karbala through northern Iraq to Aleppo in 1605. This part of his journey is
recounted in Chapters 2-9 (p. 17-89) where he gives a graphic account of his journey
and of the places he visited on his 'Journey from India to Italy'. Little is known of the
author beyond the information given in this book.

54   **The Marsh Arabs.**
     Wilfrid Thesiger.   London: Longmans, 1964; Harmondsworth,
     England: Penguin, 1967; London: Collins, 1985. 223p.

An account of the author's extended visits to the marshes of southern Iraq between
1951 and 1958 which gives a detailed portrait of the Marsh Arabs' way of life and of
the individuals whom he came to know among them. A famous account of a lifestyle
now almost certainly past.

55   **Return to the marshes.**
     Gavin Young.   London: Collins, 1977. London: Hutchinson, 1983;
     Harmondsworth, England: Penguin, 1989. 182p. bibliog.

Originally subtitled 'Life with the Marsh Arabs', this is an account of the author's
travels in the Marshes in the 1950s and of several return visits between 1973 and
1977. It provides a record of his time spent with the Marsh Arabs and observations of
their way of life, now probably vanished for ever.

# Flora and Fauna

56  **On a collection of birds from Mosul, Iraq.**
Bashir E. Allouse.  *Bulletin of the College of Arts and Sciences*
(Baghdad), no. 2 (1957), p. 162-81.

A list of species with descriptions of the specimens of the collection of birds made in
Mosul district in 1955-56 for the newly created Mosul Museum of Natural History.

57  **Plant wealth of Iraq (a dictionary of economic plants). Vol. 1.**
H. L. Chakravarty.  Baghdad: Botany Directorate, Ministry of
Agriculture and Agrarian Reform, 1976. 505p. bibliog.

The author defines as 'economic' plants: fruits and vegetables, cereal grains, pulses,
medicinal plants, sugar, fibre, gum- and fodder-yielding plants, narcotic drugs and
timber-yielding plants, minor forest resources and avenue and ornamental plants.
Botanical descriptions and notes on the properties and potential of such varieties in
Iraq are given.

58  **Recent field observations from Iraq.**
E. A. Chapman, J. A. McGeoch.  *Ibis*, vol. 98, no. 4 (1956), p. 577-94.

A systematic listing of species of birds seen and observations made in Iraq between
1952 and 1954, which notes six species not previously recorded in Iraq.

59  **Handbook of the birds of Europe, the Middle East and North
Africa: the birds of the western Palearctic.**
Chief Editor Stanley Cramp.  Oxford, London, New York: Oxford
University Press, 1977-94. 9 vols.

The coverage of species is as follows: Volume I: Ostrich to Ducks; II: Hawks to
Bustards; III: Waders to Gulls; IV: Terns to Woodpeckers; V: Tyrant Flycatchers
to Thrushes; VI: Warblers; VII: Flycatchers to Shrikes; VIII: Crows to Finches; IX:
Buntings and New World Warblers. A set of comprehensive reference books, not a
field guide, which include Iraq.

60   **Flora of Iraq.**
Edited by Evan Guest, Ali al-Rawi, C. C. Townsend (et al.).   Baghdad:
Ministry of Agriculture, 1966-85. 6 vols.
Only six out of nine projected volumes of this systematic flora were published.
Volume 1 contains an introduction to the flora of Iraq with an account of the geology,
soils, climate, ecology, a gazetteer, glossary and bibliography. Volume 2 describes
the arrangement of the volumes, and contains descriptions of Pteridophyta,
Gymnospermae and Rosaceae. Volume 3 covers Leguminales; Volume 4 Cornaceae
to Rubiaceae (pt 1) and Bignoniaceae to Resedaceae (pt 2); Volume 8
Monocotyledones (excluding Gramineae); and Volume 9 Gramineae, by N. L. Bor.

61   **The birds of Britain and Europe with North Africa and the Middle
East.**
Hermann Heinzel, Richard Fitter, John Parslow.   London: Collins,
4th ed. 1979. 313p. maps.
A field identification guide, describing itself as the complete pocket bird book, which
describes and illustrates every bird of Europe, the Middle East, and North Africa, and
includes Iraq in its coverage.

62   **The venomous snakes of the Near and Middle East.**
Ulrich Joger.   Wiesbaden, Germany: Reichert, 1984. 95p. bibliog.
maps. (Beihefte zum Tübinger Atlas des Vorderen Orients, Reihe A,
Naturwissenschaften 12).
A detailed study of the venomous species of snakes and their distribution in the
Middle East. According to the table, only four species are known for certain to occur
in Iraq: Walterinnesia Aegyptia, Cerastes Cerastes Gasperettii, Pseudocerastes
Persicus Fieldi, and Vipera Lebetina Obtusa. It is possible that Pseudocerastes
Persicus Persicus may also occur. Detailed identifications, habits, range and habitats
are given.

63   **Al-Ṭuyūr al-ʿIrāqīyah.** (Birds of Iraq.)
Bashīr al-Lūs.   Baghdad: Al-Rābiṭa, 1960-62. 3 vols. (English title-
page: *The birds of Iraq* by Bashir E. Allouse).
There is a brief introduction in English, and all the illustrations are labelled with
Latin and English names, but the descriptions are in Arabic. These volumes present a
general survey of the species of birds known to occur in Iraq according to modern
schemes of classification and nomenclature. A summary version in English was
published as *The avifauna of Iraq* by Bashir E. Allouse, by the Iraq Natural History
Museum in Baghdad in 1953.

64 **Flora iranica: Flora des iranischen Hochlandes und der umrahmenden Gebirge; Persien, Afghanistan, Teile von West-Pakistan, Nord-Iraq, Azerbaijan, Turkmenistan.** (Flora iranica: Flora of the Iranian uplands and the surrounding mountains: Iran, Afghanistan, parts of western Pakistan, northern Iraq, Azerbaijan, Turkmenistan.)
Edited by Karl Heinz Rechinger.   Graz, Austria: Akademische Druck, 1963- . In progress.

A systematic flora which includes the highlands of Iraqi Kurdistan in its coverage. In 1994, 164 fascicles describing and illustrating different plant families had been published.

65 **Flora of lowland Iraq.**
K. H. Rechinger (et al.).   Weinheim, Germany: Cranmer, 1964. 720p. bibliog.

A systematic flora of lowland Iraq, that is, the alluvial plain, the southern and western deserts, and the Jezirah except for the Persian foothills. No illustrations are included but full descriptions are given.

66 **The lepidoptera of Iraq.**
E. P. Wiltshire.   London: Nicholas Kaye, for the Government of Iraq, 1957. rev. and enlarged ed. 148p. bibliog.

The work contains an introduction and lists 906 species found in Iraq.

# Prehistory, Archaeology and Numismatics

## Prehistory and archaeology

67  **Islamic archaeology in Iraq: recent excavations at Samarra.**
Tariq al-Janabi. *World Archaeology*, vol. 14, no. 3 (February 1983),
p. 305-27.
Provides a general survey of excavations carried out at the city of Samarra which was
the capital of the Abbasid Caliphate between 836 and 892. There are a number of
illustrations.

68  **The archaeology of Mesopotamia: from the Old Stone Age to the
Persian conquest.**
Seton Lloyd.   London: Thames & Hudson, 1984. rev. ed. 238p. maps.
bibliog.
Presents the history of archaeological excavations in Iraq since the late 19th century,
and their contributions to the understanding of ancient Mesopotamian history. This
book was written as a general introduction to the archaeology of Mesopotamia.

69  **Foundations in the dust: the story of Mesopotamian exploration.**
Seton Lloyd.   London: Thames & Hudson, 1980. rev. and enlarged ed.
210p. maps. bibliog.
The first edition of this account of the Western discovery of Mesopotamia and its
antiquities was published in 1947. This is a history of archaeology in Iraq, the
decipherment of cuneiform writing and the uncovering of ancient Mesopotamian
history for the general reader.

70   **The rise of civilization: from early farmers to urban society in the ancient Near East.**
   Charles L. Redman.   San Francisco: Freeman, 1978. 322p. bibliog.
   This history of the beginnings of agriculture and civilization in ancient Mesopotamia during the period 8000 to 2000 BCE is intended primarily for students of archaeology, anthropology and ancient history. Iraq was one of the earliest centres of civilization.

71   **L'archéologie islamique en Iraq: bilan et perspectives.** (Islamic archaeology in Iraq: balance-sheet and prospects.)
   Marie-Odile Rousset.   Damascus: Institut Français de Damas, 1992. 198p. maps. bibliog.
   A useful survey of the state of research in Islamic archaeology in Iraq, outlining published work and studies currently in progress. The survey is intended as a reference work for archaeologists and contains a substantial computerized index of sites, with information about their condition and work carried out on them. There is also a general index of sites with a bibliography.

72   **Sumer.**
   Baghdad: Directorate General of Antiquities, vol. 1- , 1945- . annual.
   Published in Arabic and English, this periodical covers the history of Iraq in general, but the majority of its articles report on archaeological work and ancient history.

**Iraq.**
*See* item no. 79.

**Sumer and the Sumerians.**
*See* item no. 84.

**The rise of civilisation.**
*See* item no. 92.

**Early Mesopotamia: society and economy at the dawn of history.**
*See* item no. 95.

**The first empires.**
*See* item no. 96.

# Numismatics and seals

73   **The struggle for Syria and Mesopotamia (330-58/941-69) as reflected on Ḥamdānid and Ikhshīdid coins.**
   Ramzi Jibran Bikhazi.   *American Numismatic Society Museum Notes*, vol. 28 (1983), p. 137-86.
   Provides a survey of the history of the struggle for control of provincial areas of Syria and Iraq during the 10th century. The rule of the Abbasid Caliphs was challenged by

regional dynasties in Mosul, and the Ikhshidids of Egypt were trying to extend their influence over Syria at the expense of the Hamdanids of Aleppo. A catalogue of coins appears on p. 169-86.

## 74 First impressions: cylinder seals in the ancient Near East.
Dominique Collon. London: British Museum Publications, 1987. 197p. maps. bibliog.

Collon attempts to show what can be learned of the life and culture of the ancient Near East from cylinder seals and their impressions. Part one is called 'Cylinder seals in history'; part two 'Cylinder seals in society' and part three 'Subjects and themes on cylinder seals'. The work is extensively illustrated.

## 75 Une monnaie ʿalide d'al-Baṣrah datée de 145 H. (762-3 après J.-C.).
(An ʿAlid coin from Basra dated 145 A.H. (AD 762-3).)
N. M. Lowick. *Revue Numismatique*, vol. 21 (1979), p. 218-24.

Lowick describes a coin from the early years of the Abbasid Caliphate. It was struck in Basra in the name of a local Shiʿi ruler and its historical significance is discussed.

## 76 Ancient Near Eastern cylinder seals from the Marcopoli Collection.
Beatrice Teissier. Berkeley: University of California Press, 1984. 383p. map. bibliog.

An illustrated catalogue of the collection with a valuable introduction discussing the history of cylinder seals in the ancient Near East. Part one contains Mesopotamian, Assyrian, and Iranian seals; Part two Anatolian, Cypriot, and Levantine seals.

## 77 A hoard of Osman Turkish silver coins from Baḥrayn minted at Basra in 982-1032 A.H. = 1574-1623 A.D.
Christopher Toll. In: *Turcica et Orientalia: studies in honour of Gunnar Jarring on his eightieth birthday, 12 October 1987.* Stockholm: Swedish Research Institute in Istanbul, 1988, p. 149-66. (S.R.I.I. Transactions, 1).

Toll gives descriptions of 77 Ottoman coins from the Basra mint with a catalogue.

# History

## General

78 **Land behind Baghdad: a history of settlement on the Diyala plains.**
Robert McC. Adams.  Chicago, London: University of Chicago Press,
1965. 183p. + plates.

Based on field reconnaissance archaeology carried out in 1957-58 and historical
sources, this study presents a continuous account of human settlement and patterns of
irrigation and agriculture in southern Iraq from approximately 4000 BC to 1900 CE.
Part 1 'The contemporary setting'; Part 2 'The changing patterns of ancient
occupance'.

79 **Iraq.**
London: British School of Archaeology in Iraq, vol. 1- , 1934- .
annual.

A periodical devoted to the study of Iraq's history, archaeology, religion, economic
and social life from earliest times to AD 1700. The majority of articles tend to deal
with ancient history and archaeology.

80 **Fondements et mécanismes de l'état en Islam: l'Irak.** (Foundations
and mechanisms of the state in Islam: Iraq.)
Falih Mahdi.  Paris: Harmattan, 1991. 223p. bibliog.

A multi-disciplinary study of early state power in Iraq from the Sumerians in ancient
times up to the 10th century CE when Islamic government had been consolidated. This
book discusses the theory and exercise of state power in Islam, the Islamic
administration system and socio-economic structure.

81    **Iraq: from Sumer to Saddam.**
Geoff Simons.    Basingstoke, England: Macmillan, 1994. 375p.
bibliog.
A concise account of Iraq's history from ancient to modern times, concentrating on
the political, social and economic developments of the 20th century and taking the
story up to the aftermath of the Gulf War of 1991.

**Sumer.**
*See* item no. 72.

**Nisibe: métropole syriaque orientale et ses suffragants des origines à nos
jours.**
*See* item no. 504.

**Mossoul chrétienne: essai sur l'histoire, l'archéologie et l'état actuel des
monuments chrétiens de la ville de Mossoul.**
*See* item no. 776.

# Ancient history

82    **Gods, demons, and symbols of ancient Mesopotamia: an illustrated
dictionary.**
Jeremy Black, Anthony Green.    London: British Museum
Publications, 1992. 190p. map. bibliog.
A dictionary for ancient Mesopotamian cultures, with many drawings and some
photographs illustrating the entries. It is designed for non-specialists and contains an
explanatory introduction. The entries begin with 'abzu' – zone of a freshwater ocean
beneath the earth – and end with 'zodiac', by way of 'alcohol', 'afterlife', 'creation',
'flood', 'griffin', and 'underworld' and many others.

83    **The Cambridge ancient history.**
Edited by I. E. S. Edwards (et al.).    Cambridge: Cambridge University
Press, 1970-  .
A standard history and reference work, dated in places, which has appeared under
various editors. The first edition was begun in 1916 and numbered twelve volumes.
The second edition, begun in 1931, has been published up to Volume VIII: Rome and
the Mediterranean to 133 BC. The third edition began publication in 1970 and is still
in progress. The first volume starts with 'Pre-history' and the subsequent volumes
provide a comprehensive coverage of the whole region through ancient history and up
to the end of the classical period. Substantial bibliographies are provided for each
chapter.

## 84 Sumer and the Sumerians.
Harriet Crawford.   Cambridge: Cambridge University Press, 1991,
rp. 1993. 174p. maps. bibliog.

A survey of the history and development of civilization on the southern
Mesopotamian plain between about 3800 to 2000 BC, written for students beginning
to study the archaeology and history of the ancient Near East. It is organized
thematically and the chapters are headed: 'The rediscovery of the ancient Near East:
the physical environment'; 'History, chronology and social organisation'; 'Patterns of
settlement and agriculture'; 'Town planning and temple architecture'; 'Public
buildings and private housing'; 'Life, death and the meaning of the universe';
'Manufacturing industry and trade'; 'Writing and the arts'; 'Conclusions: the
development of Sumerian society'.

## 85 Myths from Mesopotamia: creation, the flood, Gilgamesh and others.
Translated with an introduction and notes by Stephanie Dalley.
Oxford: Oxford University Press, 1989, rp. 1990; pbk ed. 1991. 331p.
map. bibliog.

Translations of myths from the ancient Akkadian texts, with notes and brief
introductions to each tale.

## 86 Gilgamesh: a new rendering in English verse.
David Ferry.   New York: Farrar, Strauss & Giroux; Newcastle upon
Tyne: Bloodaxe, 1993. 99p.

A translation into English of the ancient Mesopotamian epic.

## 87 The art and architecture of the ancient Orient.
Henri Frankfort.   Harmondsworth, England: Penguin, 1977. 411p.
bibliog. (Pelican History of Art).

Originally published in 1970, this is an illustrated survey of the art and architecture of
the ancient Near East. Part one covers Mesopotamia in considerable detail. Part two
deals with the neighbouring areas.

## 88 The ancient Near East: a history.
William W. Hallo, William Kelly Simpson.   New York: Harcourt
Brace Jovanovich, 1971. 302p. maps. bibliog.

A basic history of the ancient Near East. Part one is entitled 'Mesopotamia and the
Asiatic Near East' (p. 1-83) and deals with the period from prehistory to
approximately 539 BCE. The final chapter in the section offers a survey of
Mesopotamian culture. Part two describes ancient Egypt.

## 89 The history and culture of ancient Western Asia and Egypt.
A. Bernard Knapp.   Belmont, CA: Wadsworth, 1988. 284p. maps.
bibliog.

A political history of the ancient Near East which includes a social and economic
perspective. The chapters deal with rise of civilization (approximately 9000-3000

BCE), the third millennium, the second millennium, and the first millennium BCE. Each chapter has a section on Mesopotamia, and others on Egypt, Syria/Palestine, and, in the penultimate chapter, Persia. Each chapter is followed by a list of suggested further reading.

90　**A dictionary of ancient Near Eastern mythology.**
Gwendolen Leick.　London: Routledge, 1991. 175p. bibliog.
Descriptions and explanations of gods, goddesses, names and themes of myths, presented in dictionary form. Myths are 'very broadly defined as narratives featuring divine or heroic protagonists'.

91　**The ancient Near East.**
P. R. S. Moorey.　Oxford: Ashmolean Museum Publications, 1987.
54p. maps. bibliog.
A general introduction to the ancient Near East, including Mesopotamia, illustrated from the Ashmolean Museum's own collections. Part one is called 'The legacy of the ancient Near East and its rediscovery', part two 'A diversity of peoples', and part three 'Aspects of daily life'.

92　**The rise of civilisation.**
David Oates, Joan Oates.　Oxford: Elsevier–Phaidon Turnhout Press, 1976. 136p. map. bibliog. (The Making of the Past).
Traces the origins of farming throughout the ancient Near East, concentrating on Mesopotamia where an urban society first developed and influenced large areas of the Fertile Crescent. This book is based mainly on archaeological evidence and takes the story up to the invention of writing when this society emerged into history as the Sumerian civilization. Many illustrations are included.

93　**Babylon.**
Joan Oates.　London: Thames & Hudson, rev. ed. 1986, rp. 1994.
210p. maps. bibliog.
Intended to provide an introduction to the history and archaeology of Babylonia throughout the time span of its greatest city. The account ends with the periods of Persian and Greek rule. Many black-and-white illustrations.

94　**Ancient Mesopotamia: portrait of a dead civilization.**
A. Leo Oppenheim, revised ed. completed by Erica Reiner.　Chicago, IL: Chicago University Press, 1977. 418p. map.
Presents for the general reader the civilization of Babylonia and Assyria. Chapter one describes the making of Mesopotamia, and the following chapters discuss the social and economic structures, the history of Babylonia and Assyria, religious beliefs, writing and documentary and creative literature, medicine, mathematics and astronomy, crafts and art.

95   **Early Mesopotamia: society and economy at the dawn of history.**
J. N. Postgate.   London: Routledge, 1992. 330p. maps. bibliog.

Postgate states in the preface that it is intended to describe 'an early state in terms sufficiently broad for the general reader, but with enough detail to help the specialist' and asserts that the result is more history than archaeology. The period covered is from 3000 to 1500 BC, based mainly on the written sources. Part one is entitled 'Setting the scene'; part two 'The institutions', part three 'The economic order', and part four 'The social order'.

96   **The first empires.**
Nicholas Postgate.   Oxford: Elsevier Phaidon, 1977. 149p. maps. bibliog.

A volume in the series called 'The Making of the Past' describing the early history of the world as revealed by archaeology and related disciplines. The chapters cover 'Civilization in context'; 'The rediscovery of Mesopotamia'; 'Mesopotamian archaeology in the 20th century'; 'Sumer and Akkad'; 'The second millennium'; 'The Assyrian and Babylonian empires'. There are many illustrations.

97   **The ancient Near East in pictures relating to the Old Testament.**
Edited by James B. Pritchard.   Princeton, NJ: Princeton University Press, 1954. 340p. maps.

Presents black-and-white photographs, and some drawings, illustrating events and cultures from ancient Mesopotamia and other parts of the Near East which are related to descriptions in the Old Testament of the Christian Bible. The illustrations are grouped under the following headings: 'Peoples and their ideas'; 'Daily life'; 'Writing'; 'Scenes from history and monuments'; 'Royalty and dignitaries'; 'Gods and their emblems'; 'The practice of religion'; 'Myth, legend, and ritual on cylinder seals'; 'Views and plans of excavations'; 'Maps'; 'Catalogue'. The maps are explanatory; the catalogue gives full descriptions of the items illustrated. A supplement to this volume, organized in the same fashion *The ancient Near East: supplementary texts and pictures relating to the Old Testament*, was published in 1969.

98   **Ancient Near Eastern texts relating to the Old Testament.**
Edited by James B. Pritchard.   Princeton, NJ: Princeton University Press, 1969. 3rd ed. with supp. 676p. maps. bibliog.

Contains translations of texts from Sumerian, Akkadian, Babylonian and Assyrian cultures related to events or literature in the Old Testament of the Christian Bible, as well as from other cultures of the ancient Near East. The book is organized by subject under the following headings: 'Myths, epics, and legends'; 'Legal texts'; 'Historical texts'; 'Rituals and incantations, and descriptions of festivals'; 'Hymns and prayers'; 'Didactic and wisdom literature'; 'Lamentations'; 'Secular songs and poems' – only from Egypt; 'Letters'; 'Miscellaneous texts'. A supplement to this volume, *The ancient Near East: supplementary texts and pictures relating to the Old Testament*, was published in 1969.

99  **Assyrian sculpture.**
Julian Reade.    London: British Museum Publications, 1983, rp. 1992.
72p.
A guide to Assyrian sculpture in the British Museum which also presents a general introduction to the subject, placing the pieces in their archaeological and historical context. Many illustrations are included.

100  **Mesopotamia.**
Julian Reade.    London: British Museum Publications, 1991, rp. 1993.
69p. map. bibliog.
An illustrated introduction to the history of ancient Mesopotamia down to the early second millennium BCE.

101  **'Your thwarts in pieces, your mooring rope cut': poetry from Babylonia and Assyria.**
Erica Reiner.    Ann Arbor: Horace H. Rackham School of Graduate Studies at the University of Michigan, 1985. 120p.
Contains an introduction and a selection of translations from various types of Babylonian and Assyrian literature presented for the general public.

102  **Cultural atlas of Mesopotamia and the ancient Near East.**
Michael Roaf.    New York: Facts on File, 1990. 223p. maps. bibliog.
A lavishly illustrated introduction for the general reader to ancient Mesopotamia. Part one is called 'Villages'; part two 'Cities'; and part three 'Empires'. Numerous special features sections cover archaeology, the origins of writing, religious beliefs, technology, architecture, and other aspects of cultural life.

103  **Ancient Iraq.**
Georges Roux.    Harmondsworth, England: Penguin, 1992. 3rd ed.
428p. maps. bibliog.
Widely regarded as one of the best general introductions to the history of ancient Iraq, this book describes the geographical setting, the history and state of archaeological research, the early development of civilization, the rise and decline of the Sumerians, Akkadians, Amorites, Assyrians, Babylonians, and other peoples, down to the Hellenistic and Parthian period.

104  **The greatness that was Babylon: a survey of the ancient civilization of the Tigris–Euphrates valley.**
H. W. F. Saggs.    London: Sidgwick & Jackson, 1988. rev. and updated ed. 468p. maps. bibliog.
Babylonian history, culture and civilization are here presented for the general reader. The chapters cover the history of Babylon under the Sumerians and Assyrians, Nebachudnezzar and his successors, and the nature of the state and its government, social and economic life, religious beliefs, literature, mathematics, astronomy and medicine.

105 **The might that was Assyria.**
H. W. F. Saggs. London: Sidgwick & Jackson, 1984. 323p. maps. bibliog.

Written for the non-specialist, part one covers the history of the Assyrian empire from its beginnings to its imperial prime, ending with Sennacherib. Part two describes the culture – domestic, agricultural, economic, technological, religious, artistic, military and medical – of the Assyrians. The last chapter deals with the modern rediscovery of the Assyrians and archaeology in Iraq.

106 **The art of Mesopotamia.**
Eva Strommenger, photographs by Max Hirmer. London: Thames & Hudson, 1964. 463p. bibliog.

A large-format book with 44 colour illustrations, 280 black-and-white photographs and 70 text figures. The text explains the political background, and the disappearance and rediscovery of Mesopotamia, and the plates and illustrations are systematically arranged to show the range of art of ancient Western Asia, and the relevant sites.

107 **Trésors du Musée de Bagdad des origines à l'Islam.** (Treasures of the Baghdad Museum from the earliest times to Islam.)
Paris: Ministère d'Etat Affaires Culturelles, 1966. 128p. map. bibliog.

A catalogue of the exhibition sent to Paris in 1966 with a historical introduction and some illustrations. Ceramics, statues, frescos and other objects formed the main content of the exhibition.

108 **Cuneiform.**
C. B. F. Walker. London: British Museum Publications, 1987. 62p. bibliog. (Reading the Past Series).

A short book introducing the cuneiform script for the general reader. It contains an introduction, and chapters about the origin and development of the script, tablets and monuments, scribes and libraries, the geographical spread of the script's use, the history of its decipherment, sample texts and, lastly, fakes.

**The rise of civilization: from early farmers to urban society in the ancient Near East.**
*See* item no. 70.

**The encyclopaedia of Middle Eastern mythology and religion.**
*See* item no. 815.

# Byzantine and early Islamic rule

109 **Al-Kūfa: naissance de la ville islamique.** (Al-Kūfah: birth of the Islamic city.)
Hichem Djaït. Paris: Maisonneuve et Larose, 1986. 331p. maps. bibliog. (Islam d'Hier et d'Aujourd'hui, 29).
A study of the development and characteristics of the Islamic city as exhibited by Kufah, the garrison town built soon after the Islamic conquest of Iraq, charting its form, influences and urban evolution from its foundation in 638 to its demise at the hands of marauding Bedouin about six centuries later.

110 **The early Islamic conquests.**
Fred McGraw Donner. Princeton, NJ: Princeton University Press, 1981. 437p. maps. bibliog.
Donner argues that Islam revolutionized the ideological bases and political structures of Arabian society, giving rise for the first time to a state capable of organizing and executing an expansionist movement. Chapter four describes the conquest of Iraq (p. 157-220), and chapter five includes Iraq in its discussion of migration and settlement (p. 221-50).

111 **Tribal settlement in Basra during the First Century** A.H.
Fred M. Donner. In: *Land tenure and social transformation in the Middle East*, edited by Tarif Khalidi. Beirut: American University of Beirut, 1984, p. 97-120.
The author discusses the impact and pattern of movement of Arabs into Basra after the Islamic conquest.

112 **Byzantium and the early Islamic conquests.**
Walter E. Kaegi. Cambridge: Cambridge University Press, 1992. 287p. bibliog.
Attempts to examine actual Byzantine efforts to defend Palestine, Syria, and Byzantine Mesopotamia against the Muslims, and the nature, causes and consequences of their failure. See in particular Chapter seven 'The brief struggle to save northern Syria and Byzantine Mesopotamia', but Mesopotamia is mentioned throughout.

113 **A study of conversion to Islam with reference to Egypt and Iraq: a survey of Western sources.**
Talip Küçükcan. *Islamic Quarterly*, vol. 35, no. 4 (1991), p. 225-31.
Reviews Western scholarship and speculation on the subject of conversion to Islam after the Islamic conquest in Egypt and Iraq, and highlights differences of approach to a subject for which evidence is scanty.

27

114 **Arab settlement and economic development of Iraq and Iran in the age of Umayyad and early Abbasid caliphs.**
Ira M. Lapidus. In: *The Islamic Middle East, 700-1900: studies in economic and social history,* edited by A. L. Udovitch. Princeton, NJ: Darwin, 1981, p. 177-208.
Lapidus attempts to reconstruct the early history of economic development in Iraq and Iran after the Islamic conquest in the seventh century CE, and to chart the pattern of Arab settlement.

115 **The shaping of ʿAbbāsid rule.**
Jacob Lassner. Princeton, NJ: Princeton University Press, 1980. 304p. maps. bibliog.
A history of the foundation of the Abbasid government in medieval Iraq in 750 AD and the relationship between the ruling family and the civilian bureaucracy and imperial army through which it maintained control over its empire during the first fifty years. Part one is entitled 'The political setting – power struggles', and part two 'The physical setting (Baghdad topography)'.

116 **Commerce in early Islamic Iraq.**
Michael Morony. *Asia, Afrika, Lateinamerika,* vol. 20, no. 4 (1993), p. 699-720.
Studies the role of commerce in the developing Islamic society of Iraq in the first four centuries after the Islamic conquest and notes the continuity of late Sasanian conditions, as well as the effect of the establishment of a unified market in the whole Islamic world.

117 **Iraq after the Muslim conquest.**
Michael G. Morony. Princeton, NJ: Princeton University Press, 1984. 536p. bibliog.
A study of the development of a local form of Islamic civilization in an area which had been under Persian Sasanian rule until the 7th century CE. Part 1 is called: 'Administration'; part 2 'People'; and part 3 'Religious communities'. See also by the same author 'Land holding and social change: Lower al-ʿIrāq in the early Islamic period' in *Land tenure and social transformation in the Middle East,* edited by Tarif Khalidi (Beirut: American University of Beirut, 1984, p. 209-22).

118 **Christianity among the Arabs in Pre-Islamic times.**
J. Spencer Trimingham. London, New York: Longman; Beirut: Librairie du Liban, 1979. 316p. bibliog. maps.
A useful survey of the history of the Arabs of the Fertile Crescent and the Arabian Peninsula in the first six centuries after Christ until the Islamic conquest. The main body of the study concerns the northern Arabs of Syria and Mesopotamia, and describes the spread of Christianity under Roman rule and its growing influence.

**Jalons pour une histoire de l'église en Iraq.**
*See* item no. 503.

# Abbasid Caliphate to 1258

119    **Two queens of Baghdad: mother and wife of Hārūn al-Rashīd.**
Nabia Abbott.    London: Al Saqi, 1986. new ed. 264p. map.
First published in Chicago in 1946, this book was written by a well-known scholar of
medieval history for a general audience to give a picture of court and harim life in the
Abbasid Empire by telling the stories of Khayzuran, the mother of Caliph Harun
al-Rashid, and Zubaydah, his wife.

120    **Social life under the Abbasids, 170-289** AH, **786-902** AD.
Muhammad Manazir Ahsan.    London: Longman, 1979. 296p. bibliog.
An essay in the social history of the Abbasid Caliphate at its most glorious stage,
concentrating on the Caliph's court and life in Baghdad, with some information about
. rural and provincial conditions. Chapter one surveys the sources, and the following
chapters deal with costume, food, housing, hunting, indoor and outdoor games, and
festivals and festivities.

121    **De l'iqta' étatique à l'iqta' militaire: transition économique et
changements sociaux à Baghdad, 247-447 de l'Hégire / 861-1055
ap.J.** (From state Iqta' to military Iqta': economic transition and social
change in Baghdad 247-447 H / 861-1055 CE.)
Habib Ben Abdallah.    Uppsala: [Uppsala University] distrib.
Almqvist & Wicksell, Stockholm, 1986. 204p. bibliog. (Studia
Historica Upsaliensia, 142).
A study of the economic and social changes in Baghdad in the early period of the
Abbasid Caliphate, based on historical sources. *Iqta'* was a variety of long-term land
concession to state officials by the state proprietor (i.e. the Caliph) who owned all
land. It functioned as a means of payment, since the office-holder took his
remuneration from the income derived from the land conceded to him, but the Caliph
could rescind the concession at any moment. The peasantry who worked the land
were effectively serfs and were transferred with it. *Iqta'* proved bad for crop
production, which led to a decline in income supporting the state while the lack of
food supplies led to rising prices, social unrest and revolts. Increasingly, therefore,
*Iqta'* lands were given to military officers, who were expected to maintain order.

122    **Chalif und Grosskönig: die Buyiden im Iraq (945-1055).** (Caliph
and Great King: the Buyids in Iraq (945-1055).)
Heribert Busse.    Beirut, in Kommission bei Franz Steiner Verlag,
Wiesbaden, 1969. 542p. bibliog. (Beiruter Texte und Studien, 9).
This is an all-round study of the period during which the Buyid (Buwayhid) dynasty
ran the Islamic Empire under the nominal control of the Abbasid Caliph. The political
context, relations at Court, the running of the state and the bureaucracy, the armed
forces, the economy, cultural life, and the relations between Muslims, Christians,
Jews, Zoroastrians and Manicheans are described. It contains an English summary.

123 **Harun al-Rashid and the world of the thousand and one nights.**
André Clot. London: Saqi, 1989. 257p.

First published in French in 1986, this is a social history of Harun al-Rashid's life and times, his court, the city of Baghdad and rural and urban conditions of the Abbasid empire at the height of the Abbasid Caliphate.

124 **Mesopotamian trade from the tenth to the fifteenth centuries C.E.**
Fred M. Donner. *Asien, Afrika, Lateinamerika*, vol. 20, no. 5 (1993), p. 1095-112.

Donner disusses commerce and general economic conditions during the period between the breakdown of the Abbasid empire and the incorporation of Iraq into the Safavid empire of Iran and later the Ottoman empire based in Istanbul. The author distinguishes two phases: Buyid and Seljuk (10th–13th centuries) and Mongol and Turkoman (13th–15th centuries).

125 **Haroon al Rasheed and the great Abbasids.**
John Bagot Glubb. London: Hodder & Stoughton, 1976. 359p. maps. bibliog.

A history of the Abbasid Caliphate at its apogee, based on Arabic sources, but written for the general reader.

126 **Continuity and change in religious adherence: ninth-century Baghdad.**
Wadi Z. Haddad. In: *Conversion and continuity: indigenous Christian communities in Islamic lands eighth to eighteenth centuries*, edited by Michael Gervers, Ramzi Jibran Bikhazi. Toronto: Pontifical Institute of Mediaeval Studies, 1990, p. 33-53.

Discusses the evidence for conversion from Christianity to Islam after the Islamic conquest, and presents three texts from the ninth century CE soliciting, accepting, and condemning such conversions. The author argues that these texts show that there was a certain amount of popular pressure to convert, and that stalwart Christians wished to stem the tide.

127 **The Buwayhid dynasty of Baghdad (334/946-447/1055).**
Mafizullah Kabir. Calcutta: Iran Society, 1964. 213p. bibliog.

A detailed study of the rise of the Buwayhid (Buyid) dynasty based near the Caspian Sea. They took power in Baghdad in 945 and reduced the Abbasid Caliphs to the status of puppet-kings until the Seljuks displaced them in 1055. Part one is headed 'Political history' and part two 'Administration and cultural and religious life'.

128 **The early Abbasid Caliphate.**
Hugh Kennedy. London: Croom Helm, 1981. 221p. maps. bibliog.

A history of political struggles and processes from the establishment of the Abbasid Caliphate in 750 through the period of Harun al-Rashid to the time of the great civil war in the early 8th century.

129  **Humanism in the renaissance of Islam: the cultural revival during the Buyid age.**
Joel L. Kramer.  Leiden, The Netherlands: Brill, 1986. 288p. bibliog.
A study of the Abbasid empire under the rule of the Buyid (Buwayhid) dynasty in the 10th-11th centuries. Originally local lords from Daylam in northern Iran, the Buyids fostered the intellectual study of philosophy, science, poetry and belles-lettres, even though their rule coincided with a period of social crisis and economic decline.

130  **The topography of Baghdad in the early Middle Ages. Text and studies.**
Jacob Lassner.  Detroit, MI: Wayne State University Press, 1970.
298p. maps. bibliog.
A translation of the text describing the topography of Baghdad as the Abbasid capital written by the classical historian Khatib al-Baghdadi in his *Tarikh Baghdad*, with a discussion of the text in part two.

131  **Baghdad during the Abbasid Caliphate from contemporary Arabic and Persian sources.**
G. Le Strange.  Oxford, 1990, rp. Frankfurt am Main: Institute for the History of Arabic–Islamic Science at the Johann Wolfgang Goethe University, 1993. 256p. maps. (Publications of the Institute for the History of Arabic–Islamic Science: Islamic Geography, 84).
Le Strange presents descriptions culled from medieval accounts of the foundation of Baghdad and its development under the Abbasids from 754 up to 1258 when it was sacked by the Mongols.

132  **Islamic taxation in the classic period with special reference to circumstances in Iraq.**
Frede Løkkegaard.  Copenhagen: Branner & Korch, 1950. 266p.
bibliog.
A study of the system of public finance and taxation in Islamic Iraq based on legal sources, surviving documents and classical literature. The concluding chapter provides a summary of the administration of medieval Islamic Iraq.

133  **Badr al-Dīn Lu'lu' and the establishment of a Mamluk government in Mosul.**
Douglas Patton.  *Studia Islamica*, vol. 74 (1991), p. 79-103.
Badr al-Din Lu'lu' was named ruler of Mosul in 1233 by the Abbasid Caliph al-Mustansir, thus supplanting the Zangid dynasty which had held power there for more than a century. Lu'lu' managed to rise from the position of Mamluk of the last Zangid sultan to become sultan himself by adroit transferral of his loyalty to the rising dynasty of the Ayyubids centred in Syria. His rule over Mosul was abruptly terminated by the Mongol invasion, culminating in the sack of Baghdad in 1258.

### 134 Badr al-Dīn Lu'lu': Atabeg of Mosul, 1211-1259.
Douglas Patton. Seattle: University of Washington Press, 1991. 91p. bibliog. (Middle East Center, Jackson School of International Studies, University of Washington Occasional Papers, 3).

An account of the rise to power of a local lord in Mosul during the unsettled times of the end of the Abbasid Caliphate. His years of independent rule were terminated by the Mongol conquest of Mosul.

### 135 La révolte des esclaves en Iraq au IIIe/IXe siècle. (The slave revolt in Iraq in the 3rd/9th century.)
Alexandre Popovic. Paris: Geuthner, 1976. 201p. map. bibliog.

The author describes the revolt by slaves in the Basra area which presented a serious threat to the Caliphate before it was finally crushed. Its origins, leadership, expansion and suppression are all examined.

### 136 Mouvements populaires à Bagdad à l'époque ʿAbbaside, IXe-XIe siècles. (Popular movements in Baghdad during the age of the Abbasids, 9th-11th centuries.)
Simha Sabari. Paris: Maisonneuve, 1981. 152p. bibliog.

A portrait of Baghdadi society, popular demonstrations and religious and secular movements among the lower ranks of Baghdadi life beyond the Court circle.

### 137 Agriculture in Iraq during the 3rd century, A.H.
Ḥusām Qawām El-Sāmarrāie. Beirut: Librairie du Liban, 1972. 210p. bibliog.

Based on a PhD thesis which discusses the history of agriculture in Iraq during the 9th century CE when it was under Abbasid rule, this work describes irrigation and technology, land tenure and crop production, cultivation and implements, floods, pests and diseases, the agricultural policy pursued by the state, and agricultural taxation and revenue.

### 138 Cereals, bread and society: an essay on the staff of life in medieval Iraq.
David Waines. *Journal of the Economic and Social History of the Orient*, vol. 30 (1987), p. 255-85.

An essay in social history dealing with the subject of food preparation and consumption in Abbasid Iraq, based on evidence in the medieval sources.

### 139 Baghdad: metropolis of the Abbasid Caliphate.
Gaston Wiet, translated by Seymour Feiler. Norman, OK: University of Oklahoma Press, 1971. 178p. map. bibliog.

A history of the Abbasid Caliphate ruled from its capital in Baghdad from 750 to 1258. Written for the general reader, this account describes the Abbasid golden age and its later decline. It was extinguished by the Mongol conquest.

The struggle for Syria and Mesopotamia (330-58/941-69) . . .
*See* item no. 73.

The shaping of ʿAbbāsid rule.
*See* item no. 115.

Chrétiens syriaques sous les Abbasides, surtout à Baghdad (749-1258).
*See* item no. 501.

# Mongol and Ottoman rule 1258-1917

140 **L'oeuvre missionaire en Irak: un aperçu historique.**
(Missionary work in Iraq: a historical view.)
Waad Alkhazraji. *L'Afrique et l'Asie Modernes*, no. 157 (Summer 1988), p. 103-16.
Iraq was the scene of considerable missionary effort by the Roman Catholic Church from the 18th century until the First World War. French missionaries played a major part in this work, and French was taught in a number of mission schools. Mosul and Baghdad, with their local Christian populations, were the principal scene of missionary work.

141 **Land tenure in Egypt and the Fertile Crescent, 1800-1950.**
Gabriel Baer. In: *The economic history of the Middle East 1800-1914*, edited by Charles Issawi. Chicago, IL: University of Chicago Press, 1966, p. 79-90.
Presents a previously unpublished article by Gabriel Baer entitled 'The evolution of private landownership in Egypt and the Fertile Crescent' which discusses the history of large landholdings in private ownership under Ottoman rule and its legacy for Iraq's development in the 20th century.

142 **British policy in Mesopotamia, 1903-1914.**
London: Ithaca Press, for the Middle East Centre, St. Antony's College, Oxford, 1976. 322p. maps. bibliog.
Examines official British interest in Mesopotamia before the First World War, and the decision-making of British officials involved. The book concentrates on British motives and actions, but provides a good deal of information about the political and economic situation in Iraq at the time, and British interest in developing irrigation and river transport systems.

143 **Mesopotamia in British strategy, 1903-1914.**
Stuart Cohen. *International Journal of Middle East Studies*, vol. 9, no. 2 (May 1978), p. 171-81.
Cohen reviews British strategic interest in Mesopotamia in the early 20th century, and the reasons for Britain's limited interest in the hinterland of the Gulf before the First World War.

144 **Mafia, mob and Shiism in Iraq: the rebellion of Ottoman Karbala 1824-1843.**
J. R. I. Cole, Moojan Momen. *Past and Present*, vol. 112 (August 1986), p. 112-43.
Describes the virtual rebellion by local élites and their gangs in Karbala against central government rule in the mid-19th century, which led to a catastrophic invasion by Baghdad-based Ottoman Turkish forces in January 1843 to bring it under control.

145 **The struggle against Shiism in Hamidian Iraq: a study in Ottoman counter-propaganda.**
Selim Deringil. *Die Welt des Islams*, vol. 30 (1990), p. 45-62.
During the reign of Abdülhamid II (1876-1909) the Ottomans placed much emphasis on the ideology of unity of the Empire under the Ottoman Sultan as Commander of the Faithful of Islam. The Shiʿi Qajar rulers of Iran were their principal rivals for the allegiance of Muslims in Iraq and both struggled for credibility in the eyes of the Iraqi people. The Ottomans sent Sunni religious officials to educate Iraqis and warn them of the evils of Shiʿism, and to send back reports on seditious Shiʿi elements among the population.

146 **The historiography of modern Iraq.**
Marion Farouk-Sluglett, Peter Sluglett. *American Historical Review*, vol. 96, no. 5 (December 1991), p. 1408-21.
The authors review the literature on the 19th- and 20th-century history of Iraq which has been written since 1900.

147 **The Mongol conquest of Baghdad: medieval accounts and their modern assessments.**
Muhammad al-Faruque. *Islamic Quarterly*, vol. 32, no. 4 (1988), p. 194-206.
Discusses the historical acounts of the conquest of Baghdad in 1258 by Hülegü Khan, and reviews modern historians' assessments of their reliability, and of the consequences of the sack of Baghdad for the local population and for Muslim civilization.

148 **The politics of the grain trade in Iraq c.1840-1917.**
Hala Fattah. *New Perspectives on Turkey*, vol. 5-6 (Fall 1991), p. 151-65.
Fattah describes the prevalence of famine, both natural and man-made, in the province of Iraq during the 19th and early 20th centuries.

149 **The historical geography of Iraq between the Mongolian and Ottoman conquests.**
Muhammad Rashid al-Feel. Najaf, Iraq: Al-Adab Press, 1967.
2 vols. maps. bibliog.
Originally a PhD thesis based on historical sources, this study discusses the socioeconomic state of Iraq from 1258 to 1534.

150  **The social origins of the modern Middle East.**
Haim Gerber.   London: Mansell; Boulder, CO: Rienner, 1987. 212p.
bibliog.
A study of the mechanisms of Ottoman landholding and administration as they
evolved in the 19th century. Iraq is discussed in general and comparative terms in the
second half of the book and this provides a guide to the social background of modern
Iraqi society.

151  **The Euphrates expedition.**
John S. Guest.   London: Kegan Paul International, 1992. 169p.
bibliog.
An account of the expedition led by F. R. Chesney in 1835 to sail two paddle-
steamers up the Euphrates to prove that the river was navigable for a regular steamer
service. The British government mounted the expedition because officials feared
Russian expansion in the area, but the idea was abandoned after the failure of the
experiment made clear that the design of the vessels was inappropriate for conditions
along the river.

152  **Iraq before World War I: a case of anti-European Arab
Ottomanism.**
Mahmoud Haddad.   In: *The origins of Arab nationalism*, edited by
Rashid Khalidi, Lisa Anderson, Muhammad Muslih, Reeva S. Simon.
New York: Columbia Press, 1991, p. 120-50.
Discusses the period between 1908 and 1914, and argues that feelings in Iraq were
not so much anti-Turkish as anti-European and pro-Arab nationalist, although some
resentment at Turkish dominance was present.

153  **The Fertile Crescent 1800-1914: a documentary economic history.**
Charles Issawi.   New York: Oxford University Press, 1988. 480p.
bibliog.
This book contains statistics and official documents from a variety of sources in
English translation. After Chapter one 'The Fertile Crescent in the Middle Eastern
economy', each chapter has a short general introduction and is divided into sections
for Syria and Iraq respectively and organized under six main headings: 'General and
social developments' (Iraq, p. 93-125); 'Trade' (Iraq, p. 173-202); 'Transport' (Iraq,
p. 246-67); 'Agriculture' (Iraq, p. 343-66); 'Industry' (Iraq, p. 395-406); 'Finance and
public finance' (Iraq, p. 450-76).

154  **Aspects of land tenure and social change in Lower Iraq during
late Ottoman times.**
Albertine Jwaideh.   In: *Land tenure and social transformation in the
Middle East*, edited by Tarif Khalidi.   Beirut: American University of
Beirut, 1984, p. 333-56.
Discusses the impact of the Ottoman Land Code introduced into the Baghdad Wilayat
by Midhat Pasha in 1869, and the changes in the pattern of landholding.

155 **Midhat Pasha and the land system of lower Iraq.**
Albertine Jwaideh. *St. Antony's Papers*, 16 (1963), p. 106-36.
(*Middle Eastern Affairs*, 3).

On the consequences of Midhat Pasha's efforts to apply the Ottoman Land Code of 1869 in Iraq. The rights to the land were bought by families who thereby became big landowners, but who could enforce their rights only through the old tribal authorities. Tribal relations were reduced to merely economic relations between landlord and tenant. The new state of affairs was later enshrined by the British, who took the side of the landlords because it ruled through them.

156 **Power and knowledge in Jalili Mosul.**
Percy Kemp. *Middle Eastern Studies*, vol. 19, no. 2 (April 1983), p. 201-12.

On intellectual and cultural life in Mosul when it was ruled by the Jalili family under Ottoman suzerainty in the 18th century. The same author published a further account of this period as 'History and historiography in Jalili Mosul' in *Middle Eastern Studies*, vol. 19, no. 3 (July 1983), p. 345-76.

157 **Oil and empire: British policy and Mesopotamian oil 1900-1920.**
Marian Kent. London: Macmillan, for the London School of Economics and Political Science, 1976. 249p. bibliog.

Examines the crucial years when oil became a major source of energy for the British economy and Mesopotamia was seen as an important source for Britain's oil needs. Part 1: 'The background'; part 2: 'Examination of the British government's involvement in the Mesopotamian oil concession negotiations, 1912-14'; part 3: 'Exigencies of war and provision for peace: oil policy and territorial desiderata'. The appendices contain documents, statistics and related information.

158 **The introduction of commercial agriculture in the Province of Mosul and its effects on the peasantry, 1750-1850.**
Dina Rizk Khoury. In: *Landholding and commercial agriculture in the Middle East*, edited by Caglar Keyder, Faruk Tabak. Albany: State University of New York Press, 1991, p. 155-71.

A detailed study of the economic history of Mosul which attempts to distinguish changes in the rural sector in the 18th century before the Ottoman Empire was fully integrated into the world market. The author concludes that the development of commercial agriculture in Mosul did not grow into agrarian capitalism because of the precarious position of the landowners whose fortunes remained closely tied to their political position. A second conclusion is that commercial agriculture did not lead to the development of wage labour in the countryside around Mosul.

159 **Merchants and trade in early modern Iraq.**
Dina Rizk Khoury. *New Perspectives on Turkey*, vol. 5-6 (Fall 1991), p. 53-86.

Discusses economic conditions and trade in Iraq in the 16th and 17th centuries, and the structure of commerce in Basra and Mosul.

160 **Four centuries of modern Iraq.**
Stephen Hemsley Longrigg.   Oxford: Clarendon Press, 1925,
rp. Beirut, 1968. 352p. maps. bibliog.
A history of Iraq covering the period from the conquest by the Ottomans in the 16th
century up to the end of the 19th century, which charts the struggle for control of the
area between the Persians and the Ottomans, and the rise and decline of various local
dynasties. Somewhat dated, but useful because it covers the whole period of Ottoman
rule.

161 **La formation de l'Irak contemporain: le rôle politique des ulémas
chiites à la fin de la domination ottomane et au moment de la
créaion de l'état irakien.** (The formation of contemporary Iraq: the
political role of the Shi'i ulama at the end of Ottoman domination and
the moment of creation of the Iraqi state.)
Pierre-Jean Luizard.   Paris: CNRS, 1991. 524p. bibliog.
Describes the political orientation and activities of the Shi'i religious hierarchy in Iraq
at the end of the 19th century and during the first two decades of the 20th century.
Although the clerics had religious ties with Shi'i Iran, they accepted the idea of an
Iraqi state promoted by the British after the First World War, as long as it was an
independent Islamic state. However they were finally driven to rebel against British
rule during the dispute over Mosul.

162 **The population of Ottoman Syria and Iraq, 1878-1914.**
Justin McCarthy.   *Asian and African Studies* (Haifa), vol. 15, no. 1
(March 1981), p. 3-44.
A broad analysis of the populations of Ottoman Syria and Iraq, based mainly on
published Ottoman sources. The author notes that the Ottomans had less involvement
with and less secure control over Iraq, so that while their records for Syrian provinces
are fairly accurate, they had only a very imperfect idea of the numbers of people in
Iraq.

163 **The British Residency in the nineteenth century: a social study.**
Margaret Makiya.   *Bulletin of the College of Arts* (Baghdad), no. 11
(1968), p. 5-31.
Describes Residency life in Baghdad, its domestic arrangements and social style,
including the wives, and intercourse with the rest of the foreign community.

164 **The Svoboda diaries.**
Margaret Makiya.   *Bulletin of the College of Arts* (Baghdad), no. 12
(1969), p. 37-67.
Describes the life of one part of Iraqi society as illuminated by the diaries kept by
Joseph Matthia Svoboda from 1862 to 1908. He was the son of a Hungarian, born in
Baghdad, and married into a local Christian family. He moved within a mainly
Christian milieu with close connections with the European community in Baghdad,
where he eventually died. He earned his living working as a clerk on the river
steamers which plied between Baghdad and Basra.

165 **The Ottoman centuries in Iraq: legacy or aftermath? A survey study of Mesopotamian hydrology and Ottoman irrigation projects.**
Rhoads Murphy. *Journal of Turkish Studies*, no. 11 (1987), p. 17-29.
Murphy reconsiders the Ottoman record in building irrigation canals, flood control and water supply structures on the Tigris and Euphrates rivers from the 17th to the 19th centuries, and enumerates some of the schemes undertaken.

166 **Politics and society in early modern Iraq: Mamlūk Pashas, tribal shayks and local rule between 1802 and 1831.**
Tom Nieuwenhuis. The Hague: Nijhoff, 1982. 215p. maps. bibliog.
A study of the period of local lordships in Iraq, which was ended by restored Ottoman centralization and assertion of Turkish control in the early 19th century. The parts are headed 'A litany of disasters'; 'The structure of Mamlūk power'; 'The rural world'; Résumé: the background of Iraqi state formation'. A valuable source for a little-studied period.

167 **Regional trade and 19th-century Mosul: revising the role of Europe in the Middle East economy.**
Sarah D. Shields. *International Journal of Middle East Studies*, vol. 23, no. 1 (1991), p. 19-37.
Discusses the economy and commerce of Mosul and its hinterland under Ottoman rule. The area had a local market and was not wholly dependent on the European trade.

168 **The education of an Iraqi Ottoman army officer.**
Reeva S. Simon. In: *The origins of Arab nationalism*, edited by Rashid Khalidi, Lisa Anderson, Muhammad Muslih, Reeva S. Simon. New York: Columbia Press, 1991, p. 151-66.
Describes the education received by Iraqi officers of the Ottoman military in the late 19th and early 20th centuries and argues that 'there is evidence that attendance at distinctive secondary schools was a most influential experience for many who later achieved political power in the Middle East'.

169 **The role of Lieutenant Muḥammad Sharīf al-Fārūqī – new light on Anglo-Arab relations during the First World War.**
Eliezer Tauber. *Asian and African Studies* (Haifa), vol. 24, no. 1 (January 1990), p. 17-50.
Discusses the role of Faruqi, an Iraqi officer who deserted from the Ottoman army in 1915, in the negotiations between Britain and Sharif Husayn of Mecca regarding British support for the Arab Revolt against the Turks and the promises made by the British. Faruqi evidently played a less than honest role as Husayn's representative, but was largely responsible for initiating British interest in an Arab revolt.

170 **The Euphrates Expedition.**
   M. E. Yapp.   In: *The Islamic world from classical to modern times: Essays in honor of Bernard Lewis*, edited by C. E. Bosworth, Charles Issawi, Roger Savory, A. L. Udovitch.   Princeton, NJ: Darwin Press, 1989, p. 891-95.
Describes the political, economic and historical background to the 1835-37 expedition which was intended to investigate the suitability of the Euphrates River for steam navigation. The author concludes that the true origin of the expedition lay in the personal ambition of the leader, Col. F. R. Chesney, and his colleagues, Lt. Robert Taylor and Henry Bosse Lynch.

171 **Mosul in 1909.**
   Wilkie Young.   *Middle Eastern Studies*, vol. 7, no. 2 (May 1971), p. 229-35.
Presents a British consular despatch written in January 1909 describing the social composition of Mosul, and the political situation there at a time between the *coups d'état* of July 1908 and April 1909 when the state's authority was somewhat shaken, and local aspirations came into play.

**Gazetteer of Arabia: a geographical and tribal history of the Arabian Peninsula.**
*See* item no. 23.

**Mesopotamian trade from the tenth to the fifteenth centuries C.E.**
*See* item no. 124.

**'Iraq, 1900 to 1950: a political, social, and economic history.**
*See* item no. 213.

**Population movements.**
*See* item no. 411.

**"Indian money" and the Shi'i shrine cities of Iraq 1786-1850.**
*See* item no. 468.

**Rabbi Yaakob Elyichar and his Megillat Paras on the history of the Basra community . . . 1775-1779.**
*See* item no. 479.

**The Jews of Baghdad in 1910.**
*See* item no. 489.

**Chrétiens syriaques sous les Mongols . . .**
*See* item no. 502.

**The transformation of land tenure and rural social structure in central and southern Iraq, c. 1870-1958.**
*See* item no. 522.

**The Middle East in the world economy 1800-1914.**
*See* item no. 604.

**The role of foreign trade in the economic development of Iraq, 1864-1964.**
*See* item no. 616.

# British occupation and the Mosul Dispute 1917-26

172 **Iraq 1908-1921: a socio-political study.**
Ghassan R. Atiyyah.   Beirut: Arab Institute for Research &
Publishing, 1973. 391p. bibliog.

Describes the political and social structure of Iraq during the last years of Ottoman rule and the early years of British administration up to the revolt of 1920, and the changes that were taking place. The appendices contain documents and statistics.

173 **'A tedious and perilous controversy': Britain and the settlement of the Mosul dispute, 1918-1926.**
Peter J. Beck.   *Middle Eastern Studies*, vol. 17, no. 2 (April 1981),
256-76.

The fate of Mosul province was unresolved at the end of the First World War in 1918, and remained as a dispute between Britain and Turkey until it was allocated to Iraq under the Treaty of Ankara in 1926. The author argues that Britain was not only concerned to retain Mosul province for the oil, but also sought to defend the economic and political interests of Iraq as a state.

174 **The letters.**
Gertrude Bell, selected and edited by Lady F. Bell.   London: Benn,
1927, rp. Harmondsworth, England: Penguin, 1987. 626p.

Gertrude Bell was appointed Oriental Secretary to the British High Commissioner in Iraq in 1915 and spent the rest of her life in Iraq. She took a particular interest in the antiquities of the country, in addition to her official duties. This book contains letters written between 1874 and 1926 from the Middle East, of which those from 1917-26 were from Baghdad, where she died in 1927. The introduction is by Jan Morris.

175 **Kurds, Turks and Arabs: politics, travel and research in north-eastern Iraq 1919-1925.**
C. J. Edmonds.   London: Oxford University Press, 1957. 440p. maps.

A vivid picture of political intrigue and socio-economic conditions in Iraqi Kurdistan after the First World War, based on the author's own experiences as a British Political Officer.

176    **Wartime in Baghdad 1917. Eleanor Franklin Egan's** *The war in the cradle of the world.*
Eleanor Franklin Egan.    New York, 1918; London, 1919,
rp. Cambridge: Allborough, 1991. 312p.
Reprint of an account by an American journalist who witnessed the British invasion of Mesopotamia in 1917, with a new Introduction.

177    **Arabian adventures: ten years of joyful service.**
John Glubb.    London: Cassell, 1978. 217p. maps.
A personal account of his time as a British officer serving with the Royal Engineers in southern Iraq from 1920 to 1930, in the early years of British rule.

178    **A soldier in Kurdistan: Rupert Hay's** *Two years in Kurdistan* **with an introduction by Paul Rich.**
Rupert Hay.    London: Sidgwick & Jackson, 1921, rp. Cambridge:
Allborough, 1991. 324p.
A reprint with a new Introduction of the personal account of his experiences administering the largely Kurdish region of Arbil for the Indian Political Service from 1918 to 1920. The British tried to create a civil administration in the area after the collapse of Ottoman rule.

179    **ʿIraq: a study in political development.**
Philip Willard Ireland.    London: Cape, 1937. 471p. maps. bibliog.
A detailed account of the domestic political scene in Iraq during the First World War and under British rule up to the formal termination of the Mandate in 1932. It is still useful for its intimate description of the personalities, both British and Iraqi, and the intricate political manoeuvrings of the period.

180    **'Only by the sword': British counter-insurgency in Iraq, 1920.**
Mark Jacobsen.    *Small Wars and Insurgencies*, vol. 2, no. 2 (August
1991), p. 323-63.
Jacobsen discusses the nationwide revolt against Britain which broke out in Iraq in 1920, and which required approximately four divisions of British and Indian troops six months to stamp out.

181    **Arabic source material for the political history of modern Iraq.**
Rasheeduddin Khan.    *International Studies*, vol. 2 (1961),
p. 298-316.
A survey of primary source material in Arabic in the form of official publications, documentary material published by semi-governmental or private institutions, diaries and memoirs, and secondary sources such as newspapers for the period 1914-58.

182 **Iraq and imperialism: Thomas Lyell's *The ins and outs of
Mesopotamia.***
Thomas Lyell, with an introduction by Paul Rich. London, 1923,
rp. Cambridge: Allborough, 1991. 192p.

A reprint with a new Introduction of the account by Thomas Lyell of the occupation
of Iraq by the British following the invasion of Mesopotamia during the First World
War. Paul Rich describes it as 'outrageously prejudiced and bigoted'. In spite of its
author's convictions, it provides a view of the state of Iraq, and British activities at
the time.

183 **Imperial quest for oil: Iraq 1910-1928.**
Helmut Mejcher. London: Ithaca, for the Middle East Centre,
St. Antony's College, Oxford, 1976. 183p. bibliog.

An account of the period during which Britain's interest in Iraqi oil was consolidated,
British power and rule over the country was established, and Iraq's northern boundary
was finally determined so that the oil-bearing region around Mosul was allocated to
Iraq and came under British control.

184 **Iraq's external relations 1921-26.**
Helmut Mejcher. *Middle Eastern Studies*, vol. 13, no. 3 (October
1977), p. 340-58.

A study of Iraq's place in Britain's strategic plans in the Middle East, and of the
struggle of Iraq's government to gain some control of power in spite of Britain's
determination to retain its dominance.

185 **The Churchill–Cox correspondence regarding the creation of the
State of Iraq: consequences for British policy towards the
nationalist Turkish government, 1921-1923.**
Robert Olson. *International Journal of Turkish Studies*, vol. 5, no. 1
& 2 ( Winter 1990-91), p. 121-36.

Winston Churchill, as British Colonial Secretary in 1921, evidently favoured the
creation of a separate state in Kurdistan after the end of the First World War, but Sir
Percy Cox, the British Resident in the Persian Gulf who was setting up a new state in
Mesopotamia under British auspices, won the argument for incorporating the oil-
bearing areas north of Mosul into the British-administered state of Iraq.

186 **Britain in Iraq, 1914-1932.**
Peter Sluglett. London: Ithaca Press, for the Middle East Centre,
St. Antony's College, Oxford, 1976. 331p. maps. bibliog.

A standard text providing an assessment of Anglo-Iraqi relations and Britain's role in
Iraqi affairs during the British military occupation of Iraq and the Mandate period.
Part one is headed 'Iraq under British occupation and mandate'; Part two 'Aspects of
policy and administration'.

187 **Supremacy and oil: Iraq, Turkey and the Anglo-American world order, 1918-1930.**
William Stivers. Ithaca, NY: Cornell University Press, 1982. 199p. map. bibliog.

Stivers charts the course of the competition between Great Britain and the United States for control over Iraqi oil, and their response to rising forces of nationalism in Iraq and Turkey after the First World War.

188 **The struggle for Dayr al-Zur: the determination of borders between Syria and Iraq.**
Eliezer Tauber. *International Journal of Middle East Studies*, vol. 23, no. 3 (1991), p. 361-85.

Describes the skirmishing which took place in the Dayr al-Zur area of eastern Syria between 1918 and 1920 when Iraqi nationalists serving the Arab government of King Faysal in Damascus took steps to ensure that the region should become part of independent Arab (as it then was) Syria, rather than part of British-controlled Iraq. In Ottoman times the area had formed part of the Iraqi province, and today it is part of the modern state of Syria.

189 **The 1920 revolt in Iraq reconsidered: the role of tribes in national politics.**
Amal Vinogradov. *International Journal of Middle East Studies*, vol. 3, no. 2 (April 1972), p. 123-39.

Re-examines the origins of the revolt against British rule in 1920 and the methods by which Britain sought to repress it and to install a Arab government through which it could exercise control.

190 **The clash of cultures in Iraq after the First World War.**
Ali Wardi. *Rocznik Orientalistyczny*, vol. 43 (1984), p. 171-78.

A sociological analysis of the impact on Iraqis of the opening up of the country to European civilization after the First World War, in contrast to the very limited contact previously experienced.

191 **Loyalties: Mesopotamia, 1914-1917, a personal historical record.**
Sir Arnold Wilson. London: 1930, rp. New York: Greenwood, 1969. 323p.

A personal account of a senior British official's involvement in the military and political events which culminated in the capture of Baghdad from the Ottomans and occupation of lower Iraq by the British in the First World War.

192 **Mesopotamia 1917-1920: a clash of loyalties, a personal and historical record.**
Sir Arnold Wilson. Oxford: Oxford University Press, 1931. 400p. map.

A first-hand account by a British official of the British victories in Iraq during the First World War and their political consequences for Iraq and the dispute over Mosul with the Turks.

193   **Gertrude Bell.**
H. V. F. Winstone.   London: Constable, 1993. 298p. maps. bibliog.
First published in 1978 by Cape, this paperback edition is revised with a new Preface.
This is a detailed study of Gertrude Bell's life which includes her travels in
Mesopotamia, and later career as Oriental Secretary to the British administration in
Baghdad in which she played an instrumental role in defining the boundaries of
modern Iraq and setting up a government and political system.

**Oil and empire: British policy and Mesopotamian oil 1900-1920.**
*See* item no. 157.

**ᵒIraq, 1900 to 1950: a political, social, and economic history.**
*See* item no. 213.

# British and Hashimi rule 1917-58

194   **The elections for the constituent assembly in Iraq, 1922-4.**
M. M. al-Adhami.   In: *The integration of modern Iraq*, edited by
Abbas Kelidar.   London: Croom Helm, 1979, p. 13-31.
The author examines the first elections held in Iraq under the British Mandate
established in 1920 and the difficulties encountered in holding them.

195   **The intellectual origins and ideas of the Ahali group.**
Mudhafar Amin, Edmund Ghareeb.   In: *Law, personalities, and
politics of the Middle East: essays in honor of Majid Khadduri*, edited
by J. Piscatori, G. S. Harris.   Boulder, CO: Westview Press & Middle
East Institute, 1987, p. 140-65.
Discusses the emergence of the Ahali group which appeared on the Iraqi political
scene in 1932 with the publication of its newspaper, and which, according to the
authors, represented the 'first Iraqi group to articulate a well-developed ideology
linked to a strong social conscience and a concept of economic progress'.

196   **Iraq: the Fertile Crescent dimension.**
H. G. Balfour-Paul.   In: *Iraq: the contemporary state*, edited by Tim
Niblock.   London: Croom Helm; New York: St. Martin's Press, 1982,
p. 7-26.
Discusses the idea of the Fertile Crescent (stretching in an arc from Basra to
Beersheba) as a political concept in Iraqi perspectives between 1920 and the
revolution of 1958.

197 **Incertain Irak: tableau d'un royaume avant la tempête,
1914-1953.** (Uncertain Iraq: portrait of a kingdom before the storm
1914-53).
Jacques Dauphin.   Paris: Geuthner, 1991. 259p. map. bibliog.
Written by an Agence France Presse journalist who was posted to Baghdad in 1950,
this gives a general picture of Iraq in the first half of the 20th century.

198 **Three kings in Baghdad, 1921-1958.**
Gerald De Gaury.   London: Hutchinson, 1961. 223p. map. bibliog.
A history of the Hashimi dynasty in Iraq: Faysal I, Ghazi, and Faysal II. The Hashimi
kings were installed by the British, and the 1958 revolution overthrew the monarchy
and created a republic.

199 **Iraqi politics and regional policies, 1945-49.**
Michael Eppel.   *Middle Eastern Studies*, vol. 28, no. 1 (January
1992), p. 108-19.
Examines the trends and contradictions in Iraq's foreign policy between the formation
of the Arab League in 1945 and the coming of the Cold War to the Middle East in
1949, and argues that Nuri al-Said played a dominant role in policy formation, even
when out of office and acting behind the scenes.

200 **Iraq under General Nuri: my recollection of Nuri al-said,
1954-1958.**
Waldemar J. Gallman.   Baltimore, MD: Johns Hopkins, 1964. 231p.
bibliog.
Written by the American Ambassador to Iraq during the period 1954-58. He
evidently respected Nuri al-Said's achievements as ruler of Iraq, and wrote this
political memoir of the period.

201 **Prerevolutionary Iraq in the light of contemporary Iraqi
historiography.**
Eduard Gombár.   *Archiv Orientalni*, vol. 58, no. 2 (1990), p. 152-55.
A review article discussing the view of 20th-century Iraq offered by Iraqi
historiography, writing both in English and in Arabic.

202 **Rashid Ali al-Gailani and the Nationalist Movement in Iraq 1939-
1941: a political and military study of the British campaign in Iraq
and the national revolution of May 1941.**
Walid M. S. Hamdi.   London: Darf, 1987. 265p. maps. bibliog.
A detailed account of the Iraqi nationalist revolt in 1941, its leader Rashid Ali al-
Gaylani and the consequences of their attempt to overthrow British rule. Based on the
author's PhD thesis.

203 **Road through Kurdistan: the narrative of an engineer in Iraq.**
A. M. Hamilton. London: Faber & Faber, 1958. rev. ed. 251p. maps.
First published in 1937, this is an account by the engineer in charge of building the
road from Arbil to Rowanduz through the mountains of Kurdistan, a task which was
begun in 1928. It includes much on the local politics and social tensions of the area at
the time.

204 **The Third Reich and the Arab East.**
Łukasz Hirszowicz. London: Routledge & Kegan Paul, 1966. 381p.
bibliog.
Originally published in Polish, this account deals with Nazi Germany's relations with
all the eastern Arab countries, but for Iraq see in particular: chapters 6, 'Iraq on the
eve of rebellion'; 7, 'The Germans and the Iraq revolt'; and 8, ' Uprising in Iraq' on
p. 95-172. The author argues that because of Hitler's attack on the Soviet Union, Iraqi
nationalists received little aid from Germany to compensate for the weakness of the
Iraqi army during the nationalist uprising of 1941. As a result Germany failed to gain
an ally and lost an opportunity in wartime Iraq.

205 **Social structures and the new state 1921-1958.**
Derek Hopwood. In: *Iraq: power and society*, edited by Derek
Hopwood, Habib Ishow, Thomas Koszinowski. Oxford: Ithaca, for
St. Antony's College, 1993, p. 1-17.
A useful survey of social and political developments in Iraq under British (and
Hashimi) rule.

206 **The Assyrian affair of 1933.**
Khaldun S. Husry. *International Journal of Middle East Studies*,
vol. 5, no. 2 (April 1974), p. 161-76; vol. 5, no. 3 (June 1974),
p. 344-60.
Challenges the accepted presentation of the massacre of Assyrian Christians in Iraq in
1933 just after Independence. The author discusses the local background and the
recruitment of the Assyrian refugees from Turkey into the British forces, a factor
which soured their relations with the population of Iraq. See also the response to this
article by John Joseph, 'The Assyrian affair: a historical perspective', in vol. 6, no 1
(January 1975), p. 115-17.

207 **The political ideas of Yunis al-Sab'awi.**
Khaldun S. al-Husry. In: *Intellectual life in the Arab East*, edited by
Marwan R. Buheiry. Beirut: American University of Beirut, 1981,
p. 165-75.
Yunis al-Sab'awi was born in Mosul on 24 March 1910 into a poor family. He entered
politics, rising to become Minister of Economics in Rashid 'Ali al-Gaylani's
nationalist cabinet in 1941, but was captured by the British in Iran after the fall of
Gaylani, and hanged by the authorities in Baghdad on 5 May 1942. This essay
considers his political ideas, and his view of politics in Iraq.

208 **The Baghdad Pact: Cold War or colonialism?**
Richard L. Jasse. *Middle Eastern Studies*, vol. 27, no. 1 (January 1991), p. 140-56.
Jasse argues that Great Britain's motive in setting up the mutual assistance pact signed by Iraq and Turkey in February 1955, joined by Britain in April 1955 and commonly known as the 'Baghdad Pact' was the maintenance of its strategic paramountcy in the Middle East.

209 **Anti-Shiism in Iraq under the monarchy.**
Elie Kedourie. *Middle Eastern Studies*, vol. 24, no. 2 (April 1988), p. 249-53.
Presents a memorandum dispatched to the Foreign Office by Sir Henry Mack from Baghdad on 13 December 1950 describing increasing Shiʿi discontent with their subordinate position in the State during the last years of the monarchy. A short article which is effectively an appendix to this item was published by the same author as 'The Shiʿite issue in Iraqi politics, 1941' in *Middle Eastern Studies*, vol. 24, no. 4 (October 1988), p. 495-500.

210 **Confidential U.S. diplomatic post records: Middle East Iraq, 1925-1941.**
Edited by Paul Kesaris. Frederick, MD: University Publications of America, 1984. 24 microfilm reels, printed guide, 45p.
Documents from the records of the US State Department files of station reports from Iraq on the country's political, social and economic affairs. Further sets of the diplomatic post records for Iraq have been made available on microfilm for the years *1942-44*, and *1945-54*.

211 **Independent Iraq, 1932-58: a study in Iraqi politics.**
Majid Khadduri. Oxford: Oxford University Press for the Royal Institute of International Affairs, 1960. 2nd ed. 381p. map.
A study of domestic politics in the era immediately after Iraq became officially independent, but was still much under British influence. The appendixes contain documents.

212 **The use of German and British archives in the study of the Middle East: the Iraqi *coup d'état* of 1936.**
H. H. Kopietz. In: *The integration of modern Iraq*, edited by Abbas Kelidar. London: Croom Helm, 1979, p. 46-62.
Kopietz discusses the nature of German archive material and in particular sources concerning the *coup d'état* in Iraq in 1936, with whose perpetrators the German Ambassador, Dr F. Grobba, was in close contact.

213  **'Iraq, 1900 to 1950: a political, social, and economic history.**
Stephen Hemsley Longrigg.   Oxford: Oxford University Press for the
Royal Institute of International Affairs, 1953. rp. 1956. 400p. map.
bibliog.

A general history of Iraq during the last years of Ottoman rule, and under the British.
The author was at one time an official in the British administration of Iraq. The work
is becoming somewhat dated.

214  **Axioms reconsidered: the rethinking of British strategic policy in
Iraq during the 1930s.**
Liora Lukitz.   In: *Britain and the Middle East in the 1930s: security
problems, 1935-39*, edited by Michael J. Cohen, Martin Kolinsky.
Basingstoke, England: Macmillan, in association with King's College,
1992, p. 113-27.

Reviews changing British–Iraqi relations in the 1930s when Britain was determined
to retain part of its Air Force in Iraq in order to secure its strategic interests and
control. It was this that drove Iraqi nationalists to stage a coup in 1941 and to
cooperate with the Germans from 1936 onwards.

215  **The development of a nationalist ideology in Iraq, 1920-1941.**
Phebe Marr.   *Muslim World*, vol. 75, no. 2 (April 1985), p. 85-101.

Examines the origins, development, and content of the Arab nationalist ideology
which was dominant in Iraq during the period of British rule. This article also
considers the means by which this ideology was institutionalized in Iraq's education
system, thereby perpetuating its influence.

216  **The modern history of Iraq.**
Phebe Marr.   London: Longman; Boulder, CO: Westview, 1985.
341p. maps. bibliog.

A detailed history of the period from 1920 to the 1980s told chronologically and
divided in the following manner: 1920-1932; 1932-1945; 1946-1958; 1958-1963;
1963-1968. The final chapter 'The Ba'th in power' takes the account up to the early
years of the Iran–Iraq war.

217  **Air power and colonial control: the Royal Air Force 1919-1939.**
David E. Omissi.   Manchester: Manchester University Press, 1990.
244p. maps. bibliog.

Explores the relationship between British air power and indirect imperialism. The
British created an Arab monarchy in Iraq in order to deflect nationalist Iraqi criticism
of British rule and to provide the political preconditions for a reduction in British
military spending. The British Air Force was able to quell local unrest by bombing
rebellious villages without the need for expensive British ground troops. Britain was
thereby able to suppress rebellion against the Arab King and keep him in power and
the Air Force was able to demonstrate its usefulness to British politicians and ensure
its own future as an independent service. See, in particular, Chapter 2: 'Iraq and the
survival of the RAF 1920-25' (p. 18-38).

218 **Iraq: international relations and national development.**
Edith Penrose, E. F. Penrose.  London: Benn, 1978. 548p. bibliog.
Sets out to interpret the political and economic development of Iraq from its
foundation as a state. Part 1 'A new state is formed'; part 2 'The years of an
independent monarchy'; part 3 'The 14th July revolution, 1958-63'; part 4 'Post-
Revolutionary Iraq: political developments after February 1963'; part 5 'Economic
policy after 1963'; part 6 'The summing up'.

219 **From elite to class: the transformation of Iraqi political
leadership.**
David Pool.  In: *The integration of modern Iraq*, edited by Abbas
Kelidar.  London: Croom Helm, 1979, p. 63-87.
Analyses the political system in Iraq before 1958 and the transformation of a ruling
élite into a ruling class operating the political institutions in its own political and
economic interest. On a similar theme see the author's article 'From elite to class: the
transformation of Iraqi leadership 1920-1939' in *International Journal of Middle East
Studies*, vol. 12, no. 3 (November 1980), p. 331-50.

220 **Power elite in Iraq – 1920-1958.**
Ayad al-Qazzaz.  *Muslim World*, vol. 51, no. 4 (October 1971),
p. 267-83.
The author analyses the educational and social background of the cabinet members of
the monarchic period and concludes that the élite which dominated the scene was a
small one which was largely blind to the feelings of the ordinary people and to the
problems of the large Shi'i population of Iraq.

221 **Faisal's ambitions of leadership in the Fertile Crescent:
aspirations and constraints.**
A. Shikara.  In: *The integration of modern Iraq*, edited by Abbas
Kelidar.  London: Croom Helm, 1979, p. 32-45.
Shikara discusses King Faysal's attitudes and role in the Arab nationalist movement
from 1916 to 1930 and his efforts to achieve Iraqi–Syrian unity between 1930 and
1933.

222 **Iraqi politics 1921-41: the interaction between domestic politics
and foreign policy.**
Ahmed Abdul Razzaq Shikara.  London: LAAM, 1987. 208p.
bibliog.
Describes the efforts made by King Faysal to develop a unified Iraqi state with some
political equilibrium, and the manner in which it was shattered after his death in 1933
by infighting among his supporters and the ruling élite. At the same time, the
emergence of new political forces advocating Arab nationalist and anti-British
politics was characterized by a series of coups from 1936 to 1941.

223 **Britain's informal empire in the Middle East: a case study of Iraq, 1929-1941.**
Daniel Silverfarb. New York: Oxford University Press, 1986. 184p. map. bibliog.

An account of Anglo-Iraqi relations from the time of Britain's decision in 1929 to grant Iraq independence until the conclusion of hostilities between the two countries in 1941. The author tries to show how Britain attempted to maintain its political influence, economic ascendancy and strategic position in Iraq after granting independence.

224 **Iraq between the two world wars: the creation and implementation of a nationalist ideology.**
Reeva S. Simon. New York: Columbia University Press, 1986. 209p. bibliog.

Discusses why a group of army officers who had seized control in Iraq in 1941 proceeded to launch a disastrous and futile war against Britain while seeking support from Germany.

225 **The role of the military in politics: a case study of Iraq to 1941.**
Mohammad A. Tarbush. London: Kegan Paul International, 1982. 268p. map. bibliog.

This study of the political history of Iraq in the first two decades after its creation in 1921 analyses the reasons for the Iraqi army's involvement in politics and coups from 1931 to 1941.

**Iraq: its people, its society, its culture.**
*See* item no. 4.

**The historiography of modern Iraq.**
*See* item no. 146.

**Arabic source material for the political history of modern Iraq.**
*See* item no. 181.

**Britain in Iraq, 1914-1932.**
*See* item no. 186.

**Jordan and Iraq: efforts at intra-Hashemite unity.**
*See* item no. 313.

**Nuri al-Saʿid's Arab unity programme.**
*See* item no. 317.

**The Kurdish revolt: 1961-1970.**
*See* item no. 444.

**The photography of Kamil Chadirji 1920-1940: social life in the Middle East.**
*See* item no. 514.

**The Iraq Development Board and British policy, 1945-50.**
*See* item no. 587.

**The Iraq Development Board: administration and program.**
*See* item no. 589.

**Economic policy in Iraq 1932-1950.**
*See* item no. 608.

**The role of foreign trade in the economic development of Iraq, 1864-1964.**
*See* item no. 616.

**Anglo-Japanese competition in the textile trade in the inter-war period . . . 1932-1941.**
*See* item no. 621.

# The Revolution and Ba'th rule 1958-

226 **Iraq reborn: a firsthand acount of the July 1958 revolution and after.**
Ismail al-Arif. New York: Vantage, 1982. 117p.
An account of the 1958 Revolution in Iraq, its motivation and the ambitions of the Free Officers who led it. The author also considers the Free Officers' endeavours to ensure that Iraq moved in a new direction. The story is written in the third person by one of the Colonels who took part in the plot.

227 **Culture, history and ideology in the formation of Ba'thist Iraq, 1968-89.**
Amatzia Baram. Basingstoke, England: Macmillan, in association with St. Antony's College, Oxford, 1991. 182p. bibliog.
This study of Ba'th rule in Iraq discusses the Ba'th Party's use of folklore and ancient Mesopotamian culture to build a local Iraqi nationalist identity in place of the emphasis on Pan-Arabism and supra-national ideology which characterized the early years of the Party's rule.

228 **The Egyptian, Syrian and Iraqi revolutions: some observations on their underlying causes and social character.**
Hanna Batatu. Washington, DC: Center for Contemporary Arab Studies, Georgetown University, [1984]. 29p.
Batatu compares the social and political background of the revolutions in Egypt, Syria and Iraq. He then examines the impact they had on various sectors of society in their respective countries, and the benefits they brought to different groups.

229 **Ba'thi Iraq in search of identity: between ideology and praxis.**
Ofra Bengio. *Orient* (Opladen), vol. 28, no. 4 (December 1987),
p. 511-18.
Bengio considers the Ba'th regime's attempts to tackle Iraq's lack of collective
national identity and its approach to more concrete political, socio-economic and
ideological problems of government.

230 **The development of internal politics in Iraq from 1958 to the
present day.**
May Chartouni-Dubarry. In: *Iraq: power and society*, edited by
Derek Hopwood, Habib Ishow, Thomas Koszinowski. Oxford:
Ithaca, for St. Antony's College, 1993, p. 19-36.
The author describes the military regime brought to power by the Revolution of 1958,
the later coups and the rise of the Ba'th Party.

231 **Iraq under Qassem: a political history 1958-1963.**
Uriel Dann. London: Praeger, 1969. 380p. maps. bibliog.
A detailed study of the political background and of developments in the political
scene during 'Abd al-Karim Qasim's regime from 1958 to its downfall in 1963.

232 **Iraq since 1958: from revolution to dictatorship.**
Marion Farouk-Sluglett, Peter Sluglett. London: Tauris, 1990.
new ed. 326p. bibliog.
First published by KPI in 1987, the new edition has an added postscript entitled 'Iraq
since 1986'. This is a solidly researched study of the political history of Iraq and its
domestic development since the revolution of 1958. It is organized chronologically
into periods: before 1958; 1958-63; 1963-68; 1968-72; 1972-75; 1975-80; Economy
and society since 1958; Epilogue: the war between Iraq and Iran.

233 **"Socialist" Iraq 1963-1978. Towards a reappraisal.**
Marion Farouk-Sluglett. *Orient* (Opladen), vol. 23, no. 2 (June
1982), p. 206-19.
Sets out to provide 'a preliminary assessment of the nature and consequences of the
"socialist" policies initiated by the various Iraqi governments which have come to power
since 1963, and in particular of the effect of these policies upon the private sector'.

234 **The Iraqi revolution of 1958: the old social classes revisited.**
Edited by Robert A. Fernea, Wm. Roger Louis. London: I.B. Tauris,
1991. 222p.
A collection of twelve essays which refer to the subject matter of Hanna Batatu's
book (item no. 513). The contents are: 'Contemporary perceptions of the revolution in
Iraq on 14 July 1958' by Norman Daniel (p. 1-30); 'The British and the origins of the
Iraqi revolution' by Wm Roger Louis (p. 31-61); 'Reflections on US foreign policy
towards Iraq in the 1950s' by Nicholas G. Thacher (p. 62-76); 'US support for the
British positions in pre-revolutionary Iraq' by Frederick W. Axelgard (p. 77-94); 'The
Soviet Union, the Great Powers & Iraq' by Joe Stork (p. 95-105); 'The impact of the

Iraqi revolution on the Arab world' by Rashid Khalidi (p. 106-17); 'The social classes and the origins of the revolution' by Marion Farouk-Sluglett and Peter Sluglett (p. 118-41); 'State and tribe in southern Iraq: the struggle for hegemony before the 1958 revolution' by Robert A. Fernea (p. 142-53); 'Class and class politics in Iraq before 1958: the "colonial and post-colonial state"' by Roger Owen (p. 154-71); 'The struggle for cultural hegemony during the Iraqi revolution' by Abdul-Salaam Yousif (p. 172-96); 'Community, class and minorities in Iraqi politics' by Sami Zubaida (p. 197-210); 'The old social classes revisited' by Hanna Batatu (p. 211-22).

235 **Iraq and the Kurdish question 1958-1970.**
Sa'ad Jawad. London: Ithaca Press, 1981. 349p. bibliog.
Based on a PhD thesis, this book provides a history of Iraqi attempts to deal with the rebellious Kurdish population of northern Iraq after the Iraqi Revolution of 1958. The book is organized chronologically and describes the differing attitudes to the problem taken by Qasim, 'Abd al-Salam 'Arif, 'Abd al-Rahman 'Arif and the Ba'th Party.

236 **Republican Iraq: a study in 'Iraqi politics since the revolution of 1958.**
Majid Khadduri. Oxford: Oxford University Press, for the Royal Institute of International Affairs, 1969. 305p. map.
Khadduri discusses the reasons for the fall of the old regime in 1958, and describes the new forces and élite which reshaped the political system after the Revolution.

237 **Socialist Iraq: a study in Iraqi politics since 1968.**
Majid Khadduri. Washington, DC: Middle East Institute, 1978. 260p.
Examines domestic political developments in Iraq, the success of the Arab Socialist Movement in attaining power under the aegis of the Ba'th Party and the subsequent power struggle among its leaders and ideological groups in the 1970s. The appendixes contain documents.

238 **Iraq: its revolutionary experience under the Ba'th.**
Phebe Marr. In: *Ideology and power in the Middle East: studies in honor of George Lenczowski*, edited by Peter J. Chelkowski, Robert J. Pranger. Durham, NC: Duke University Press, 1988, p. 185-209.
Surveys the changes which have taken place in Iraq under Ba'th rule, the institutionalization of the Party, the role of the political élite and of ideology, and the economic and social policies which have been implemented. The author concludes that 'Iraq in the 1980s is a very different country from what it was in the 1960s'.

239 **The beginning of parliamentary democracy in Iraq – a case study.**
Abida Samiuddin. *Middle Eastern Studies*, vol. 18, no. 4 (October 1982), p. 444-48.
Samiuddin considers the general elections for the National Assembly held in 1980 and concludes that nature of its composition and powers mean that the Assembly 'cannot be supposed to function as a deliberative body in the Western sense. It is more of a sounding board' and was intended to consolidate the leadership of the Ba'th Party in power.

240   **Irak: aux origines du régime militaire.** (Iraq: the beginning of the military regime.)
      Alaa Tahir.   Paris: L'Harmattan, 1989. 301p. maps. bibliog.
A detailed account of the Revolution of 14 July 1958, of the military regime of ʿAbd al-Karim Qasim, and the political struggles which culminated in the coup of 8 February 1963.

**The historiography of modern Iraq.**
*See* item no. 146.

**The modern history of Iraq.**
*See* item no. 216.

**Iraq: international relations and national development.**
*See* item no. 218.

**The Kurdish question in Iraq.**
*See* item no. 434.

**The anti-Jewish Farhūd in Baghdad, 1941.**
*See* item no. 481.

**The Jewish minority in Iraq: a comparative study of economic structure.**
*See* item no. 482.

**The connection between the bombings in Baghdad and the emigration of the Jews from Iraq: 1950-51.**
*See* item no. 484.

**Iraq and the legislation on Jewish emigration: March 1950.**
*See* item no. 485.

**Operation Babylon.**
*See* item no. 488.

**The transformation of land tenure and rural social structure . . . 1870-1958.**
*See* item no. 522.

**Iraq: the eternal fire: 1972 Iraqi oil nationalization in perspective.**
*See* item no. 628.

**Baathism in practice: agriculture, politics and political culture in Syria and Iraq.**
*See* item no. 668.

# The Iran–Iraq war 1980-88

241  **Khomeini's forgotten sons: the story of Iran's boy soldiers.**
Ian Brown.   London: Grey Seal, 1990. 187p.
Describes the appalling conditions in which teenaged Iranian soldiers who were taken
prisoner in the war (1980-88) were held in Iraq, often for several years. The author
worked for Terre des Hommes, a Swiss children's rights organization, which supplied
teachers and materials to educate and train these prisoners of war.

242  **The Gulf War: its origins, history and consequences.**
John Bulloch, Harvey Morris.   London: Methuen, 1989. 294p. map.
bibliog.
A political history of the Iran–Iraq war, considering the motives and driving forces
on either side, the progress of the military effort, and the diplomatic and political
moves.

243  **Iran and Iraq at war.**
Shahram Chubin, Charles Tripp.   London: Tauris, 1988, rp. 1991.
305p. map. bibliog.
Considers the domestic effect of the Iran–Iraq war on the two countries and the way
in which the nature of their societies affected the onset and conduct of the war in
terms of domestic politics, economy, and foreign relations. Appendixes give
chronologies of political and military events and data on the armed forces of each
country. Shahram Chubin also published 'The last phase of the Iran–Iraq war: from
stalemate to ceasefire' in *Third World Quarterly*, vol. 11, no. 1 (1989), p. 1-14.

244  **The lessons of modern war. Volume 2: The Iran–Iraq war.**
Anthony H. Cordesman.   Boulder, CO: Westview; London: Mansell,
1990. 600p. maps. bibliog.
This account by a military analyst and historian focuses on military events and
lessons of the Iran–Iraq war and discusses the political side only to the extent
necessary to understand the strategy and progress of the war.

245  **Oil on troubled waters: Gulf wars, 1980-91.**
John Creighton.   London: Echoes, 1992. 140p. maps.
An account of the Iraq–Iran war from 1980 to 1988 and of the subsequent invasion of
Kuwait in 1990 and the Allies' war against Iraq in 1991.

246  **The Gulf War of 1980-1988: the Iran–Iraq war in international
legal perspective.**
Edited by Ige F. Dekker, Harry H. G. Post.   Dordrecht,
The Netherlands: Nijhoff, 1992. 299p. bibliog.
A collective volume. Part 1 '*Casus belli* and the *ius ad bellum*' has: 'Border conflicts
between Iraq and Iran: review and legal reflections' by Harry Post (p. 7-50); ' "Ius
ad bellum": legal implications of the Iran–Iraq war' by Kaiyan Homi Kaikobad

(p. 51-94). Part two 'The *Ius in bello*' has: 'Prohibitions or restrictions on the use of methods and means of warfare' by Frits Kalshoven (p. 97-128); 'Combatants and non-combatants' by Paul Tavernier (p. 129-49). Part three 'Armed conflict at sea and neutrality' has: 'Targeting theory in the law of armed conflict at sea: the merchant vessel as a military objective in the tanker war' by Francis V. Russo, Jr (p. 153-204); 'Neutrality at sea' by Michael Bothe (p. 205-19); 'The law of neutrality: third states' commercial rights and duties' by A. Gioia, N. Ronzitti (p. 221-46). Part four 'Criminal responsibility: an Islamic international legal order?' has: 'Criminal responsibility and the Gulf War of 1980-1988: the crime of aggression' by Ige F. Dekker (p. 249-76); 'The Gulf War of 1980-1988 and the Islamic conception of international law' by Mohammed Bedjaoui (p. 277-99). The first eight chapters are followed by comments on the essays by other authors.

247  **The Iran–Iraq war: a bibliography.**
J. Anthony Gardner.  London: Mansell, 1988. 107p.
An annotated bibliography of the war, published shortly before it ended. It contains 509 entries in English and other Western languages, Arabic and Persian.

248  **The Iran–Iraq war (1980-1988) and the law of naval warfare.**
Andrea de Guttry, Natalino Ronzitti.  Cambridge: Grotius, 1993. 573p.
Collected documents and political statements relating to navigation and naval warfare during the Iran–Iraq war. Each part is introduced by a short commentary, and the parts are headed as follows: Introduction; Iran; Iraq; United States; United Kingdom; France; Italy; Belgium and the Netherlands; International organizations and other international forums.

249  **The longest war: the Iran–Iraq military conflict.**
Dilip Hiro.  London: Grafton, 1989, rp. 1990. 300p. maps.
A detailed account of the political and military developments of the Iran–Iraq war, 1980-88. Appendixes contain a detailed chronology, statistics and documents.

250  **Pakistan and the Iran–Iraq war.**
Suroosh Irfani.  *Journal of South Asian and Middle Eastern Studies*, vol. 9, no. 2 (Winter 1985), p. 55-66.
Pakistan maintained a position of neutrality throughout the Iran–Iraq war which it considered a futile struggle between Islamic states, one of which is a neighbour of Pakistan. The war threatened Pakistan's relations with the Arab states.

251  **The Persian Gulf war: lessons for strategy, law, and diplomacy.**
Edited by Christopher C. Joyner.  Westport, CT: Greenwood Press, 1990. 240p. map. bibliog. (Contributions in Military Studies, 99).
A collective volume about the Iran–Iraq war. The contents are: Introduction: 'The geography and geopolitics of the Persian Gulf' by the editor (p. 1-17); Part One 'Strategic and political dimensions' contains: 'The roots of crisis: Iraq and Iran' by Edmund Ghareeb (p. 21-38); 'Strategic and political objectives in the Gulf War: Iran's view' by Eric Hooglund (p. 39-58); 'The Iran–Iraq war: the view from Iraq' by

Phebe Marr (p. 59-73); 'Israel and the Iran–Iraq war' by Bernard Reich (p. 75-90); 'The Gulf Cooperation Council and the Gulf War' by Joseph A. Kechichian (p. 91-110); 'U.S. policy and the Gulf War: a question of means' by Thomas L. McNaugher (p. 111-25); 'The role of U.S. military force in the Gulf War' by Maxwell Orme Johnson (p. 127-38); 'Moscow and the Gulf War' by Mark N. Katz (p. 139-49). Part two 'Diplomatic and legal dimensions' contains: 'Choice and duty in foreign affairs: the reflagging of the Kuwaiti tankers' by David D. Caron (p. 153-72); 'The laws of maritime warfare and neutrality in the Gulf War' by Boleslaw Adam Boczek (p. 173-90); 'The role of the United Nations in the Iran–Iraq war' by Anthony Clark Avend (p. 191-208); 'Iran, Iraq, and the cease-fire negotiations: contemporary legal issues' by Charles C. Macdonald (p. 209-23); 'Peace and security in the Persian Gulf: a proposal' by R. K. Ramazani (p. 225-40). The 'Selected bibliography' is compiled by Bryan R. Daves (p. 241-46).

252 **Geopolitical determinism: the origins of the Iran–Iraq war.**
Efraim Karsh. *Middle East Journal*, vol. 44, no. 2 (Spring 1990), p. 256-68.
Karsh argues that the war began because Iraq, the weaker of the two states, attempted to resist Iran's hegemonic aspirations to reshape the region in its own revolutionary image, after the fall of the Shah. The war was the product of the immediate geopolitical situation, not merely of the historical antipathy of Iranians and Arabs.

253 **The Iran–Iraq war: impact and implications.**
Edited by Efraim Karsh. Basingstoke, England: Macmillan, in association with the Jaffee Center for Strategic Studies, Tel-Aviv University, 1989. 295p. bibliog.
Papers from a conference held in Tel Aviv in 1988, revised and updated after the end of the war in early 1989. Part 1: 'The war and the belligerents' contains: 'Iran and the war: from stalemate to ceasefire' by Shahram Chubin (p. 13-25); 'From ideological zeal to geopolitical realism: the Islamic republic and the Gulf' by Efraim Karsh (p. 26-41); 'Iran: doctrine and reality' by David Menashri (p. 42-57); 'The conse-quences of the Iran–Iraq war for Iraqi politics' by Charles Tripp (p. 58-77); 'Iraq: between East and West' by Amazia Baram (p. 78-97). Part 2 'Regional implications' contains: 'The impact on the Arab world' by Itamar Rabinovitch (p. 101-9); 'The war and the spread of Islamic fundamentalism' by Robin Wright (p. 110-20); 'The Gulf States and the Iran–Iraq war' by Barry Rubin (p. 121-32); 'The silent victor: Turkey's role in the Gulf War' by Henri J. Barkey (p. 133-53); 'Israel and the Iran–Iraq war' by Joseph Alpher (p. 154-68). Part 3 'The war and the world' contains: 'Walking tightropes in the Gulf' by Thomas L. McNaugher (p. 171-99); 'The Soviet Union and the Iran–Iraq war' by Robert S. Litwak (p. 200-14); 'Europe and the Iran–Iraq war' by John Chipman (p. 215-28). Part 4 'The economics of war' contains: 'Economic implications for the region and world oil market' by Eliahu Kanovsky (p. 231-52). Part 5 'Strategic and military implications' contains: 'A military-strategic overview' by Chaim Herzog (p. 255-68); 'The arms race after the Iran–Iraq war' by Geoffrey Kemp (p. 269-79); 'Escalation in the Iran–Iraq war' by Philip A. G. Sabin (p. 280-95).

### 254 The Gulf war: the origins and implications of the Iraq–Iran conflict.

Majid Khadduri.   New York: Oxford University Press, 1988. 230p.

Describes the historical background and cumulation of events leading to the outbreak of war in 1980 in the context of tension between the two countries ever since Iraq came into existence as a modern state. The Appendixes contain documents.

### 255 International mediation and the Gulf War.

Edited by Mohammed H. Malek.   Glasgow: Royston, 1991. 202p. maps. bibliog.

Contains: 'Iran–Iraq war: historical perspective and regional context' by Mohammed H. Malek (p. 1-35); 'The US military intervention in the Persian Gulf 1987-1988' by Mohammad E. Saify (p. 36-109); 'Iran–Iraq war: some legal issues' by S. H. Amin (p. 110-57); 'The Security Council and the Gulf War: a case study of double standards' by Mohammed H. Malek and Mark F. Imber (p. 158-202).

### 256 The Gulf war.

Edgar O'Ballance.   London: Brassey's, 1988. 217p. maps.

Written in 1987 just before the Iran–Iraq war ended, but the conclusions remain largely valid. This is an useful account of the course of the war by a military historian.

### 257 Iraq's military containment of Iran.

Andrew T. Parasiliti.   *Journal of South Asian and Middle Eastern Studies*, vol. 13, no. 1-2 (Fall/Winter 1989), p. 128-45.

Assesses the impact of the war with Iran on Iraq's domestic (political and economic) and foreign policies which were aimed at containing the Iranian revolution and enhancing Iraq's own status as a regional power. The author considers that Iraq regarded the 1989 ceasefire as a victory, since it had indeed contained the revolutionary threat from Iran, and that at that point Iraq's society showed more cohesion than ever before.

### 258 The Iran–Iraq war: chaos in a vacuum.

S. C. Pelletiere.   New York: Praeger, 1992. 154p. maps. bibliog.

Describes the origins and course of the war. A readable narrative of the events and the motivations of the participants.

### 259 The Iran–Iraq war: the politics of aggression.

Edited by Farhang Rajaee.   Gainesville: University Press of Florida, 1993. 227p.

Part one 'Genesis, development, and implication' contains: 'Iraqi attitudes and interpretation of the 1975 Agreement' by Ibrahim Anvari Tehrani (p. 11-23); 'Analyses of the risks of war: Iran–Iraq discord, 1979-1980' by Keith McLachlan (p. 24-31); 'The war of the cities' by S. Taheri Shemirani (p. 32-40); 'Cultural identity in danger' by Mehdi Hojjat (p. 41-46); 'The war's impact on Iraq' by Laith Kubba (p. 47-54); 'War and responsibility: governments or individuals?' by Abdolrahman Alem (p. 55-65). Part two 'Superpowers, international law, and politics' contains: 'The USSR and the Iran–Iraq war: from Brezhnev to Gorbachev' by Mohiaddin Mesbahi (p. 69-102); 'Saudi Arabia and the United States: partnership in the Persian Gulf' by A. Reza Sheikholeslami (p. 103-22); 'U.S. reflagging of Kuwaiti tankers' by Elizabeth Gamlen, Paul Rogers (p. 123-51); 'International law: observations and violations' by Bahman Baktiari (p. 152-66); 'The UN Secretary-General: attitudes and latitudes' by Paul Tavernier (p. 167-80). Part three 'Theoretical aspects and meaning' contains: 'The inherent right of individual self-defense in the Iran–Iraq war' by Djamchid Momtaz (p. 183-90); 'The problem of retaliation in modern warfare from the point of view of *fiqh*' by Hamid Algar (p. 191-97); 'Morale vs. technology: the power of Iran in the Persian Gulf war' by James A. Bill (p. 198-209); 'Aggression in historical perspective' by Richard Bulliet (p. 210-16); 'The need for modification and development of the laws in war in modern international law' by Saeid Mirzaee Yengejeh (p. 217-27).

260   **The Iran–Iraq war.**
      Behrouz Souresrafil.   Plainview, NY: Guinan Lithographic Co., 1989.
      165p. bibliog.
The author argues that Ayatollah Khomeini needed this war in 1980 in order to save his revolution and regime which had reached a dead end and was on the verge of collapse. The chapters deal with the reasons for the outbreak of war, the benefits to the Iranian regime, the forces in power and their role in the war, the ideological aspects of the war, and its consequences for the Muslim world.

261   **The Iran–Iraq war and the Iraqi state.**
      Charles Tripp.   In: *Iraq: power and society*, edited by Derek
      Hopwood, Habib Ishow, Thomas Koszinowski.   Oxford: Ithaca, for
      St. Antony's College, 1993, p. 91-115.
Tripp considers the nature of Saddam Husayn's rule and the means by which he mobilized the population in the long-drawn-out war against Iran.

**Iraq, the Gulf states & the war: a changing relationship 1980-1986 and beyond.**
*See* item no. 315.

**Saddam's closest ally: Jordan and the Gulf War.**
*See* item no. 324.

**The Soviet Union and the Iran–Iraq War, 1980-88.**
*See* item no. 339.

**The forgotten war: the Iraqi army and the Iran–Iraq war.**
*See* item no. 349.

**The Anfal Campaign in Iraqi Kurdistan . . .**
*See* item no. 424.

**Winds of death: Iraq's use of poison gas against its Kurdish population.**
*See* item no. 430.

**The economic consequences of the Gulf War.**
*See* item no. 600.

**Infitah, agrarian transformaton and elite consolidation in contemporary Iraq.**
*See* item no. 669.

# Invasion of Kuwait, Gulf War and aftermath 1990-91

262  **Report of Mr. Martti Ahtisaari concerning his visit to Iraq.**
Martti Ahtisaari.   New York: United Nations, 1991.
The official report to the United Nations by the mission sent to Iraq after the Gulf War of 1991 to report on the urgent humanitarian needs of Iraq. The report covers the areas of food and agriculture, water, sanitation and health, refugees and other vulnerable groups, logistics, transportation, communications and energy.

263  **The Gulf crisis: an attempt to understand.**
Ghazi A. Algosaibi.   London: Kegan Paul International, 1993. 156p.
An account of the Iraqi invasion of Kuwait, the positions taken in the Arab world, and the Arab political environment in which the Gulf war of 1991 was carried out. The author is a long-standing member of the Saudi political élite, and was Saudi Arabia's ambassador to Bahrain at the time of the crisis. This book provides an insider's view of the situation in the Arab world, Saddam's calculations and the reactions of other Arabs. First published in Arabic in 1991 as *Azmat al-Khalīj*.

264  **Crisis in the Arabian Gulf: an independent Iraqi view.**
Omar Ali.   Westport, CT: Praeger, 1993. 154p. bibliog.
Gives an account of the crisis following the Iraqi invasion of Kuwait in 1990 and the international response. The author argues that the crisis would not have been possible if the Iraqi and Kuwait governments had been less despotic and their citizens had been able to monitor and restrain the policies which led to Iraq's economic crisis and the desperate solution of taking over Kuwait.

265  **Iraq's road to war.**
Edited by Amatzia Baram, Barry Rubin.   Basingstoke, England: Macmillan, 1994. 291p.
A collective volume setting the invasion of Kuwait in the context of Iraq's political and economic situation in the years preceding it. Part one 'Iraq's politics, economics and society: why Iraq invaded Kuwait and lost the Gulf War' contains: 'The Iraqi invasion of Kuwait: decision-making in Baghdad' by Amatzia Baram (p. 5-36); 'Iraq's army: military weakness, political utility' by Mark A. Heller (p. 37-50); 'Iraq's Shi'a and Kurdish communities: from resentment to revolt' by Ofra Bengio (p. 51-66); 'Iraq's economy and international sanctions' by Patrick Clawson

(p. 69-83); 'Iraq and the world oil market: oil and power after the Gulf War' by Robert J. Lieber (p. 85-99). Part two 'Iraq's foreign relations' contains: 'Kuwait: confusing friend and foe' by Joseph Kostiner (p. 105-16); 'Saudi Arabia: the bank vault next door' by Jacob Goldberg (p. 117-34); 'Jordan's relations with Iraq: ally or victim' by Joseph Nevo (p. 135-48); 'Iraq and the PLO: brother's keepers, losers weepers' by Barry Rubin (p. 149-62); 'A modus vivendi challenged: the Arabs in Israel and the Gulf War' by Ilan Pappé (p. 163-75); 'Syria: Iraq's radical nemesis' by Michael Eppel (p. 177-89); 'Egypt in the Gulf crisis' by Yoram Meital (p. 191-202); 'Turkey: Iraq's European neighbour' by David Kushner (p. 205-17); 'Iran: war ended, hostility continued' by David Kushner (p. 219-31); 'Israel faces Iraq: the politics of confrontation' by Avner Yaniv (p. 233-51); 'The United States and Iraq: from appeasement to war' by Barry Rubin (p. 255-72); 'Western Europe and Iraq: the cases of France and West Germany' by Helmut Hubel (p. 273-85); 'The Gulf crisis in historical perspective' by P. J. Vatikiotis (p. 287-91).

## 266 Gulf crisis chronology.
Compiled by BBC World Service. Harlow, England: Longman, 1991. 287p.

The Preface states that the chronology is intended to provide a detailed record of the sequence of events. The time-span covered is from 2 August 1990, the date of Iraq's invasion of Kuwait, to 3 March 1991, when the ceasefire between allied and Iraqi military leaders was signed. There are detailed Name and Subject indexes, which include Iraqi leaders and Iraq. The chronology provides a succinct story of the unfolding of events, but does not attempt any evaluation or analysis.

## 267 America and the Iraqi crisis, 1990-1992.
Lester H. Brune. Claremont, CA: Regina Books, 1993. 188p. bibliog.

Brune discusses United States policy towards Iraq before and after the invasion of Kuwait in August 1990, and assesses American management of the crisis.

## 268 The Gulf conflict: a political and strategic analysis.
Roland Dannreuther. London: Brassey's, for the Institute for Strategic Studies, 1992. 88p. (Adelphi Paper, 264).

A concise and sober attempt to assess why Iraq invaded Kuwait in 1990, why the West and the Arab world failed to avert the invasion, what were the political and military objectives of the anti-Iraq coalition, and to what extent they were realized.

## 269 The Gulf conflict, 1990-1991: diplomacy and war in the new world order.
Lawrence Freedman, Efraim Karsh. London: Faber, 1993. 485p. maps. bibliog.

A scholarly study of the background to and immediate causes of the Iraqi invasion of Kuwait in August 1990, of the unfolding of the crisis and war in 1991, including its aftermath up to July 1991. This is probably the most considered account of events, with a dispassionate analysis.

270 **The Iraqi occupation of Kuwait: an eyewitness account.**
Shafeeq Ghabra. *Journal of Palestine Studies*, vol. 20, no. 2 / 78
(Winter 1991), p. 112-25.
An account of the invasion of Kuwait by a Palestinian who was living there at the time, and of his decision to leave after a brief experience of Iraqi rule.

271 **Endless torment: the 1991 uprising and its aftermath.**
Eric Goldstein, edited by Andrew Whitley. New York: Middle East
Watch, 1992. 66p.
A report based on interviews with Iraqi refugees which describes human rights abuses under the Iraqi regime, the repercussions of the failed uprising in the south and the outcome of the uprisings in the north. See also the short report *Unquiet graves: the search for the disappeared in Iraqi Kurdistan* by Eric Stover, edited by Andrew Whitley (New York: Middle East Watch & Physicians for Human Rights, 1992) which attempts to document deaths in Iraqi Kurdistan at the hands of the Iraqi government during the 1980s from evidence uncovered after Kurdish autonomy was effectively achieved in 1991.

272 **Iraq, the Gulf conflict and the world community.**
Edited by James Gow. London: Brassey's, for the Centre for
Defence Studies, 1993. 200p. map.
The volume is described as a set of case-studies, written shortly after the end of the war in 1991, which show the differing perspectives which shaped the international response to the Gulf conflict. The contents are: 'Introduction' by James Gow (p. 1-15); 'Iraq and the war for Kuwait' by Charles Tripp (p. 16-33); 'American objectives in the crisis' by Jo-Anne Hart (p. 34-54); 'The Arab states and the Middle East balance of power' by Anoushiravan Ehteshami (p. 55-73); 'Reactions in North America' by George Joffé (p. 74-88); 'Europeans, the EC and the Gulf' by Trevor C. Salmon (p. 89-106); 'An Iranian perspective' by Elahe Mohtasham (p. 107-20); 'The Soviet involvement' by James Gow (p. 121-37); 'The military option' by Julian Thompson (p. 138-61); 'The economic implications' by Susan Willett (p. 162-82); 'The war and the New World Order' by Lawrence Freedman (p. 183-200).

273 **The Gulf War: how many Iraqis died?**
John G. Heidenrich. *Foreign Policy*, no. 90 (1993), p. 108-25.
Heidenrich assesses the evidence and argues that the loss of life among Iraqi soldiers and civilians during the 1991 Gulf War was considerably lower than the widely quoted estimate of 100,000 Iraqi dead.

274 **Illusions of triumph: an Arab view of the Gulf War.**
Mohamed Heikal. London: HarperCollins, 1992. 338p.
An assessment of the causes of Iraq's invasion of Kuwait in 1990, the diplomatic and political run-up to the crisis, Arab and other attempts to mediate, and Arab responses to the West's victory. Mohamed Heikal is an Egyptian journalist.

275 **Desert Shield to Desert Storm: the second Gulf War.**
Dilip Hiro. London: HarperCollins, 1992. 560p. maps. bibliog.
An account of the development of the international crisis after the invasion of Kuwait
by Iraq in 1990 and the war against Iraq in 1991, with a detailed narrative of political
and military events.

276 **Martyrs' day: chronicle of a small war.**
Michael Kelly. London: Macmillan London, 1993, 354p. map.
Described as an 'impressionistic account' of the Gulf War of 1991 intended to convey
some feeling of the 'oddities and terrors of even a modest war', this book grew out of
the author's four long visits to the region between November 1990 and November
1991 as a free-lance writer covering events leading up to the war, the war itself and
its aftermath. He also attempts to give some impression of local attitudes to the war.

277 **The Kuwait crisis: basic documents.**
Edited by E. Lauterpacht. Cambridge: Grotius, 1991. 330p. map.
(Cambridge International Documents Series, 1).
Reproduces texts of relevant documents, including background material on border
delineation, and the United Nations' reaction to the invasion of Kuwait in 1990.
Further volumes of documents were published as *The Kuwait crisis: sanctions and
their economic consequences*, edited by D. L. Bethlehem, 1991 (Cambridge
International Documents Series, 2), and *Iraq and Kuwait: the hostilities and their
aftermath*, edited by M. Weller, 1993 (Cambridge International Documents Series, 3).

278 **Cruelty and silence: war, tyranny, uprising, and the Arab world.**
Kanan Makiya. London: Cape; New York: Norton, 1993. 357p.
An indictment of the Iraqi regime, of its brutality, despotism and disregard of the
most elementary human rights, and in particular of its behaviour in crushing the
uprising in southern Iraq after the Gulf War of 1991. The author also castigates those
Arab intellectuals who supported Saddam Husayn during the crisis. This author, here
publishing under his own name, published his earlier books under the pseudonym of
Samir al-Khalil.

279 **The Gulf conflict and international relations.**
K. Matthews. London: Routledge, 1993. 325p. maps.
An international relations perspective on the Gulf War of 1991, written with the
objective of understanding the motives of the actors and the reasons for the choices
made during the crisis and war.

280 **Crisis in the Gulf: enforcing the rule of law.**
John Norton Moore. New York: Oceana, 1992. 633p. maps.
(Terrorism: Documents of International & Local Control, first volume,
second series).
A monograph by a specialist in international law which analyses the illegality of
Iraq's actions in Kuwait, the legality of the international response and the terms on
which the conflict was ended. The appendixes on pages 399-633 contain texts of
relevant documents.

281 **Der Golfkrieg (1990/91). Eine Auswahlbibliographie.** (The Gulf
War (1990/91): a selected bibliography.)
Ingeborg Otto, Marianne Schmidt-Dumont. Hamburg: Deutsches
Übersee-Institut, 1992. 288p. (Dokumentationsdienst Vorderer Orient /
Near and Middle East Documentation Service, Reihe/Series A, 20).

An annotated bibliography of 288 items in Western languages and in Arabic about the
invasion of Kuwait and the 1991 Gulf War, with an introduction in German. There are
indexes of authors and of periodicals cited.

282 **The Gulf War assessed.**
John Pimlott, Stephen Badsey and members of the Department of War
Studies, Royal Military Academy, Sandhurst. London: Arms &
Armour, 1992. 278p. maps.

A sober assessment of the military operations and political conduct of the Gulf War
against Iraq. The contents are: 'Saddam Hussein and the Iraqi army' by Sean
McKnight (p. 13-34); 'The Gulf crisis and world politics' by John Pimlott (p. 35-56);
'The doctrines of the coalition forces' by Stephen Badsey (p. 57-79); 'The build-up'
by Duncan Anderson (p. 81-104); 'The air war' by Ray Sibbald (p. 105-24); 'The
naval war' by Andrew Lambert (p. 125-46); 'The land war' by Francis Toase (p. 147-
72); 'The failure of the Iraqi forces' by Sean McKnight (p. 173-92); 'The
international ramifications' by John Pimlott (p. 193-217); 'The media war' by
Stephen Badsey (p. 219-45); 'The Gulf War and the environment' by Ray Sibbald
(p. 247-59); 'Conclusion' (p. 261-73). Each chapter is followed by a list of 'Further
reading', and at the end of the book is a 'Chronology of the Gulf crisis and war'.

283 **Invasion Kuwait: an Englishwoman's tale.**
Jehan S. Rajab. London: Radcliffe, 1993. 204p.

An eye-witness account of the Iraqi invasion of Kuwait in August 1990, and
subsequent problems of life under Iraqi rule by an resident English citizen.

284 **Hollow victory: a contrary view of the Gulf War.**
Jeffrey Record. Washington, DC: Brassey's (US), 1993. 172p.
bibliog.

The author discusses the broader political, military and strategic issues raised by the
Gulf War of 1991 and its aftermath from a critical perspective.

285 **The Gulf war aftermath: an environmental tragedy.**
Muhammad Sadiq, John C. McCain, Texas Christian University.
Dordrecht, The Netherlands: Kluwer, 1993. 278p. (Environment &
Assessment, 4).

Assesses the impact of the war on the marine environment, the impact of the Kuwait
oil fires and military operations on air pollution and land resources, and the general
cost of the war to human health.

286    **Secret dossier: the hidden agenda behind the Gulf War.**
Pierre Salinger with Eric Laurent, translated by Howard Curtis.
Harmondsworth, England: Penguin, 1991. 241p.
First published in French in the same year, the prefatory matter states that it is not a
book about the war, but a book that shows how the war could have been avoided. It
argues that Iraq's huge armament was entirely the responsibility of the Soviet Union
and the Western powers, and that the signals sent by the USA from the beginning of
1990 were not understood by Saddam Husayn who believed that military action
against Kuwait would not provoke an American reaction.

287    **Needless deaths in the Gulf war: civilian casualties during the air
campaigns and violations of the laws of war.**
(Virginia N. Sherry et al.).    New York: Human Rights Watch, 1991.
402p. maps. (Middle East Watch Report).
States that the report applies the rules of war governing international armed conflicts
to examine civilian casualties and damage to civilian objects from bomb and missile
attacks during the Gulf War of 1991. The contents are: Part one 'The legal standards';
Part two 'The air war against Iraq'; Part three 'Iraq's missile attacks against Israel
and the Gulf States'.

288    **From the house of war: John Simpson in the Gulf.**
John Simpson.    London: Hutchinson, 1991. 389p. maps. bibliog.
A personal account of the Gulf War as experienced by the BBC journalist reporting
from Baghdad. The story includes reports of the uprisings following the war and the
immediate aftermath. A detailed chronology of events is appended.

289    **Class, state and politics in Iraq.**
Joe Stork.    In: *Power and stability in the Middle East*, edited by
Berch Berberoglu.    London: Zed, 1989, p. 31-54.
A carefully argued article exploring the motives behind Saddam's invasion of
Kuwait, and the evolution of the diplomatic crisis.

**Oil on troubled waters: Gulf wars, 1980-91.**
*See* item no. 245.

**Unholy Babylon: the secret history of Saddam's war.**
*See* item no. 335.

**The death lobby: how the West armed Iraq.**
*See* item no. 355.

**The Kurds of Iraq: tragedy and hope.**
*See* item no. 435.

**Effect of the Gulf War on infant and child mortality in Iraq.**
*See* item no. 547.

**Mass flight in the Middle East: involuntary migration and the Gulf conflict, 1990-1991.**
*See* item no. 577.

**Iraq: economic consequences of the 1991 Gulf War and future outlook.**
*See* item no. 581.

**On the way to the market. Economic liberalization and Iraq's invasion of Kuwait.**
*See* item no. 584.

**Gulf War reparations: Iraq, OPEC and the transfer problem.**
*See* item no. 601.

# Iraq since the second Gulf War July 1991-

290 **The Gulf war, sanctions and the lives of Iraqi women.**
Louise Cainkar. *Arab Studies Quarterly*, vol. 15, no. 2 (Spring 1993), p. 15-52.

Attempts to provide a picture of the way in which Iraqi households coped during and after the 1991 Gulf War, and the impact of sanctions and impoverishment on women in Iraq. The author notes that the sale of household goods and personal jewellery for food has undermined women's security for the future.

291 **Hunger and poverty in Iraq, 1991.**
Jean Drèze, Haris Gazdar. London: Development Economics Research Programme, London School of Economics, 1991. 62p. bibliog. (Discussion Paper Series, DEP 32).

Discusses the effect of international sanctions on Iraq after more than one year of embargo and the war and subsequent internal conflicts. The paper considers the effects on Iraqi employment and incomes, the public distribution system, and hunger and poverty.

292 **From food security to food insecurity: the case of Iraq, 1990-91.**
J. O. Field. *GeoJournal*, vol. 30, no. 2 (1993), p. 185-94.

Field has written here a paper on the impact of the sanctions imposed on Iraq after the invasion of Kuwait in 1990 on Iraq's internal food supplies for its population.

293  A *de facto* **Kurdish state in northern Iraq.**
Michael M. Gunter.  *Third World Quarterly*, vol. 14, no. 2 (1993),
p. 295-319.
Gunter describes developments in Iraqi Kurdistan which enjoyed autonomous
government after the Kurdish rebellion following Iraq's defeat in the Gulf War of
1991.

294  **Iraq since the Gulf War: prospects for democracy.**
Edited by Fran Hazleton, for CARDRI.   London: Zed, 1994. 252p.
Prepared by the Committee Against Repression and for Democratic Rights in Iraq,
this volume contains the following essays: 'Cultural totalitarianism' by Fatima
Mohsen (p. 7-19); 'State terror and the degradation of politics' by Isam al-Khafaji
(p. 20-31); 'Ba'thist ideology and practice' by Zuhair al-Jaza'iri (p. 32-51); 'Saddam
as hero' by Kamil Abdullah (p. 52-59); 'Women: honour, shame and dictatorship' by
Suha Omar (p. 60-71); 'Economic devastation, underdevelopment and outlook' by
Abbas Alnasrawi (p. 72-96); 'Why the *Intifada* failed' by Faleh 'Abd al-Jabbar (p. 97-
117); 'The Kurdish parliament' by Falaq al-Din Kakai (p. 118-33); 'Suppression and
survival of Iraqi Shi'is' by Hussein al-Shahristani (p. 134-40); 'Destruction of the
southern marshes' by Hamid al-Bayati (p. 141-46); 'Human rights, sanctions and
sovereignty' by Leila Kubba (p. 147-52); 'The opposition' by Rend Rahim Francke
(p. 153-77); 'Attitudes to the West, Arabs and fellow Iraqis' by Ayad Rahim (p. 178-
93); 'Intolerance and identity' by Kanan Makiya ('Samir al-Khalil') (p. 194-204);
'Charter 91' by Arif Alwan (p. 205-10); 'Federalism' by Ali Allawi (p. 211-22); 'The
rule of law' by Ahmad Chalabi (p. 223-31); 'Playing by the rules' by Dlawer
Ala'Aldeen (p. 232-43).

295  **Two years after the Gulf War: a status report on Iraq and the
region.**
Shireen T. Hunter.  *Security Dialogue*, vol. 24, no. 1 (March 1993),
p. 21-36.
The author discusses the objectives of the Gulf War of 1991, the economic state of
Iraq and the humanitarian cost of the war, and considers the political position of
Saddam Husayn, of the Iraqi opposition, and of Iraqi Kurdistan two years after Iraq's
defeat.

296  **Difficult reconstruction in northern Iraq.**
Cristina Karrer.  *Swiss Review of World Affairs*, vol. 42, no. 9
(December 1992), p. 18-19.
Karrer reports on efforts to reconstruct the Kurdish area of northern Iraq which for
practical purposes has been autonomous since 1991.

297  **The United Nations and Iraq: verification in the face of
obstruction.**
Tim Trevan.   In: *Verification 1993*, edited by J. B. Poole, R. Guthrie.
London: Brassey's (UK), 1993, p. 171-80.
Reports on the efforts of the United Nations Special Commission to ascertain Iraq's
holdings of banned weapons and the extent to which it has engaged in weapons

research and production, in the face of obstruction and deceit by the Iraqi government, after Iraq's defeat in the Gulf War of 1991.

### 298 Living short, with dignity: in Iraqi Kurdistan.
Stuart Weir. *New Politics*, N.S. vol. 4, no. 2 (Winter 1993), p.129-39.

A report on the political scene and the difficulties faced by the local people in Iraqi Kurdistan in May 1992, after the Gulf War of 1991 and the revolt against the Iraqi regime.

**Hidden death: land mines and civilian casualties in Iraqi Kurdistan.**
*See* item no. 443.

**The creation of a Kurdish state in the 1990s?**
*See* item no. 445.

**Iraq: economic consequences of the 1991 Gulf War and future outlook.**
*See* item no. 581.

**Economic development in Iraq. Factors underlying the relative deterioration of human capital formation.**
*See* item no. 597.

# Foreign Relations

## General

**299  The dialectics of domestic environment and role performance: the foreign policy of Iraq.**
Ahmad Yousef Ahmad.  In: *The foreign policies of Arab states.*
Bahgat Korany, Ali E. Hillal Dessouki (et al.).  Boulder, CO:
Westview, 1984, p. 147-73.
Ahmad considers that the influence of domestic factors has played a major role in shaping Iraq's foreign policy. The serious ethnic and religious cleavages in the population mean that the government must accommodate dissatisfied or unsympathetic sectors of the population in pursuit of its goals.

**300  What price Arabism? Aspects of Iraqi foreign policy since 1968.**
Marion Farouk-Sluglett.  In: *Foreign policy issues in the Middle East: Afghanistan – Iraq – Turkey – Morocco*, edited by R. Lawless.
Durham, England: University of Durham, Centre for Middle Eastern and Islamic Studies, 1985, p. 24-42.
Argues that, in spite of the rhetoric of Pan-Arabism, anti-imperialism, and anti-Zionism, the Iraqi government has in practice pursued policies entirely subservient to the interests of the regime itself since 1968.

**301  Iraq as a regional power.**
Thomas Koszinowski.  In: *Iraq: power and society*, edited by Derek Hopwood, Habib Ishow, Thomas Koszinowski.  Oxford: Ithaca, for St. Antony's College, 1993, p. 283-301.
Surveys Ba'th Party ideology and practice from the 1970s to 1990 in the matter of foreign policy.

302 **A diplomatic history of modern Iraq.**
Abid A. al-Marayati.   New York: Speller, 1961. 206p. bibliog.
Considers the conduct of diplomacy, as contrasted with the evolution of foreign
policy over the period between 1920 and 1959 when Iraq began to participate in
international organizations such as the League of Nations and later the United
Nations. This study discusses the practical side of diplomacy and the need for able
and qualified people to carry it out.

303 **Iraq's voice at the United Nations 1959-69: a personal record.**
Adnan Pachachi.   London: Quartet, 1991. 460p.
A personal account of his service at the United Nations in the years following the
Iraqi revolution by the Iraqi Representative.

**Pakistan and the Iran–Iraq war.**
*See* item no. 250.

# Arab world

304 **Operation Vantage: British military intervention in Kuwait 1961.**
Mustafa M. Alani.   Surbiton, England: LAAM, 1990. 283p. bibliog.
Discusses British military action in support of Kuwait in July 1961 and the Iraqi
claim to sovereignty over Kuwait. The main part of the book studies relations
between Britain, Kuwait and Iraq, and British actions during the crisis.

305 **Baathi Iraq and Hashimite Jordan: from hostility to alignment.**
Amatzia Baram.   *Middle East Journal*, vol. 45, no. 1 (Winter 1991),
p. 51-70.
Baram traces the changing relationship of Jordan and Iraq from the 1970s to 1991.

306 **War and peace in the Gulf: domestic politics and regional
relations into the 1990s.**
Anoushiravan Ehteshami, Gerd Nonneman with Charles Tripp.
Reading, England: Ithaca, 1991. 269p. maps. bibliog. (Exeter Middle
East Monographs, 5).
An assessment of the balance of power and Iraq's relations with Iran and the Gulf
states up to the time of the invasion of Kuwait. Chapter one describes the post-
Khomeini power structure in Iran. Chapter two is 'Domestic politics in Iraq: Saddam
Hussein and the autocrat's fallacy' by Charles Tripp (p. 19-34); The remaining
chapters are by the other two authors and are entitled: 'Iraq and the Arab States of the
Gulf: full circle'; 'The military balance in the Gulf: one step forward, two steps
back'; 'Defence investment and military procurement strategies of Iran and Iraq';
'Documents from the Algiers Agreement 1975 to 1990, UN Resolutions on the
Kuwait Crisis'; 'Chronology of Gulf events 1980-1991'.

307   **Shifting lines in the sand: Kuwait's elusive frontier with Iraq.**
David H. Finnie.   Cambridge, MA: Harvard University Press, 1992.
214p.
A history of the efforts made to define the boundary between Iraq and Kuwait and the
various claims advanced from 1899 to 1991.

308   **Les relations de la Jordanie avec l'Irak: de l'embarras à
l'ambiguïté, de l'ambiguïté au recentrage.** (Jordan's relations with
Iraq: from embarrassment to ambiguity, from ambiguity to recentring.)
Frédéric Gratier.   *Monde Arab Maghreb-Machrek,* no. 141
(July-August 1993), p. 37-52.
Describes how Jordan distanced itself from Iraq after its support during the Gulf War
of 1991 and moved closer to the United States of America.

309   **Relations between Iraq and Kuwait.**
Habib Ishow.   In: *Iraq: power and society,* edited by Derek
Hopwood, Habib Ishow, Thomas Koszinowski.   Oxford: Ithaca, for
St. Antony's College, 1993, p. 303-18.
A survey of Iraq's relations with Kuwait throughout the 20th century.

310   **The Arab Cold War: Gamal 'Abd al-Nasir and his rivals
1958-1970.**
Malcolm Kerr.   London: Oxford University Press, 1971. 3rd ed.
156p. bibliog.
An essay for the general reader on Nasser's career as a pan-Arab leader and the
rivalry between Egypt, Syria and Iraq in the years after the 1958 Revolution in Iraq.
The Arab nationalist ideology espoused by Nasser was taken up in Syria and Iraq and
a number of attempts were made to unite the Arab countries, but with little success.
This book explains why.

311   **Ba'th v. Ba'th: the conflict between Syria and Iraq 1968-1989.**
Eberhard Kienle.   London: Tauris, 1990, rp. 1991. 211p. bibliog.
Describes the tortured relationship between the rival Baʿth regimes in Syria and Iraq
from 1968 to the 1980s in which they moved from attempts to unite their countries to
open conflict.

312   **The limits of Fertile Crescent unity: Iraqi policies towards Syria
since 1945.**
Eberhard Kienle.   In: *Iraq: power and society,* edited by Derek
Hopwood, Habib Ishow, Thomas Koszinowski.   Oxford: Ithaca, for
St. Antony's College, 1993, p. 357-79.
Charts the variable relationship between Iraq and Syria which has included
declarations of union and open hostility as a result of the two Baʿth regimes' rivalry
for regional status and hegemony.

313 **Jordan and Iraq: efforts at intra-Hashemite unity.**
Bruce Maddy-Weitzman. *Middle Eastern Studies*, vol. 26, no. 1 (January 1990), p. 65-75.
Describes the attempts made by the Hashimite family to associate their kingdoms of Jordan and Iraq, though more effort was directed at involving Syria which became a republic after independence from France in 1943. The article deals with the years 1946-58 when the revolution in Iraq put an end to Hashimite rule there.

314 **Iraqi policies towards the Arab states of the Gulf, 1958-1981.**
Tim Niblock. In: *Iraq: the contemporary state*, edited by Tim Niblock. London: Croom Helm; New York: St. Martin's Press, 1982, p. 125-49.
Charts the development of Iraq's relations with its Arab neighbours in the Gulf from the Iraqi revolution to the war with Iran.

315 **Iraq, the Gulf states & the war: a changing relationship 1980-1986 and beyond.**
Gerd Nonneman. London: Ithaca, 1986. 198p. maps. bibliog. (Exeter Middle East Politics, 1).
A chronological account of Iraq's relations with Saudi Arabia, Kuwait and the other Gulf States from the beginning of the war with Iran in 1980 through its various stages to 1986, and the changing attitudes that accompanied Iraq's declining fortunes.

316 **Iraq, King Fayṣal the First and Arab unity.**
Yehoshua Porath. In: *Studies in Islamic history and civilization in honour of Professor David Ayalon*, edited by M. Sharon. Jerusalem: Cana; Leiden, The Netherlands: Brill, 1986, p. 237-65.
The author examines King Faysal's initiatives towards Syria in the late 1920s and his efforts to build a circle of support among Arab countries to shore up his regime in Iraq.

317 **Nuri al-Saʿid's Arab unity programme.**
Yehoshua Porath. *Middle Eastern Studies*, vol. 20, no. 4 (October 1984), p. 76-98.
An account of Nuri al-Said's efforts to promote regional Arab unity in order to secure Hashimi rule in Iraq and strengthen the regime's hold over the country.

318 **Iraq–UAR relations 1958-63: the genesis, escalation and culmination of a propaganda war.**
Haggay Ram. *Orient* (Opladen), vol. 34, no. 3 (September 1993), p. 421-38.
Traces the war of words between Iraq and Egypt which was waged on the radio and in the newspapers after the 1958 coup in Iraq. After the initial few months of amicability, a vicious antagonism developed which peaked in March 1959 and finally subsided after Qasim's fall from power in February 1963.

319 **Iraq and Saudi Arabia: from rivalry to confrontation.**
Andreas Rieck. In: *Iraq: power and society*, edited by Derek
Hopwood, Habib Ishow, Thomas Koszinowski. Oxford: Ithaca, for
St. Antony's College, 1993, p. 319-39.
Rieck considers the changing relationship between the two countries during the 20th
century.

320 **Economic relations between Iraq and other Arab Gulf States.**
Naomi Sakr. In: *Iraq: the contemporary state*, edited by Tim
Niblock. London: Croom Helm; New York: St. Martin's Press, 1982,
p. 150-67.
Discusses Iraq's economic relationship with Kuwait, Saudi Arabia, the United Arab
Emirates, Qatar and Bahrain from 1975 onwards, when Iraq began to show an interest
in developing ties and cooperation with its southern neighbours.

321 **Arabian boundaries: primary documents, 1853-1957.**
Edited by Richard Schofield, Gerald Blake. Farnham Common,
England: Archive Editions, 1988. 25 vols. maps.
A series of volumes reproducing original documents. Volumes 1 and 2 deal with
general issues of political control and sovereignty. Volumes 7 and 8 cover the
boundary between Kuwait and Iraq; volume 9 covers Saudi Arabia–Kuwait, and
Saudi Arabia–Iraq. Volumes 23-25 contain maps.

322 **Kuwait and Iraq: historical claims and territorial disputes.**
Richard Schofield. London: Royal Institute of International Affairs,
1991. 137p. maps.
Reviews the history of border delineation and associated disputes between Kuwait
and Iraq from the 18th and 19th centuries up to 1990. A clearly set out chronological
survey.

323 **The question of delimiting the Iraq–Kuwait boundary.**
Richard N. Schofield. *Boundary Bulletin*, [no. 1 (1991)?], p. 5-13.
Describes the history of boundary-drawing and agreements from the 1913 Anglo-
Ottoman Gulf settlement up to 1990, and all the exchanges between Kuwait, Britain,
and Iraq from the 1920s onwards. A sequel 'The United Nations' settlement of the
Iraq–Kuwait border, 1991-1993' was published in a later issue after the bulletin
changed its name to *Boundary and Security Bulletin*; see vol. 1, no. 2 (July 1993),
p. 70-82.

324 **Saddam's closest ally: Jordan and the Gulf War.**
W. Andrew Terrill. *Journal of South Asian and Middle Eastern
Studies*, vol. 9, no. 2 (Winter 1985), p. 43-54.
Outlines Jordan's practical, political and military support for Iraq during the Iran–Iraq
war, when it functioned as a major supply route to Iraq.

**Turkey, Syria, Iraq: the Euphrates.**
*See* item no. 25.

**Iraq's road to war.**
*See* item no. 265.

# Iran

325 **Iraq and Iran: the years of crisis.**
J. M. Abdulghani. London: Croom Helm, 1984. 244p.

Examines Iraq's relations with Iran from the time of the Ba'th Party's accession to power in 1968, and the phases of Cold War confrontation and rivalry over the Gulf (1968-75); tensions over the Shatt al-'Arab boundary dispute and the Kurdish question; the temporary rapprochement in 1975, and the subsequent return to Cold War and confrontation.

326 **Iran–Iraq boundaries: a legal analysis.**
Sayed Hassan Amin. In: *Hannoversche Beiträge zur Geschichte des Mittleren Ostens*, edited by Ahmad Mahrad. Frankfurt am Main, Germany: Lang, 1985, p. 55-90. (Europäische Hochschulschriften: Reihe 3, Geschichte und ihre Hilfswissenschaften, 279).

Analyses the background of the unsettled question of the Iran–Iraq marine boundary, and the territorial claims on off-shore areas and continental shelf boundaries of the two countries.

327 **Relations between Iraq and Iran.**
Paul Balta. In: *Iraq: power and society*, edited by Derek Hopwood, Habib Ishow, Thomas Koszinowski. Oxford: Ithaca, for St. Antony's College, 1993, p. 381-97.

A survey of relations between the two countries during the 20th century, taking the story up to 1992.

328 **The Shatt-al-Arab river boundary: a note.**
Gideon Biger. *Middle Eastern Studies*, vol. 25, no. 2 (April 1989), p. 248-52.

Biger examines the 1975 Algiers Agreement concerning delineation of the southern frontier between Iraq and Iran which was broken in September 1980 when the war began.

329 **The legal status of the Shatt-al-Arab (Tigris and Euphrates) river basin.**
Dante A. Caponera. *Austrian Journal of Public and International Law*, vol. 45, no. 2 (1993), p. 147-58.
Considers the legal obligations regarding water resources shared between countries, and the political and practical problems surrounding Iraq's rivers (the Tigris and Euphrates). Iraq's relationships during the last few decades with Turkey and Syria upstream, and with Iran to the East, are discussed.

330 **The Shatt-al-Arab boundary question: a legal reappraisal.**
Kaiyan Homi Kaikobad. Oxford: Clarendon Press, 1988. 142p. maps. bibliog.
A study by an international law expert of the background to the history, politics, diplomacy and law of the dispute over the Iran–Iraq boundary down the Shatt al-ʿArab.

331 **Iran and Iraq: changing relations and future prospects.**
Andrew T. Parasiliti. In: *Iran and the Arab world*, edited by Hooshang Amirahmadi, Nader Entessar. Basingstoke, England: Macmillan, 1993, p. 217-43.
Analyses the relationship between Iran and Iraq since 1979 in terms of the geopolitical and ideological challenges which the two states pose to each other. The discussion covers the Iran–Iraq war and the consequences of Iraq's invasion of Kuwait in 1990. Three other articles in this volume deal with the Iran–Iraq war: 'The ideological context of the Iran–Iraq war: Pan-Islamism versus Pan-Arabism' by Mohssen Massarrat (p. 28-41), 'The Iran–Iraq war' by Dilip Hiro (p. 42-68), and 'Revolutionary Iran's Persian Gulf policy: the quest for regional supremacy' by Bahman Baktiari (p. 69-93). Iran's response to the invasion of Kuwait and subsequent war are discussed in 'Iran and the Persian Gulf crisis' by Hooshang Amirahmadi (p. 94-125).

332 **Evolution of the Shatt al-ʿArab boundary dispute.**
Richard N. Schofield. Wisbech, England: Middle East and North African Studies Press, 1986. 86p. maps. bibliog.
Describes the general problems surrounding boundary demarcation in the Middle East, the particular problems with the Shatt al-ʿArab river boundary between Iraq and Iran, the position in international law, and the economic importance and levels of utilization of the Shatt al-ʿArab in the twentieth century.

**A bibliography of the Iran–Iraq borderland.**
*See* item no. 18.

**War and peace in the Gulf: domestic politics and regional relations into the 1990s.**
*See* item no. 306.

# Turkey

333 **De Mossoul à Kirkouk: la Turquie et la question du Kurdistan irakien.** (From Mosul to Kirkuk: Turkey and the question of Iraqi Kurdistan.)
François Gorgeon. *Maghreb-Machrek*, 132 (April-June 1991), p. 38-49.

Turkey's relations with Iraq are affected by Kurdish insurgency in their common border area. This article summarizes the history of the dispute over Mosul between Turkey and British-ruled Iraq from 1918 to 1925 and the renewed problem of Kurdish resurgence in Iraqi Kurdistan from 1986 to 1991.

334 **Relations between Iraq and its Turkish neighbour: from ideological to geostrategic constraints.**
Elizabeth Picard. In: *Iraq: power and society*, edited by Derek Hopwood, Habib Ishow, Thomas Koszinowski. Oxford: Ithaca, for St. Antony's College, 1993, p. 341-56.

Surveys 20th-century relations with Turkey which in the 1920s were dominated by the Mosul Dispute, but concentrates on more recent decades since 1970, up to and including the 1991 Gulf War.

**Turkey, Syria, Iraq: the Euphrates.**
*See* item no. 25.

# United States of America and Western Europe

335 **Unholy Babylon: the secret history of Saddam's war.**
Adel Darwish, Gregory Alexander. London: Gollancz, 1991. 317p. maps. bibliog.

Describes Saddam Husayn, his rise to power, and the political, economic and industrial assistance which the West made available to him. The book states that the authors conceived it a month before the invasion of Kuwait with the intention of exposing the unpleasant nature of Saddam's regime and Western complicity in his arms build-up.

336 **Terrorist: the inside story of the highest-ranking Iraqi terrorist ever to defect to the West.**
Steven A. Emerson, Cristina Del Sesto. New York: Villard Books, 1991. 233p.

Claims to be the story of a Palestinian who became part of a terrorist group which was directed by a high-ranking member of the Iraqi government but who later defected to the USA in 1982. The book accuses the US government of ignoring the information supplied by this man about terror activities, in favour of doing business with the Iraqi government until 1990.

337 **Die Bundesrepublik Deutschland und der Irak: eine Bilanz.** (The relations between the Federal Republic of Germany and Iraq.)
Rüdiger Robert. *Orient* (Opladen), vol. 22, no. 2 (1981), p. 195-218.

Reviews the course of Iraqi relations with West Germany which improved considerably after 1974, facilitated by greater pragmatism in Iraq's foreign policy and Germany's increasing willingness to appreciate Arab views on the Arab–Israeli conflict. There is an English summary on p. 336-37.

338 **United States–Iraq relations: a spring thaw.**
Barry Rubin. In: *Iraq: the contemporary state*, edited by Tim Niblock. London: Croom Helm; New York: St. Martin's Press, 1982, p. 109-24.

Describes the course of US–Iraqi relations from the 1960s to the 1980s.

**America and the Iraqi crisis, 1990-1992.**
*See* item no. 267.

# Union of Soviet Socialist Republics and Eastern Europe

339 **The Soviet Union and the Iran–Iraq War, 1980-88.**
James Clay Moltz, Dennis B. Ross. In: *Soviet strategy in the Middle East*, by George W. Breslauer (et. al.). Boston, MA; London: Unwin Hyman, 1990, p. 123-50.

Describes the vagaries in Soviet policy towards the Iran–Iraq war close to its southern borders, which began by favouring Iran, tilted back toward neutraliy in 1982-83, then favoured Iraq in 1984-85, and from 1986 to the end of the war in 1988 adopted a sort of middle stance.

340    **Soviet–Iraqi relations, 1968-1988: in the shadow of the Iraq–Iran conflict.**
Haim Shemesh.    Boulder, CO: Rienner, 1992. 265p. bibliog.
Shemesh charts the course of relations between the Soviet Union and Iraq from the installation of the Baʿth regime to the end of the war with Iran, which coincided with the beginning of the collapse of Soviet power.

341    **The USSR and Iraq: the Soviet quest for influence.**
Oles M. Smolansky, with Bettie M. Smolansky.    Durham, NC: Duke Press, 1991. 331p. bibliog.
Discusses the nature of the relationship between the Soviet Union and Iraq and its vicissitudes from 1968 to the Iran–Iraq war. Part one deals with domestic issues in Iraq: the nationalization of the oil industry, the Kurdish question and the Iraqi Communist Party; part two with regional problems in the Gulf, and the Iran–Iraq war.

# Armed Forces and
# National Security

342 **China's arms sales in the Gulf: a research note.**
Amitav Acharya. *Middle East Strategic Studies Quarterly*, vol. 1,
no. 3 (Autumn/Winter 1989), p. 118-30.
The author reviews China's sales of arms to Iran and Iraq between 1980 and 1987 in
terms of quality and proportion of total supply.

343 **Reflections on human rights issues in prewar Iraq.**
Roger Bartram. *Journal of Palestine Studies*, vol. 20, no. 3 / 79
(Spring 1991), p. 89-97.
Sketches the atmosphere inside Iraq where informants told of twelve different police
services, and domestic spying on families and individuals to ensure support for, or at
least acquiescence in, the Ba‘th Party, the government and the person of Saddam
Husayn. Some case-histories are included. The article notes that in spite of a sorry
human rights record, the regime does tolerate freedom of expression for all religions
in Iraq, and greater liberty is afforded to women than in many other Middle Eastern
countries. This article was written before the invasion of Kuwait.

344 **Weapons of mass destruction in the Middle East.**
Anthony H. Cordesman. London: Brassey's, 1991. 209p. bibliog.
Part one describes patterns in the conventional arms race in the Middle East. Part two
'Current trends in the proliferation of weapons of mass destruction' includes case-
studies of Iran and Iraq (p. 35-112) and deals with rockets, surface-to-surface
missiles, chemical and biological weapons and Iraq's efforts to acquire nuclear
weapons. Part three treats the impact of the arms race in the Middle East.

### 345    Guns, lies and spies: how we armed Iraq.

Chris Cowley, introduction by Paul Foot.   London: Hamish
Hamilton, 1992. 273p.

This book claims to provide the full story behind the 'Supergun affair', told by the
engineer in charge of the project known as 'project Babylon'. A number of other
books have recently been published on the subject of Western arms supplies to Iraq.

### 346    Politics and the military in Iraq and Jordan, 1920-1958: the British influence.

Mark Heller.   *Armed Forces and Society*, vol. 4, no. 1 (November
1977), p. 75-99.

Examines the different behaviour with regard to politics of the armed forces in Iraq
and in Jordan. The author argues that British policy in these two countries produced
officer corps with entirely different political backgrounds and different experiences of
British rule.

### 347    The formation of the Iraqi army, 1921-33.

Paul P. J. Hemphill.   In: *The integration of modern Iraq*, edited by
Abbas Kelidar.   London: Croom Helm, 1979, p. 88-110.

Hemphill describes the process of creating a national army to defend the new state of
Iraq after the imposition of the British mandate when the country lacked any national
identity or consensus.

### 348    Arms and the man: Dr. Gerald Bull, Iraq and the supergun.

William Lowther.   London: Macmillan, 1991. 288p.

Published as *Iraq and the supergun: Gerald Bull – the true story of Saddam
Hussein's Dr Doom*, by Pan in 1992, this is a biography of the weapons engineer
whose work on the Iraqi Supergun project led to his assassination in 1989.

### 349    The forgotten war: the Iraqi army and the Iran–Iraq war.

Sean McKnight.   *Small Wars and Insurgencies*, vol. 2, no. 1 (April
1991), p. 91-102.

Considers developments in the Iraqi Army and efforts to improve its professionalism
and efficiency during the protracted war against Iran (1980-88) which led to gradual
improvements in its performance after years of suffering from political interference
and manipulation.

### 350    Prisoner in Baghdad.

Daphne Parish, with Pat Lancaster and contributions from Michelle de
Vries.   London: Chapman, 1992. 200p.

A personal account of her experience by the British nurse who took in her car the
*Observer* newspaper reporter Farhad Barzoft to investigate a secret Iraqi military
complex where an explosion was rumoured to have occurred in 1989. Both were
imprisoned as a result of this excursion and Barzoft was executed while Parish was given
a heavy prison sentence. This book tells the story of her acquaintance with Barzoft, her
trial and experiences in the women's prison, and her sudden release in early 1990.

351    **The changing patterns of the politics of the Iraqi army.**
A. al-Qazzaz.   In: *On military intervention*, edited by Morris
Janowitz, Jacques van Doorn.   Rotterdam: Rotterdam University
Press, 1971, p. 335-57.
Discusses the background and formation of military officers who played prominent
roles in coups and politics in Iraq from 1958 to 1968, and their ambitions and goals.

352    **The role of the army in the national, social and political
development of Iraq.**
Faisal Al Samir.   In: *The military as an agent of social change*, edited
by Claude Heller.   [Mexico]: Colegio de México, 1981, p. 107-26.
(XXX International Congress of Human Sciences in Asia and North
Africa).
Traces the development of the Iraqi army under British rule, its expansion to take in
new recruits from other backgrounds in the 1930s, and its subsequent involvement in
political issues.

353    **The road to Osiraq: Baghdad's quest for the bomb.**
Jed C. Snyder.   *Middle East Journal*, vol. 37, no. 4 (Autumn 1983),
p. 565-93.
Traces the development of Iraq's interest in nuclear energy and pursuit of a high-
technology research reactor which would produce plutonium, potentially for use in
atomic weapons. The account covers the years from 1959 to Israel's destruction of the
advanced reactor at Osiraq on 7 June 1981, thus setting back Iraq's nuclear
programme by several years.

354    **Circle of fear.**
Hussein Sumaida, with Carole Jerome.   London: Hale, 1992. 295p.
A gripping account of subversion and espionage in Ba'thist Iraq. The author claims to
be the son of a high-ranking member of the Ba'thist ruling clique, who early became
disillusioned with the Party's rule and became an undercover agent for Israel and the
CIA. He was protected by his father's position for many years until he defected to the
United States. This book provides a convincing picture of Iraq's police state, and the
lifestyle of the ruling élite.

355    **The death lobby: how the West armed Iraq.**
Kenneth R. Timmerman.   London: Fourth Estate, 1992. 443p.
First published in Boston by Houghton & Mifflin in 1991, this is an account of how
Western businessmen and governments helped Iraq to build a formidable arsenal in
the years leading up to the invasion of Kuwait in 1990.

356 **Iraq.**
John S. Wagner. In: *Fighting armies: antagonists in the Middle East: a combat assessment*, edited by Richard A. Gabriel. Westport, CT: Greenwood Press, 1983, p. 63-84.

Wagner describes the expansion of the Iraqi army between 1973 and 1980, during which time it more than doubled in size. He goes on to assess its capabilities, equipment, officer training and operational performance during the Kurdish conflict and the early stages of the war with Iran, launched in 1980.

# Politics

357 **Report and recommendations of an Amnesty International Mission to the Government of the Republic of Iraq, 22-28 January 1983, including the government's response and Amnesty International comments.**
London: Amnesty International, 1983. 74p.
A report on the treatment of political prisoners in Iraq by the international human rights organization.

358 **The June 1980 elections to the National Assembly: an experiment in controlled democracy.**
Amatzia Baram. *Orient* (Opladen), vol. 27, no. 3 (September 1981), p. 391-412.
Baram analyses the political background of the elections, the constitution of the National Assembly and the social and political composition of its newly elected members.

359 **The ruling political elite in Ba'thi Iraq, 1968-1986: the changing features of a collective profile.**
Amatzia Baram. *International Journal of Middle East Studies*, vol. 21 (1989), p. 447-93.
Assesses the gradual change in the élite leadership of Iraq from a military background in the 1960s to a generation with a political party background in the mid-1980s. The new generation is drawn from a wider range of regions of Iraq, and from rural lower classes rather than from the urban lower middle classes which formed the military leadership.

360 **Political society and social structure in Syria and Iraq.**
Hanna Batatu. In: *Arab society: continuity and change*, edited by
Samih K. Farsoun. London: Croom Helm, 1985, p. 34-47.
Briefly outlines and compares political structures in Syria and Iraq and the importance
in politics of social allegiances and backgrounds.

361 **Shi'is and politics in Ba'thi Iraq.**
Ofra Bengio. *Middle Eastern Studies*, vol. 21, no. 1 (January 1985),
p. 1-14.
A study of the ruling Ba'th Party's attempts to control and defuse Shi'i distrust of the
rulers of Iraq since 1968. The author argues that the regime has perceived a greater
threat from Shi'i political disaffection since 1977 and taken more aggressive measures
to control it while offering economic and social development projects to win over the
Shi'i community.

362 **Middle Eastern political clichés: 'Takriti' and 'Sunni rule' in
Iraq; 'Alawi rule' in Syria: a critical appraisal.**
Nikolas van Dam. *Orient* (Opladen), vol. 21, no. 1 (January 1980),
p. 42-57.
Investigates the reasons for the strong representation of Sunnis, in particular from
Takrit, in the Iraqi Ba'thist regime, and of 'Alawis in the Syrian one, and argues that
in both countries 'reliance on regional and tribal ties, at present appears to be
preconditional for staying in power'.

363 **Minorities and political elites in Iraq and Syria.**
Nikolaos van Dam. In: *Sociology of "Developing societies" : the
Middle East*, edited by Talal Asad, Roger Owen. London:
Macmillan, 1983, p. 127-44, 233-34.
The author discusses the reasons for a concentration of political power in small
groups from particular sectors of society in Iraq and Syria, and compares social and
political developments in the two countries.

364 **The Ba'th Party: a history from its origins to 1966.**
John F. Devlin. Stanford, CA: Hoover Institution Press, 1976. 353p.
bibliog.
Devlin traces the rise, spread, successes and disasters of the Ba'th Party from its
foundation to the great schism in 1966 between Syrian and Iraqi sections. This book
provides a background for the behaviour of the Ba'th which took power in Iraq in
1963.

365 **Iraq.**
Marion Farouk-Sluglett, Peter Sluglett. In: *Religion in politics:
a world guide*, edited by Stuart Mews. London: Longman, 1989,
p. 116-19.
Provides a survey of the ethnic and religious structure of the Iraqi population, and the
role which religion has played in the recent history of the country.

366 **The Iraqi Baʿth Party.**
Marion Farouk-Sluglett, Peter Sluglett. In: *Political parties in the Third World*, edited by Vicky Randall. London: Sage, 1988, p. 57-74.
Provides a concise outline of the origins and growth of the Baʿth Party in Syria and Iraq, and of Baʿth rule in Iraq from 1963 to the mid-1980s.

367 **Essai sur l'histoire du Parti communiste irakien: luttes nationales et stratégie "internationaliste".** (Essay on the history of the Iraqi Communist Party: national struggles and "internationalist" strategy.)
Mohieddine Hadhri. In: *Mouvement ouvrier, communisme et nationalismes dans le monde arabe*, edited by René Gallissot. Paris: Editions Ouvrières, 1978, p. 203-29. (Cahiers du 'Mouvement Social', 3).
A history of the Communist Party from its foundation in 1922 up to its alliance with the ruling elements after the 1958 Revolution. It declined after 1961 when the Baʿth Party turned against its cadres.

368 **Political parties, institutions and administrative structures.**
Peter Heine. In: *Iraq: power and society*, edited by Derek Hopwood, Habib Ishow, Thomas Koszinowski. Oxford: Ithaca, for St. Antony's College, 1993, p. 37-49.
Heine describes the functioning of the political system in the 1980s, the Baʿth and opposition parties, and other forms of mass organization.

369 **Iraq: eastern flank of the Arab world.**
Christine Moss Helms. Washington, DC: Brookings Institution, 1984. 208p. maps.
The author explores the forces that influence policy formulation in Iraq, and considers the political and social development of Iraq which provided the background to the outbreak of war with Iran in 1980. The work is in 3 parts: Part 1 'The Iraqi nation versus the Iraqi state'; Part 2 'The Iraqi Baʿth Party'; Part 3 'Iraq goes to war'.

370 **Instant empire: Saddam Hussein's ambition for Iraq.**
Simon Henderson. San Francisco, CA: Murray House, 1991. 261p. map. bibliog.
A history of Iraq under Saddam's rule by a journalist who claims to have taken a particular interest in Iraqi politics and Saddam's personality from his rise to power up to the invasion of Kuwait in 1990.

371 **Social policy and social change: the case of Iraq.**
Jacqueline S. Ismael. *Arab Studies Quarterly*, vol. 2, no. 3 (Summer 1980), p. 235-48.
Considers Iraq's social policy, and concludes that the subordination of social policy to political and economic objectives is consistent with Baʿth Party ideology.

372 **Aziz al-Haj: a communist radical.**
A. R. Kelidar. In: *The integration of modern Iraq*, edited by Abbas Kelidar. London: Croom Helm, 1979, p. 183-92.

Kelidar here studies Aziz Al-Haj Ali Haydar and the rift in the Iraqi Communist Party which split in 1967. Aziz al-Haj publicly renounced his Communist past in Baghdad in 1969.

373 **Republic of fear: Saddam's Iraq.**
Samir al-Khalil. London: Hutchinson, 1991. 296p.

Written by Kanʿan Makiya under a pseudonym and originally published in 1989, the updated edition includes an assessment of Iraq after the war of 1991 and notes that 'the principal victims, as always, have been the long-suffering people of Iraq'. This book is an indictment of the Baʿth Party and Saddam's regime which terrorized the Iraqi people, but at the same time created in Iraq the most powerful and most stable regime in the country's modern history.

374 **Human rights in Iraq.**
Middle East Watch (D. A. Korn, edited by K. Roth, A. Whitley, E. Goldstein). New Haven, CT: Yale University Press, 1990, rp. 1991. 155p. map. bibliog. (Human Rights Watch Books, 164).

A detailed indictment of Iraq's gross infractions of human rights over two decades of rule by the Baʿth Party. The chapters cover: Background; The institutions of repression; The constitution, the judiciary, and fundamental rights; The forms of repression; The Kurdish minority; The treatment of Iranian prisoners of war; The United States and Iraq; Covering up human rights violations; Conclusions and recommendations.

375 **L'opposition irakienne: le temps des ingérences.** (The Iraqi opposition: the times of interference.)
Chris Kutschera. *Cahiers de l'Orient*, no. 25-26 (1-2nd trim. 1992), p. 57-71.

Kutschera discusses the tensions between the different elements in the Iraqi opposition, especially between the Kurds and others, and the personalities who make up the Sunni Arab opposition. A brief abstract in English appears on p. 317.

376 **Politics in Iraq.**
Edited by Shiv Lal. New Delhi: The Election Archives, 1985. 160p.

Contains three sections entitled: 'Iraq goes to the polls October 1984'; 'The Iraq constitution'; 'The interim constitution of Iraq'. This is a markedly uncritical book.

377 **Saddam Hussein's political thinking: the comparison with Nasser.**
Peter Mansfield. In: *Iraq: the contemporary state*, edited by Tim Niblock. London: Croom Helm; New York: St. Martin's Press, 1982, p. 62-74.

Mansfield attempts to identify standing themes in Saddam Hussein's strategy and political thinking.

378 **Iraq's leadership dilemma: a study in leadership trends, 1948-1968.**
Phebe Ann Marr. *Middle East Journal*, vol. 24, no. 3 (Summer 1970), p. 283-301.
Examines the ethnic, religious, social, educational and occupational background of the political leaders of Iraq in the decade before and after the 1958 Revolution, and their individual records of survival on the political scene.

379 **The political elite in Iraq.**
Phebe A. Marr. In: *Political elites in the Middle East*, edited by George Lenczowski. Washington, DC: American Enterprise Institute for Public Policy Research, 1975, p. 109-49.
A study of the group which has made decisions on public policy since the Revolution of 1958: of their historical perspective, educational and socio-economic background and occupation (military or civilian). The group comprised 125 men and two women.

380 **La nomenklatura irakienne, ou l'organisation du pouvoir en Irak.**
(The Iraqi nomenklatura, or the organization of power in Iraq.)
*Cahiers de l'Orient*, vol. 8-9 (4th qu. 1987 – 1st qu. 1988), p. 341-51.
Describing itself as 'Le Who's Who du pouvoir en Irak', this article offers brief biographical descriptions of the men around the President of Iraq who exercise power conferred by him, and on occasions, on his behalf. The names are arranged alphabetically.

381 **The postage stamp: a window on Saddam Hussein's Iraq.**
Donald Malcolm Reid. *Middle East Journal*, vol. 47, no. 1 (Winter 1993), p. 77-89.
Asserts that Saddam Husayn has personified his country since 1979 when he took over as president and that Iraqi postage stamps which have appeared since that time 'provide a significant gauge of the images Saddam Hussein wanted to project'. The stamps are classified into: Portraits, military themes, and the cult of personality; From 'colonial picturesque' to turath (heritage/folklore); Revolutionary symbols of 'the people' and industrialization; Arab nationalist / Islamic themes; Non-ideological and international themes.

382 **Saddam's Iraq: revolution or reaction?**
London: Committee Against Repression and for Democratic Rights in Iraq, CARDRI. rev. ed. 1989, rp. 1990. 254p. maps. bibliog.
A collective volume exposing the nature of Saddam Husayn's regime in Iraq and the political situation in the late 1980s. The contents are: 'Iraq to 1963' by Fran Hazleton (p. 1-29); 'Political development in Iraq 1963-1980' by U. Zaher (p. 30-53); 'Oil and the Iraqi economy' by Celine Whittleton (p. 54-72); 'The parasitic base of the Baʿthist regime' by ʿIsam al-Khafaji (p. 73-88); 'Iraqi Baʿthism: nationalism, socialism and national socialism' by Marion Farouk-Sluglett, Peter Sluglett (p. 89-107); 'Baʿth terror – two personal accounts' by an Iraqi mother and Suʿad Khairi (p. 108-19); 'Women in Iraq' by Deborah Cobbett (p. 120-37); 'The opposition' by U. Zaher (p. 138-76); 'The Kurds' by Peter Sluglett (p. 177-202); 'The Iraqi armed forces, past

and present' by A. Abbas (p. 203-28); 'Iraq in the Gulf War' by Jabr Muhsin, George Harding, Fran Hazleton (p. 229-41); 'Whither Iraq' by Celine Whittleton, Jabr Muhsin, Fran Hazleton (p. 242-52); 'UN Security Council Resolution 598' (p. 253-54).

### 383 Socialisme en Irak et en Syrie. (Socialism in Iraq and in Syria.)
A. G. Samarbakhsh. Paris: Antropos, 1980. 344p.

Examines the political background, achievements and operation of the 'home-grown' socialism of the Arab world as it has been expounded and practised by the Ba'th Party regimes in Iraq and Syria, and discusses the extent to which it deserves to be described as socialist.

### 384 Organisation et structure du pouvoir en Irak. (Organization and structure of power in Iraq.)
Antoine Sfeir. *Cahiers de l'Orient*, no. 20 (4th trim. 1990), p. 129-33.

Sfeir describes Saddam Husayn's methods of controlling the Ba'th Party and the army in Iraq since 1969.

### 385 Sunnis and Shi'is revisited: sectarianism and ethnicity in authoritarian Iraq.
Peter Sluglett, Marion Farouk-Sluglett. In: *Iraq: power and society*, edited by Derek Hopwood, Habib Ishow, Thomas Koszinowski. Oxford: Ithaca, for St. Antony's College, 1993, p. 75-90.

Reconsiders some of interpretations of the Sunni–Shi'i divide in Iraqi politics published in the 1970s and argues that 'the process of national integration was checked by an increasingly powerful totalitarian state'. Political developments since 1958 are summarized to illustrate this view.

### 386 Qasim and the Iraq Communist Party: a study in Arab politics.
Oles M. Smolansky. In: *Man, state and society in the contemporary Middle East*, edited by Jacob M. Landau. New York: Praeger, 1972, p. 151-82.

Argues that the Communist Party was a major political force in Iraq, although mostly it was forced to operate underground. After the 1958 Revolution, it came out into the open, and 'Abd al-Karim Qasim alternately courted it and pushed it away from the centres of power during his regime.

### 387 The 1968 revolution in Iraq: experience and prospects. The political report of the Eighth Congress of the Arab Ba'th Socialist Party in Iraq, January 1974.
London: Ithaca Press, 1979. 176p.

This work was first published in 1974. Book one gives the Party's official analysis of the Party's taking of power in July 1968 and the tasks which faced it in the matter of socialist transformation. Book two lays out the tasks of the phase for 1974-79.

**"Socialist" Iraq 1963-1978. Towards a reappraisal.**
*See* item no. 233.

**Iraq: ethnic minorities and their impact on politics.**
*See* item no. 420.

**The old social classes and the revolutionary movements of Iraq.**
*See* item no. 513.

**Economy and politics in the Arab world: a comparative analysis of Egypt, Iraq and Saudi Arabia since the 1950s.**
*See* item no. 603.

**Communism and agrarian reform in Iraq.**
*See* item no. 658.

# Constitution and Law

388 **Legal system of Iraq.**
S. H. Amin. Glasgow: Royston, 1989. 582p. bibliog.
A description of the Iraqi legal system intended to be useful for those with no previous knowledge of Arabic or of Iraqi law as well as for the legal profession. The sections give a general outline, the law of contracts, extra-contractual personal status, property, evidence and procedure. There is an extensive bibliography.

389 **Middle East legal systems.**
Sayed Hasan Amin. Glasgow: Royston, 1985. 419p.
See especially Chapter four 'Iraq' on p. 150-243. Amin gives a general introduction to and history of Iraqi law from before the Islamic era through to the British Mandate administration, and describes the development of the national legal system, the sources of Iraqi law, the judiciary and court structure, the legal profession, and legal education. A bibliography of Iraqi law is included which contains Arabic sources for secular and Islamic law and material in European languages.

390 **A law of personal status for Iraq.**
J. N. D. Anderson. *International and Comparative Law Quarterly*, vol. 9, no. 4 (October 1960), p. 542-64.
Provides a detailed review of the Iraqi Code of Personal Status enacted in 1959. This law created a unified code which eliminated the differences among the four recognized Sunni schools, and between Sunni and Shiʿi legal prescriptions in matters of personal status in Iraq.

391 **Business laws of Iraq.**
Translated by Nicola H. Karam. London: Graham & Trotman,
1980- . (Middle East Business Law Series).
Issued in a loose-leaf binder with periodic supplements, these are translations of laws
affecting commercial transactions. The supplements include new laws, amendments
to existing laws, or newly relevant texts of current laws.

392 **Constitutions, electoral laws, treaties of states in the Near and
Middle East.**
Helen Miller Davis. Durham, NC: Duke University Press, 1953.
2nd rev. and enlarged ed. 541p. map. rp. New York: AMS Press,
1970.
This work consists of documents, organized by country. Iraq, on p. 151-204, contains
texts of the following: Constitution (Organic law) of Iraq promulgated 21 March
1925, as amended 29 July 1925 and 27 October 1943; Electoral law of 27 May 1946;
Treaty of Alliance between the UK and Iraq 30 June 1930; Declaration of the
Kingdom of Iraq, made at Baghdad on the occasion of the termination of the
Mandatory Regime in Iraq, 30 May 1932; Note on treaties.

393 **Irakisches Arbeitsrecht: das Irakische Arbeitsgesetz nebst
Feiertagsgesetz und anderen neuen Regelungen der Irakischen
Republik.** (Iraqi labour law: the Iraqi labour statute with statutory
holidays and other regulations of the new Iraqi Republic.)
Translated by Norbert F. Küppers. Frankfurt am Main, Germany:
Verlag Kommentator, 1959. 80p.
The legal text of the Iraqi labour law translated into German.

394 **Claims against Iraq: the current status.**
Mahir Jalili. *Arab Law Quarterly*, vol. 7, no. 1 (1992), p. 64-68.
Explains the situation regarding the status of claims against Iraq arising from the
invasion and occupation of Kuwait and the arrangements made for the United Nations
Compensation Fund.

395 **Des modifications à apporter aux dispositions du code pénal
irakien sur la fixation de la peine. Etude comparative.**
(Modifications to be made to the Iraqi penal code in fixing the penalty.
Comparative study.)
Hammoudi al-Jassim. Geneva: Librairie E. Droz; Paris: Librairie
Minard, 1959. 333p. bibliog.
A highly detailed legal study discussing the fixing of the penalty in Iraqi criminal law,
the reasons for allowing mitigation and assessment of mitigating circumstances.

### 396 Essential principles of insurance contract.

Sa'doun Naji al-Kishtaini.   Baghdad: al-Ma'aref Press, 1977. 2nd ed. 164p.

A study, primarily intended for law students, of the principles of insurance-contracting in Iraq.

### 397 Personal law in Islamic countries: (history, text and comparative analysis).

Tahir Mahmood.   New Delhi: Academy of Law and Religion, 1987. 310p.

Chapter 3, 'Iraq: The code of personal status and supplementary laws 1959-1984' (p. 49-72), gives the texts of the laws with a brief introduction.

### 398 Shi'ism and Sunnism in Iraq: revisiting the codes.

Chibli Mallat.   *Arab Law Quarterly*, vol. 8, no. 2 (1993), p. 141-59.

Examines the significance of the Sunni–Shi'i divide in Iraq as manifested in the criticisms of the unified Personal Status Code of 1959 made by Muhammad Bahr al-'Ulum, a Shi'i scholar, in a treatise published in Najaf in 1963. The changes in legal practice brought in by the Code raised a number of problems in the matter of family and personal law.

### 399 Bridging the gulf.

Sabah al-Mukhtar.   *Arab Law Quarterly*, vol. 8, no. 3 (1993), p. 184-89.

The author notes changes in Iraqi laws which have been enacted since 1991 and which affect the affairs of foreign companies who were enagaged in Iraq at the time of the invasion of Kuwait in 1990 and left in a hurry. These companies either owe Iraq money or have unfulfilled obligations, or are owed money by Iraq for work carried out.

### 400 Lawyers and politics in the Arab world, 1880-1960.

Donald M. Reid.   Minneapolis, MN and Chicago, IL: Bibliotheca Islamica, 1981. 399p. bibliog. (Studies in Middle Eastern History, 5).

As part of the élite in Middle Eastern society, lawyers have played an important part in recent political history. This book surveys the role played by lawyers in the move towards national independence and constitutional governments in Egypt and the Fertile Crescent. Chapters 3 'Lawyers in the Fertile Crescent up to 1918' (p. 68-90) and 4 'Arab lawyers, political culture and social values' (p. 91-117) discuss the general situation. Chapters 11 and 12 'Iraqi lawyers, 1918-1960' parts 1 and 2 (p. 324-79) deal with Iraq in particular.

401   **Commercial arbitration in the Arab Middle East: a study in Shari'a and statute law.**
Samir Saleh.   London: Published under the patronage of the International Chamber of Commerce by Graham & Trotman, 1984. 440p.

Part 1 describes the Shari'a (Islamic religious law) and Part 2 the modern statute law concerning commercial arbitration in the Arab Middle East. Chapter 15 of Part 2 'Iraq' (p. 175-94) cites the relevant legal statutes and laws, and gives details of relevant institutions and practices.

402   **Property law in the Arab world: real rights in Egypt, Iraq, Jordan, Lebanon, Libya, Syria, Saudi Arabia and the Gulf States.**
Farhat J. Ziadeh.   London: Graham & Trotman, 1979. 203p. bibliog.

Briefly presents the history of rights in real estate and property in the countries mentioned in the title, with an indication of the sources for such rights – whether grounded in Islamic or Western law. The current legal doctrine concerning the nature and extent of real rights is given. The study is arranged by subject, with comparison and discussion of the all countries under the headings of ownership, acquisition of ownership, rights derived from right of ownership, securities and tenancy.

**Renewal of Islamic law . . .**
*See* item no. 474.

**Labor laws in the Middle East: tradition in transit.**
*See* item no. 578.

**Development of agricultural land taxation in modern Iraq.**
*See* item no. 620.

# Biographies

403 **Iraqi statesman: a portrait of Mohammed Fadhel Jamali.**
Harry J. Almond.   Salem, OR: Grosvenor Books, 1993. 165p.
bibliog.

A biography of Muhammad Jamali (b. 1902), a Shiʿi who began his career in the Ministry of Education, but from 1945 to 1958 was associated with foreign affairs. He was foreign minister five times, and prime minister for seven months. After the revolution of 1958, he spent three years in prison, but was pardoned in 1961 and lived the rest of his long life in Tunisia, teaching at the University of Tunis and writing.

404 **Jelal Talebani (Jalâl Ṭâlabânî).**
E. Franz.   *Orient* (Opladen), vol. 28, no. 1 (March 1974), p. 5-8.

A brief biography of the life and career of Jalal Talabani, the president of the Patriotic Union of Kurdistan.

405 **Saddam Hussein: a political biography.**
Efraim Karsh, Inari Rautsi.   London: Brassey's (UK), 1991. 292p.
maps. bibliog.

A well-researched and balanced biography of Saddam Husayn's rise to power and control of Iraq, of which he has been the ruler since 1974, although he became President himself only in 1979. The story is taken up to the 1991 war against Iraq.

406 **Saʿdun Hammadi (Saʿdûn Ḥammâdî). Kurzbiographien.** (Saʿdun
Hammadi. Biographical sketch.)
Thomas Koszinowski.   *Orient*, (Opladen), vol. 32, no. 1 (1991),
p. 5-9.

A brief synopsis of Hammadi's political career. Born in 1930 in Karbala, he became a member of the Baʿth Party in 1949, and has been associated with the government of Iraq since 1963.

407    **Saddam Hussein: un gaullisme arabe?** (Saddam Husayn: an Arab
       De Gaulle?).
       Charles Saint-Prot.    Paris: Albin Michel, 1987. 234p. map. bibliog.
Written by an admirer of Saddam before the invasion of Kuwait in 1990. Part one
argues that Saddam Hussein superintended the transformation of Iraq into a modern,
free and strong nation able to play its role in the international arena. Part two
describes the domestic agenda which created a nation out of a country lacking a
national identity.

# Population and Ethnic Minorities

## General

### 408 Current population trends in Iraq.
Doris G. Adams. *Middle East Journal*, vol. 10, no. 2 (Spring 1956), p. 151-65.

Adams discusses the population structure given in the results of the 1947 census, and trends in fertility and mortality.

### 409 The anthropology of Iraq.
Henry Field. Chicago, IL: Field Museum of Natural History; Cambridge, MA: Peabody Museum, 1951-52. 2 pts. (Field Museum of Natural History Anthropological Series, Vol. 30i-ii; Papers of the Peabody Museum of American Archaeology & Ethnology, Harvard University, 46i-iii).

Published as Part 1, nos 1 & 2; Part 2, nos 1-3, these papers provide the results of a detailed physical anthropological study of various ethnic types and religious communities in Iraq, including Yazidis, Turkmens, Arabs, Kurds, Assyrians, Jews, Armenians and Gypsies.

### 410 Arabs of central Iraq, their history, ethnology, and physical characters.
Henry Field. Chicago, IL: Field Museum of Natural History, 1935. 463p. map. bibliog.

A detailed anthropological study of the physical types of the Arabs and Bedouin living near Kish.

411 **Population movements.**
M. S. Hasan. In: *The economic history of the Middle East 1800-1914*, edited by Charles Issawi. Chicago, IL: University of Chicago Press, 1966, p. 154-62.

This article is reprinted with a few omissions from 'Growth and structure of Iraq's population, 1867-1947' published in the *Bulletin of the Oxford University Institute of Statistics*, vol. 20 (1958), p. 339-52 and charts the demographic development of Iraq in the late 19th and early 20th centuries. It is one of nine items reproduced in Part three 'Iraq' on p. 127-202 all of which are taken from sources not easily available. The other articles are: 'Trade in 1800' by J-B. Rousseau taken from the *Description du Pachalik de Baghdad* published in Paris in 1809; 'Projected railway to the Mediterranean, 1850s' by Edward de Warren, published in 1857; 'Steam navigation on the Tigris and Euphrates, 1861-1932' reprinted from the *Story of the Euphrates Company*, published in 1935; 'Land tenure in the nineteenth century' by Saleh Haider from a London University thesis of 1942; 'Production, transport, and foreign trade in the 1900's' by Adriano Lanzoni, translated from the Italian published in 1910; 'Taxation in the 1900's' by Saʿid Himadah, translated from the Arabic published in 1938; 'Irrigation projects in the 1900's' by Sir W. Willcocks, published in 1910; 'The struggle for oil in Iraq' by Karl Hoffmann, translated from the German published in 1927. Hasan's article is a valuable source on this subject.

412 **Zur Geschichte der Ethnologie im Iraq.** (On the history of ethnology in Iraq.)
P. Heine, R. Stipek. *Al-Rafidayn: Jahrbuch zu Geschichte und Kultur des Modernen Iraq*, vol. 1 (1991), p. 9-20.

Describes the development of anthropological and ethnological studies of Iraq. The article is followed, on p. 21-40, by a bibliography of such works, 'Bibliographie zur Ethnologie des Iraq', compiled by the two authors, along with I. Herterich-Akinpelu.

413 **Minorities in the Arab world.**
Albert H. Hourani. Oxford: Oxford University Press, 1947. 125p. maps.

This is still the clearest presentation of the population mosaic of the Middle East. See chapter 11 'Iraq' for a succinct survey of Iraq's ethnic and religious make-up as of the late 1940s. The author argues that the minority problem in Iraq is much more one of relations between Arabs and non-Arabs than is the case in other Arab countries.

414 **Internal migration in Iraq.**
Atheel al-Jomard. In: *The integration of modern Iraq*, edited by Abbas Kelidar. London: Croom Helm, 1979, p. 111-22.

Discusses the determinants of internal migration in Iraq from rural areas to the cities using census data from the 1947, 1957 and 1965 population censuses.

415　An econometric analysis of fertility: the case of Iraq.
　　　Mihssen Kadhim, J. W. Leasure. *Pakistan Economic & Social
　　　Review*, vol. 13, no. 3-4 (Autumn-Winter 1975), p. 179-87.
A demographic study of fertility in Iraq which argues that the rather high rate of
population growth will not decline significantly in the short term.

416　Iraq: a sectarian polity.
　　　M. A. Saleem Khan. *Islam and the Modern Age*, vol. 3, no. 1
　　　(February 1972), p. 76-99.
The author describes the differentiation of the Iraqi population, the tensions and
discontent shown by various sectors during British rule, and the lack of national
integration or national identity.

417　Regional variations of fertility in Iraq and factors affecting it.
　　　K. L. Kohli. *Journal of Biosocial Science*, vol. 9, no. 2 (April 1977),
　　　p. 175-82.
A demographic study of differentials in fertility of Iraq's provinces, based on the
results of the 1965 population census.

418　Iraq: changing population patterns.
　　　R. I. Lawless. In: *Populations of the Middle East and North Africa*,
　　　edited by J. I. Clarke, W. B. Fisher. London: University of London
　　　Press, 1972, p. 97-129.
Lawless presents a survey of the ethnic and religious make-up of the population of
Iraq, its spatial distribution in the country, the various lifestyles (nomadic, village and
urban), and trends in migration within Iraq during the 20th century. Statistical data
and maps are included.

419　The social characteristics of the population of Iraq.
　　　Jack S. McCrary, Mustafa Sa'eed. *Bulletin of the College of Arts*
　　　(Baghdad), no. 11 (1968), p. 71-124.
Describes the population of Iraq in terms of its size and distribution, movement, and
dynamics (fertility, mortality, marriage and divorce). Many statistical tables are
included.

420　Iraq: ethnic minorities and their impact on politics.
　　　Munir H. Nasser. *Journal of South Asian and Middle Eastern
　　　Studies*, vol. 8, no. 3 (Spring 1985), p. 22-37.
A useful description of the ethnic and religious make-up of the population of Iraq,
including some statistics, and the relations of the various communities with the state
before and after the revolution of 1958.

421 **Population in the Arab world: problems & prospects.**
Abdel-Rahim Omran. New York: U.N. Fund for Population
Activities; London: Croom Helm, 1980. 197p. bibliog.
Discusses the whole Arab world, with specific reference to individual countries
(including Iraq) where appropriate, under the headings: historical and demographic
context; demographic profiles; health and social institutions; consequences of rapid
population growth and excessive fertility; and population policy. Many charts and
tables are included.

422 **The population situation in the ECWA region: Iraq.**
Beirut: United Nations Economic Commission for Western Asia,
1980. 26p. bibliog.
An attempt to provide a survey of the population of Iraq in the late 1970s. After
discussing the sources of data, the study briefly considers in turn the size, distribution
and structure of the population, fertility, mortality, migration, growth, education, and
economic activity (years 1947-77). The appendixes provide useful lists of statistical
documents, organizations dealing with population matters, and references.

423 **Spatial diffusion of the population of al-Jazirah region in Iraq.**
Abbas F. Sa'adi. *Population Bulletin of ESCWA*, no. 35/36/37
(December 1989-December 1990), p. 99-127.
Discusses the variables affecting population diffusion and provides data at the lowest
administrative level (nahiyah) in order to illustrate the diffusion of the population of
the Jazirah region of north-west Iraq which lies between the Tigris and Euphrates
rivers and the border with Syria. The data are derived from the population censuses
held in 1977 and 1987.

**Les relations inter-communautaires en Irak.**
*See* item no. 462.

# Kurds

424 **The Anfal Campaign in Iraqi Kurdistan: the destruction of Koreme, the forced relocation of its inhabitants, the massacre and disappearance of its men and boys, the chemical weapons attack on the village of Birjinni, and the death of Farwan Tawa Mostafa, a female infant, at Beharke Camp, in the course of the 1988 Anfal Campaign against the Kurds of Iraqi Kurdistan by the Government of Saddam Hussein. Oral testimony and physical forensic evidence. A report by Middle East Watch, a division of Human Rights Watch and Physicians for Human Rights.**
Kenneth Anderson, edited by Andrew Whitley.   New York: Human Rights Watch, 1993. 116p.
Presents evidence of the Iraqi government's brutality in the course of its campaign to subdue the Kurdish population of northern Iraq in 1988.

425 **The lost peoples of the Middle East: documents of the struggle for survival and independence of the Kurds, Assyrians, and other minority races in the Middle East.**
Edited and introduced by F. David Andrews.   Salisbury, NC: Documentary Publications, 1982. 163p.
The transcriptions of documents previously classified as confidential and secret materials in the US National Archives, 1945-50. The subject matter is mainly concerned with the Iraqi Kurds and Assyrians.

426 **Principles of social organization in southern Kurdistan.**
Fredrik Barth.   Oslo: Brørene Jørgensen, 1953. 144p. bibliog.
(Universitets Etnografiske Museum Bulletin, 7).
Based on material collected in Kirkuk and Sulaymaniyah provinces in 1951, this anthropological study describes formal political organization, non-political hierarchical organization, the village scene and local social structures of the area.

427 **Les Kurdes et le Kurdistan: bibliographie critique 1977-1986.**
(The Kurds and Kurdistan: critical bibliography 1977-1986.)
Joyce Blau et collaborateurs.   Paris: Institut Français de Recherche en Iran, 1989. 146p. (Abstracta Iranica: Volumes Hors Série, 5).
A corrected and edited compilation of bibliographical citations on the Kurds extracted from the periodical *Abstracta Iranica*. The bibliographies are annotated, and include items in all languages, including Kurdish. They are reprinted as in the original volumes, but a short subject index and author index have been added.

428 **Agha, shaikh and state: the social and political structures of Kurdistan.**
Martin van Bruinessen.   London: Zed Books, 1992. 373p. maps.
bibliog.
A detailed anthropological study of the social organization of the Kurds, including those living in Iraq. This excellent PhD thesis was submitted at Utrecht in 1978, but published much later.

429 **People without a country: the Kurds and Kurdistan.**
Edited by Gerard Chaliand, translated by Michael Pallis.   London: Zed, 1993. rev. and updated ed. map. bibliog.
First published in French in Paris in 1978 as *Les Kurdes et le Kurdistan*, this book deals with the whole area where Kurds live, but see in particular: Chapter 1 'The Kurds under the Ottoman Empire' by Kendal (p. 11-37); Chapter 5 'Kurdistan in Iraq' by Ismet Sheriff Vanly (p. 139-93); Chapter 9 'The two Gulf Wars: the Kurds on the world stage, 1949-1992' by Kamran Karadaghi (p. 214-30); and Chapter 10 'Operation Provide Comfort: false promises to the Kurds' by Bill Frelick (p. 231-37). There is a chronology of Kurdistan from the 7th century CE to May 1992 and a bibliography.

430 **Winds of death: Iraq's use of poison gas against its Kurdish population. Report of a Medical Mission to Turkish Kurdistan by Physicians for Human Rights, February 1989.**
[Robert Mullen Cook-Deegan, Howard Hu].   Somerville, MA: Physicians for Human Rights, 1989. 39p. maps.
The findings of the report are that Iraqi aircraft attacked Kurdish villages in northern Iraq around Halabjah with bombs containing lethal poison gas on 25 August 1988. The report presents the evidence collected from survivors in Turkey.

431 **Hygiene and attention to personal appearance among the Iraqi Kurds.**
Leszek Dzięgiel.   *Archív Orientální*, vol. 50 (1982), p. 43-50.
Discusses personal cleanliness, and cleanliness of clothing, homes, and public areas in a part of rural Iraq inhabited by Kurds, in the context of health practice, available water and services, and the health status of the population in a rather isolated area where free medical care and modern development were made available only in 1975. The author carried out field research as part of a Polish team of experts in 1977, 1978 and 1980.

432 **Villages et petites villes kurdes dans l'Irak actuel: construction traditionnelle, formes et fonctions dans leur processus de changement culturel.** (Kurdish villages and small towns in contemporary Iraq: traditional construction, forms and functions in the process of cultural change.)
Leszek Dzięgiel.   *Studia Kurdica*, vol. 1-5 (1988), p. 127-56.
The author, an anthropologist, carried out fieldwork in 80 villages and small towns in the Dohuk, Arbil and Sulaymaniyah areas during 1977-80. This essay describes the

rural lifestyle, forms of houses and farms and the changes which had begun to affect the Kurds, economically and politically since 1970.

### 433 Kurdish ethnonationalism.
Nader Entessar. Boulder, CO: Lynne Rienner, 1992. 191p. bibliog.
Sets out to 'analyse the political and social dimension of Kurdish integration into the mainstream of sociopolitical life in Iran, Iraq and Turkey'. The author considers that ethnic conflict constitutes a major challenge to the contemporary nation-state, and charts the history of the Kurds in Iraq since the creation of the modern state in the 1920s, with some treatment also of the experience of the Kurds in Iran and Turkey.

### 434 The Kurdish question in Iraq.
Edmund Ghareeb. Syracuse, NY: Syracuse University Press, 1981. 218p. map.
Ghareeb describes the historical context of the Kurdish question in Iraq and, in particular, the Ba'th Party's attempts from 1968 to 1980 to come to an understanding with the Kurds concerning their status in northern Iraq. The author concludes that a separatist nationalism in a land-locked country cannot win against a strong government, unless it has strong foreign support. Subsequent events have not disproved this argument.

### 435 The Kurds of Iraq: tragedy and hope.
Michael M. Gunter. New York: St. Martin's Press, 1992. 152p. map.
A history of Iraqi Kurdistan from Mustafa Barzani's revolt in the 1960s up to and including the rebellion after the Gulf War in 1991 and the establishment of a degree of autonomous government.

### 436 Daughters of Allah: among Moslem women in Kurdistan.
Henny Harald Hansen. London: Allen & Unwin, 1960. 190p. maps.
Hansen describes her work as a travel book by an ethnographer who visited the area due to be flooded by the Doka dam in 1957 and carried out research in the villages. It is an account of her work and the life of the local people written for the general reader. A more formal account of her ethnographic research was published as *The Kurdish woman's life: field research in a Muslim society, Iraq* (Copenhagen, 1961).

### 437 Die kurdische Nationalbewegung im Irak: eine Fallstudie zur Problematik ethnischer Konflikte in der Dritten Welt. (The Kurdish national movement in Iraq: a case study on the problems of ethnic conflict in the Third World.)
Ferhad Ibrahim. Berlin: Schwarz, 1983. 824p. maps. bibliog. (Islamkundliche Untersuchungen, 88).
A detailed study of the history of the Kurdish nationalist movement in Iraq in the 20th century, under British rule, the monarchy and since the Revolution in 1958. The historical introduction traces its roots back to the 16th century.

438 **The Kurds: a concise handbook.**
Mehrdad R. Izady. Washington, DC: Crane Russak, 1992. 268p.
map. bibliog.
A succinct guide to the Kurdish nation, with chapters covering their land and environment, history, demography and settlement, religion, language, literature, press, society, political parties, culture and arts. Short bibliographies are appended to each section.

439 **The Kurdish problem in Iraq.**
Sa'ad N. Jawad. In: *The integration of modern Iraq*, edited by Abbas Kelidar. London: Croom Helm, 1979, p. 171-82.
Jawad reviews the history of Kurdish rebellion against central Iraqi rule up to 1975 and the government's failure to resolve it.

440 **Recent developments in the Kurdish issue.**
Sa'ad Jawad. In: *Iraq: the contemporary state*, edited by Tim Niblock. London: Croom Helm; New York: St. Martin's Press, 1982, p. 47-61.
Describes the history of the Kurdish movement since the 1958 revolution, the Ba'th Party's efforts to deal with the Kurdish problem by both peaceful and aggressive means between 1970 and 1975, and the factional differences among the Kurds themselves.

441 **The trend of population of Sulaimaniya Liwa: a case study of Kurdish population.**
Shakir Khesbak. *Bulletin of the College of Arts* (Baghdad), no. 1 (1959), p. 42-64.
A demographic study of the province which argues that its population has been largely static because a high mortality rate counterbalanced a high fertility rate, but that the death-rate can be expected to drop, leading to a population growth. The article includes many statistical tables.

442 **The Kurds: a nation denied.**
David McDowall. London: Minority Rights Publications, 1992.
141p. maps. bibliog.
A concise general history and description of the Kurds. See in particular the following chapters: 1. 'Kurdistan: the land of the Kurds'; 2. 'The basis of Kurdish society: tribes, shaikhs and aghas'; 3. 'Hidden from history: the Kurds before 1920'; 10. 'The Kurds in Iraq: from the mandate to the Ba'th'; 11. 'The Kurds in Iraq: under the Ba'th'; 12. 'Kurds between warring states: the Iran–Iraq war'; 13. 'Kurdish uprising 1991: brief victory and bitter defeat' (p. 81-120).

443  **Hidden death: land mines and civilian casualties in Iraqi Kurdistan.**
(Rae McGrath, edited by Aryeh Neier).   New York: Middle East Watch, 1992. 67p.

Millions of land-mines were laid by the Iraqi army in Iraqi Kurdistan during the Iran–Iraq war and along the borders with Turkey and Syria before the 1991 war. They do not self-destruct and their locations are not marked or recorded. After mid-1991 the Iraqi army withdrew from Kurdistan and Kurdish civilians returned to their homes and farms, where huge numbers suffered injury. This report documents the problem and concludes that the Iraqi army deliberately intended to make large tracts of land unusable for all time, and that its actions contravened International Protocols and customary International Law.

444  **The Kurdish revolt: 1961-1970.**
Edgar O'Ballance.   London: Faber & Faber, 1973. 189p. maps.

An account by a military historian of the Kurdish revolt against the Baʿthist Iraqi government in the 1960s. This book traces the course of the military action.

445  **The creation of a Kurdish state in the 1990s?**
Robert Olson.   *Journal of South Asian and Middle Eastern Studies*, vol. 15, no. 4 (Summer 1992), p. 1-25.

Olson considers the prospects for the Kurds in Iraq after the Gulf War of 1991, and the attitudes of Iran, Turkey, and Syria, which all have their own Kurdish populations, to recent developments in Iraq.

446  **The Kurds: a contemporary overview.**
Edited by Philip G. Kreyenbroek, Stefan Sperl.   London: Routledge, 1992. 233p. bibliog.

Contains several general articles about Kurdish culture and history followed by essays on the situation of the Kurds in Turkey, Iraq, Lebanon, Syria, Iran and the Soviet Union. The relevant contents are: 'The Kurdish question: a historical review' by David McDowall (p. 10-32); 'Kurdish society, ethnicity, nationalism and refugee problems' by Martin van Bruinessen (p. 33-67); 'On the Kurdish language' by Philip G. Kreyenbroek (p. 68-83); 'Humanitarian legal order and the Kurdish question' by Jane Connors (p. 84-94); 'The situation of Kurds in Iraq and Turkey: current trends and prospects' by Munir Morad (p. 115-33); 'The Kurdish movement in Iraq: 1975-88' by A. Sherzad (p. 134-42). Chapter notes are placed at the end of the book.

**Iraq and the Kurdish question 1958-1970.**
*See* item no. 235.

**A *de facto* Kurdish state in northern Iraq.**
*See* item no. 293.

**Difficult reconstruction in northern Iraq.**
*See* item no. 296.

**Living short, with dignity: in Iraqi Kurdistan.**
*See* item no. 298.

**Jelal Talebani.**
*See* item no. 404.

**An introduction to Kurdish rugs and other weavings.**
*See* item no. 795.


# Turkmens and Turks

447 **The Iraqi Turks yesterday and today.**
Fazil Demirci.   [Istanbul or Ankara?]: Turkish Historical Society
Printing Press, 1991. 82p.
An indictment of the Iraqi regime's treatment of Iraqi Turks. The chapters are headed:
Introduction, general information; The condition of the Iraqi Turks since the First
World War; Conclusion.

448 **The Turkic peoples of Iraq.**
R. I. Lawless.   In: *The Turkic peoples of the world*, edited by
Margaret Bainbridge.   London: Kegan Paul International, 1993,
p. 159-78.
A survey of the numbers, distribution, and present socio-economic situation of the
Turkmens of Iraq, who represent somewhere between two and five per cent of the
Iraqi population and live mainly in the north-eastern areas of the country.

449 **The forgotten minority: the Turkomans of Iraq.**
Zubaida Umar.   *Afkār Inquiry*, vol. 4, no. ii (1987), p. 37-43.
A brief account of the Turkmens in Iraq, their history and their present social and
economic situation.


# Bedouin and Marsh Arabs

450 **Diet and dietary habits of nomads in Iraq.**
Majeed R. al-Ani.   *Ecology of Food and Nutrition*, vol. 9, no. 1
(1980), p. 55-57.
A description of the diet of nomads in Iraq which the author considered to be
adequate. Nevertheless, the article argues that the settled Bedouin would be more at
risk nutritionally than nomadic ones because of changes in their food supply.

451   **Nomadism and sedentarisation in Iraq. A study (dealing with nomadic tribal population)** [*sic*].
Abduljabbar Araim.   Baghdad: Al-Maa'ref [*sic*] Press, 1966. 89p.
Originally written for the Technical Meeting on Nomadism and Sedentarisation convened at the request of the International Labour Office in Geneva, 1964, this general description of nomadic communities in Iraq and of official projects to settle nomads covers the social communities of Iraq, the land system, customary tribal law, and sedentarization projects.

452   **Guests of the Sheik.**
Elizabeth Warnock Fernea.   London: Hale, 1968. 346p.
A personal account of the author's experiences living in a tribal settlement on the edge of a village in southern Iraq in the mid-1950s while her husband carried out his anthropological fieldwork. This is an entertaining picture of the local society, and in particular, of the women's society in which she participated.

453   **Shaykh and effendi: changing patterns of authority among the El Shabana of southern Iraq.**
Robert A. Fernea.   Cambridge, MA: Harvard University Press, 1970. 209p. maps. bibliog.
An anthropological study of a tribal settlement near Daghara in southern Iraq, where the author was investigating the relationship between irrigation and political authority. The fieldwork was carried out in 1956-58.

454   **Bedouin of northern Arabia: traditions of the Āl-Ḍhafīr.**
Bruce Ingham.   London: KPI, 1986. 118p. map. bibliog.
Ingham's book is about the oral traditions, dialect, way of life and socio-economic position of a nomadic Arab tribe whose territory lies across the borders of Saudi Arabia and Iraq. Part of the tribe is resident in Iraq or visits relations living in that country.

455   **Die Nomadenansiedlung in der Irakischen Jezira.** (Sedentarization of nomads in the Iraqi Jezirah.)
Nafi Nasser al-Kasab.   Tübingen, Germany: Universität Tübingen, 1966. 130p. maps. bibliog.
Originally presented as a PhD thesis, this study considers the environment, settlement history, landholding, and process of nomad sedentarization in the Jazirah (north-western Iraq). The final chapter compares the process with that taking place in other countries.

456   **The manners and customs of the Rwala Bedouins.**
Alois Musil.   New York: Prague Press, 1928. 684p. map. (American Geographical Society Oriental Explorations & Studies, 6).
Alois Musil travelled in Arabia and Iraq between 1908 and 1915. This is a detailed anthropological account of the lifestyle, beliefs, traditions and culture of the Rwala Bedouin tribe whose territory extends up into Iraq from northern Arabia.

457 **Marsh dwellers of the Euphrates Delta.**
S. M. Salim. London: Athlone Press, 1962. 148p. bibliog. (London
School of Economics Monographs on Social Anthropology, 23).
An anthropological study of the 'marsh-dwelling community of Bedouin descent on
the Lower Euphrates'. The various parts describe the setting, social organization, and
economic organization.

458 **Soziologie des Nomadentums. Studie über die iraqische
Gesellschaft.** (Sociology of nomadism: a study of Iraqi society.)
Ali al-Wardi, translated by Gunter Weirauch, Ibrahim al-Haidari.
Neuwied and Darmstadt, Germany: Luchterhand, 1972. 447p. bibliog.
(Soziologische Texte, 73).
Originally published in Arabic, this book discusses the impact of nomads on Iraq and
the cultural struggle between the town and country populations in Iraq from Ottoman
times to the present. It provides a sociological study of the formation of personality
and cultural traits in antagonistic sectors of Iraqi society. This complex social
structure has influenced the modern history of the country.

459 **Die Ma'dan: Kultur und Geschichte der Marschenbewohner im
Süd-Iraq.**
Sigrid Westphal-Hellbusch, Heinz Westphal. Berlin: Duncker &
Humblot, 1962. 345p. maps. bibliog. (Forschungen zur Ethnologie und
Sozialpsychologie, 4).
A detailed ethnographic study of the way of life of the Marsh Arabs based on
fieldwork carried out in 1955-56, describing their houses, boats and equipment, social
structure, culture and folklore. This way of life has been largely destroyed by the
central Iraqi government in the wake of the uprisings after the Gulf War of 1991.

**Bedouin tribes of the Euphrates.**
*See* item no. 44.

**The Marsh Arabs.**
*See* item no. 54.

**Return to the marshes.**
*See* item no. 55.

# Other ethnic minorities

460 **Al-Kawliya's attainment of Iraqi nationality and its effect on their socioeconomic transformation: a geographical study.**
T. H. al-Hadithi. *Arab Journal of the Social Sciences*, vol. 3, no. 2 (October 1988), p. 270-93.
The Kawliya are a community of Gypsies who are Muslims (mostly Shi'is) with their own language and who were treated as resident aliens because their nationality was unknown. They formed an underprivileged group in Iraqi society, but in 1978 they were granted Iraqi nationality and by 1982 had ceased their nomadic life and settled in urban centres and rural areas. Their average income and literacy rates rose but only a small percentage of families abandoned their original occupation of dancing.

461 **Egyptian migrant peasants in Iraq.**
Camillia Fawzi el-Solh. *Arab Affairs*, vol. 1, no. 7 (Summer/Autumn 1988), p. 82-95.
An article on the experience of the Egyptian families settled at Khalsah in Iraq, their prejudices about Iraq, and their aspirations in their new homes. The scheme for settling land-poor Egyptians in relatively underpopulated Iraq was sponsored by both governments.

**Migration and the selectivity of change: Egyptian peasant women in Iraq.**
*See* item no. 545.

# Religion

## General

462 **Les relations inter-communautaires en Irak.** (Intercommunal relations in Iraq).
Joyce Blau. *Correspondance d'Orient. Etudes*, vol. 5-6 (1964), p. 87-102.
Blau describes the various communities that make up the Iraqi population. These consist of Muslims (Arabs Sunni and Shiʿi, Kurds Sunni and Shiʿi, Turkmens) and non-Muslims. These latter are Yazidis, Christians (Assyrians, Uniate Chaldeans, Jacobites, Syrian Catholics, Greek Orthodox, Greek Catholics [Melkites], Armenian Orthodox, Armenian Catholics), Sabaeans (or Mandaeans), and Jews. Relations between the communities, especially in the 20th century, are outlined.

463 **Some reflections on the Sunni/Shiʿi question in Iraq.**
Marion Farouk-Sluglett, Peter Sluglett. *British Society for Middle Eastern Studies Bulletin*, vol. 5, no. 2 (1978), p. 79-87.
A critical look at the received wisdom on the division between Sunnis and Shiʿis in analyses of contemporary Iraq, which argues that the revolution of 1958 broke the old pattern of Sunni domination, and that the preponderance of Sunni ministers over Shiʿi ones reflects the realities of power structures in the country rather than some kind of sectarian solidarity.

**Middle Eastern political clichés: 'Takriti' and 'Sunni rule' in Iraq; 'Alawi rule' in Syria: a critical appraisal.**
*See* item no. 362.

# Shiʿi Muslims

**464 The role of Muhammad Baqir al-Sadr in Shiʿi political activism in Iraq from 1958 to 1980.**
T. M. Aziz. *International Journal of Middle East Studies*, vol. 25, no. 2 (May 1993), p. 207-22.

Muhammad Baqir al-Sadr, who was executed on 8 April 1980, had openly supported Khomeini's revolutionary regime in Iran. The Iraqi government consequently considered him a threat to its own survival and moved swiftly against him because he had emerged as an anti-government leader who acted as a catalyst for anti-Baʿth activity. This article argues that Sadr was pushed into political opposition to the regime by supporters who looked to him for leadership because of his standing in the Shiʿi community, although he himself did not believe the time was right.

**465 From radicalism to radical pragmatism: the Shiʿite fundamentalist opposition movements of Iraq.**
Amatzia Baram. In: *Islamic fundamentalisms and the Gulf Crisis*, edited by James Piscatori. Chicago, IL: The Fundamentalism Project, for the American Academy of Arts and Sciences, 1991, p. 20-51.

Describes the components of the Islamic opposition to the Iraqi regime – the Islamic Daʿwah Party, the Supreme Assembly for the Islamic Revolution in Iraq, and the Organization of Islamic Action – their reaction to the Gulf Crisis of 1990-91, and the outbreak and failure of the Shiʿi uprising in southern Iraq after the war.

**466 Iraq's Shiʿa, their political role, and the process of their integration into society.**
Hanna Batatu. In: *The Islamic impulse*, edited by Barbara Freyer Stowasser. London: Croom Helm, in association with the Center for Contemporary Arab Studies, Georgetown University, Washington DC, 1987, p. 204-13.

Describes the social structure of the Shiʿi community in Iraq, its development from 1920 to the 1970s, and involvement in political parties and Shiʿi political organizations.

**467 Shiʿi organizations in Iraq: al-Daʾwah al-Islamiyah and al-Mujahidin.**
Hanna Batatu. In: *Shiʾism and social protest*, edited by Juan R. I. Cole, Nikki R. Keddie. New Haven, CT: Yale University Press, 1986, p. 179-200.

Batatu examines the two underground movements which have attracted a considerable following among the poorer Shiʿis in Iraq, and the reasons for their popularity.

468 **"Indian money" and the Shi'i shrine cities of Iraq 1786-1850.**
Juan R. I. Cole. *Middle Eastern Studies*, vol. 22, no. 4 (October
1986), p. 461-80.
A study of the political economy of the important Shi'i shrine cities of Iraq – Najaf,
Karbala and Kazimayn – which grew up around the tombs of Imams and supported a
number of Shi'i clerics in comfortable circumstances. Funds coming from the Shi'i
state of Oudh (South Asia) in the 18th-19th century paid for the building of mosques
and hostels for Indian pilgrims and gave the local clerics considerable freedom and
power. As a result, the Ottomans eventually took steps to exert their own control over
these cities.

469 **Zur Soziologie des schiitischen Chiliasmus: ein Beitrag zur
Erforschung des irakischen Passionsspiels.** (On the sociology of the
Shi'i millennium: a contribution to research on the Iraqi Passion-play.)
Ibrahim al-Haidari. Freiburg im Breisgau, Germany: Schwarz, 1975.
251p. bibliog. (Islamkundliche Untersuchungen, 31).
A sociological study of millenarianistic beliefs among the Shi'is based on the
Passion-plays put on in Iraq. The history and form of the ta'ziyah [passion-play]
together with socio-political and economic relations in Iraqi society are described,
and then the Passion-play as an expression of Shi'i millenarianism, its meaning, and
its influence on religion and society is discussed.

470 **The theological colleges of Najaf.**
Fāḍil Jamāli. *Muslim World*, vol. 50, no. 1 (January 1960), p. 15-22.
Describes the 20 or more colleges in Najaf – the main centre of Shi'i religious
education – their organization and students, and the nature of the religious instruction
given.

471 **The Shii Imami community and politics in the Arab East.**
Abbas Kelidar. *Middle Eastern Studies*, vol. 19, no. 1 (1983),
p. 3-16.
Describes the history and political organization of the Shi'is in Iraq and their place in
the political life of the country. The author argues that the natural historical
association of Shi'is with the Shi'i state of Iran bedevils the Iraqi community's
attempts to articulate their particular communal interests by laying them open to
charges of disloyalty.

472 **Continuity and change in the ulema population of Najaf and
Karbala, 1791-1904: a socio-demographic study.**
Meir Litvak. *Iranian Studies*, vol. 23, no. 1-4 (1990), p. 31-60.
Litvak describes the student and teacher populations of Najaf and Karbala which
emerged as principal centres of Shi'i learning in the 19th century, and whose ulama
[religious scholars] population increased during that time.

473 **Religious militancy in contemporary Iraq: Muhammad Baqer as-Sadr and the Sunni–Shia paradigm.**
Chibli Mallat. *Third World Quarterly*, vol. 10, no. 2 (April 1988), p. 699-729.

Mallat analyses the process of political change in Iraq from the 1950s to the 1970s and attempts to shed light on the origins of the Iran–Iraq war by considering the role and importance of the Iraqi Shiʿi scholar Muhammad Baqir al-Sadr as leader of the Shiʿi community in Iraq. The ruling regime in Iraq was alarmed by the Iranian revolution and Sadr was executed by the government in April 1980.

474 **Renewal of Islamic law: Muhammad Baqer as-Sadr, Najaf and the Shiʿi international.**
Chibli Mallat. Cambridge: Cambridge University Press, 1993. 227p. bibliog. (Cambridge Middle East Library, 29).

Discusses the way in which the leaders of the Shiʿi Islamic renewal couched their ideas of an appropriate Islamic religious and social order in terms of law and legal form. Muhammad Baqir al-Sadr was one of the most prominent thinkers of the Shiʿi intellectual renaissance in Najaf, and this book discusses some of his published ideas. Part one is headed 'Islamic law and the constitution' and part two 'Islamic law, "Islamic economics", and the interest-free bank'.

475 **The Shiʿis of Iraq.**
Yitzhak Nakash. Princeton, NJ: Princeton University Press, 1994. 288p. map. bibliog.

A history of the Shiʿi community in Iraq under Ottoman, British and independent rule. Today Shiʿis form the largest single community in Iraq. The rise of state power challenged the established centres of Shiʿi influence in Najaf and Karbala, and eventually offered alternative opportunities for political participation, although Shiʿis have resented Sunni domination of the government in Iraq.

476 **Activist Shiʿism in Iran, Iraq, and Lebanon.**
Abdulaziz A. Sachedina. In: *Fundamentalisms Observed*, edited by M. E. Marty, R. Scott Appleby. A study conducted by the American Academy of Arts and Sciences. Chicago, IL: University of Chicago Press, 1991, p. 403-56 (The Fundamentalism Project, 1).

A substantial essay on the history of activist Shiʿi movements and their modern successors in the 1970s and 1980s in Iran, Iraq and Lebanon, which sees these movements as a form of religious fundamentalism. A select bibliography is appended to the article.

477 **The Islamic movement of Iraq (1958-1980).**
Robert Soeterik. Amsterdam: Stichting MERA / Middle East Research Associates, 1991. 24p. bibliog. (Occasional Paper, 12).

This paper studies the role of the Shiʿi ulama [clerics] as the driving force behind the Islamic movement in Iraq, and, in particular, Muhammad Baqir al-Sadr and his sister, known as Bint al-Huda. The Islamic movement's ostentatious support for Ayatollah Khomeini's revolutionary government in Iran led to a confrontation with the Iraqi regime which executed both Baqir al-Sadr and Bint al-Huda in 1980. Many of their followers were rounded up, and others fled into exile.

478    **The Islamic movement of Iraqi Shi'as.**
       Joyce N. Wiley.    Boulder, CO: Lynne Rienner, 1992. 166p. bibliog.
Wiley describes the contemporary Islamic movement among the Shi'is of Iraq, and sets it in the context of Shi'i experience of state violence and social and economic disadvantage. The philosophy and political ideology of the movement are analysed.

**The struggle against Shiism in Hamidian Iraq.**
*See* item no. 145.

**La formation de l'Irak contemporain: le rôle politique des ulémas chiites ...**
*See* item no. 161.

**Anti-Shiism in Iraq under the monarchy.**
*See* item no. 209.

**Shi'is and politics in Ba'thi Iraq.**
*See* item no. 361.

**Shi'ism and Sunnism in Iraq: revisiting the codes.**
*See* item no. 398.

**Ethnicity, cultural discontinuity and power brokers in northern Iraq: the case of the Shabak.**
*See* item no. 529.

# Jews

479    **Rabbi Yaakob Elyichar and his Megillat Paras on the history of the Basra community in the years 1775-1779.**
       Meir Benayahu.    Jerusalem: [Tzur-Ot Press], 1975. 104p.
Discusses the historical background of the Elyichar family and Basra during the war with Iran 1775-79, and then describes the biography of the poet and the *Megillat Paras* [Scroll of Persia] itself which Elyichar wrote to commemorate the miracle that befell the Jews of Basra. He recounts the fall of Basra, its occupation by the Iranians, and their withdrawal from it (1775-79). A translation of the poem is included.

480    **The Jews of Kurdistan.**
       Erich Brauer, completed and edited by Raphael Patai.    Detroit, MI: Wayne State University Press, 1993. 429p. map.
A portrait of the lifestyle, folklore and customs of the Jewish communities who lived in Kurdistan. These long-established communities emigrated in the early 1950s to Israel and elsewhere.

481   **The anti-Jewish *Farhūd* in Baghdad, 1941.**
Hayyim J. Cohen.   *Middle Eastern Studies*, vol. 3, no. 1 (October 1966), p. 2-17.
Cohen argues that the outbreak of mob violence against the Jews in Baghdad in 1941 – the only one experienced by the Jews in Iraq in the last 100 years – was the result of imported anti-Jewish propaganda and did not arise from deep-seated local animosity. The government of the time could have prevented attacks on Jews, and did so effectively from 1945 to 1951, but in June 1941 it was not interested in doing so.

482   **The Jewish minority in Iraq: a comparative study of economic structure.**
Tikva Darvish.   *Jewish Social Studies*, vol. 49, no. 2 (Spring 1987), p. 175-80.
Compares and contrasts the economic structures of the Jewish communities in the three centres of Iraqi Jewry (Mosul, Baghdad and Basra) in 1947, shortly before the mass emigration to Israel.

483   **Aspects of the social life of Kurdish Jews.**
Dina Feitelson.   In: *Jewish societies in the Middle East: community, culture, and authority*, edited by Shlomo Deshen, Walter P. Zenner. Washington, DC: University Press of America, 1982, p. 251-72.
The author reconstructs the social and family life of the Jews of Kurdistan from the testimony of the women from this community now living in Israel.

484   **The connection between the bombings in Baghdad and the emigration of the Jews from Iraq: 1950-51.**
Moshe Gat.   *Middle Eastern Studies*, vol. 24, no. 3 (July 1988), p. 312-29.
Gat argues that it was probably not Zionists who were responsible for the bomb attacks against the Jews in Baghdad, but possibly some radical Arab party.

485   **Iraq and the legislation on Jewish emigration: March 1950.**
Moshe Gat.   *Asian and African Studies* (Haifa), vol. 21, no. 3 (November 1987), p. 263-79.
The author argues that the Iraqi government viewed the emigration of pro-Zionist elements among the Jews of Iraq after 1949 as a means of solving domestic problems and communal unrest, and allowing the remaining Jews to live in peace without agitation against them from pro-Arab elements. The restoration of tranquillity in Iraq would help to reduce economic stagnation.

486   **Flight from Babylon: Iraq, Iran, Israel, America.**
Heskel M. Haddad, as told to Phyllis I. Rosenteur.   New York: McGraw-Hill, 1986. 373p.
The autobiography of an Iraqi Jew who grew up in Baghdad where he was born in 1930. The first half of the book describes his childhood in Iraq, culminating in an exciting account of his escape with a group of Jews from Kurdistan across the border

to Iran in 1949, thence eventually to Israel. He left Israel after a few bitter years, and settled in the USA.

487    **Aspects of Jewish life in Baghdad under the monarchy.**
Sylvia G. Haim. *Middle Eastern Studies*, vol. 12, no. 2 (May 1976), p. 188-208.
Discusses the increasing political pressures on the large and well-established Jewish community in Baghdad during the 1940s and 1950s as nationalist passions were aroused among the Arabs and events in Palestine had repercussions on the Jews in Arab countries.

488    **Operation Babylon.**
Shlomo Hillel, translated by Ina Friedman.    London: Collins, 1988, rp. Fontana, 1989. 392p.
Hillel tells the story of his activities as a clandestine Zionist agent in Iraq attempting to arrange in secret the emigration of the Jewish community to Palestine (and later to Israel) between 1946 and 1951. The author was born in Baghdad and emigrated to Palestine himself in 1934.

489    **The Jews of Baghdad in 1910.**
Elie Kedourie. *Middle Eastern Studies*, vol. 7, no. 3 (October 1971), p. 355-61.
Kedourie presents a British consular report of February 1910 by J. G. Lorrimer entitled 'Account of the Jewish community at Baghdad' which gives a brief description of the social and economic situation of the Jews in Baghdad under late Ottoman rule.

490    **Hakham Sasson in 1949.**
Emile Marmorstein. *Middle Eastern Studies*, vol. 24, no. 3 (July 1988), p. 364-68.
The reprint of an article originally published by Marmorstein in *The Jewish Chronicle* of 30 December 1949 under the title 'Baghdad Jewry's leader resigns'. It describes the resignation of Hakham Sasson Khadouri as official leader of the Baghdad Jewish Community after a demonstration against him by members of the community. The article offers a picture of the internal organization of Iraqi Jewry at the time.

491    **Zionism in Iraq.**
Sadok H. Masliyah. *Middle Eastern Studies*, vol. 25, no. 2 (April 1989), p. 216-37.
A description of the rise and fall of Zionist organizations in the first half of the 20th century in Iraq. The author identifies three periods: the time of small enthusiastic groups 1919-35; the period of curtailment of Jewish freedoms because of problems in Palestine and the influence of Nazi propaganda 1935-41; and the attacks on Jews and arrival of Zionist emissaries which bred a new Zionist movement 1942-51.

492 **The Orbach file: visit to Iraq.**
Maurice Orbach. *New Outlook*, vol. 23 (June/July 1980), p. 70-78;
vol. 23 (August 1980), p. 40-45; vol. 24 (January 1981), p. 34-39;
vol. 24 (April 1981), p. 37-47.
A report on a visit to Iraq by the British Labour MP in the spring of 1958, ostensibly
to visit hospitals, but with the intention of finding out about and assisting the
remaining Iraqi Jews.

493 **The Jews of Iraq: 3000 years of history and culture.**
Nissim Rejwan. London: Weidenfeld & Nicolson, 1985. 266p.
bibliog.
A readable and comprehensive history of the Jews of Iraq from the earliest times to
the mass exodus to Israel in 1951. Part 1 is entitled 'From the Assyrian captivity to
the Arab conquest (731 BC – AD 641)'; Part 2 'The encounter with Islam (641-1850)';
Part 3 'A century of radical change (1850-1951)'.

494 **A history of the Jews in Baghdad.**
David Solomon Sassoon. Letchworth, England: Solomon D.
Sassoon, 1949. 218p.
Written as 'a concise and fairly popular account of the history of the Jews in the place
of my ancestors', this is the story of the community told from the earliest times to the
1940s. It describes its intellectuals and cultural life, and ends with a chapter on
'Settlements of Baghdad Jews in the Far East'.

495 **The history of the Jews in Basra.**
David S. Sassoon. *Jewish Quarterly Review*, N.S. vol. 17, no. 4
(1927), p. 407-69.
An historical survey of the Jewish community in Basra from the 9th century CE to the
20th century CE, based on documentary sources.

496 **The Baghdad connection.**
Maurice M. Sawdayee. [Locust Valley, NY: Sawdayee], 1991. 178p.
bibliog.
Originally a PhD dissertation entitled 'The impact of Western European education of
the Jewish Millet of Baghdad: 1860-1950', submitted to New York University in
1977, the author states that he has published this book in order to make the story of
Baghdad Jewry more widely known. The study describes the impact of modern
Western education provided by the schools of the Alliance Israélite Universelle in the
late 19th century which led to a resurgence in the Jewish community, brought
abruptly to an end in the 1940s by the backlash from Zionism in Palestine and rising
Arab nationalism.

497 **The lure of Zion: the case of the Iraqi Jews.**
Abbas Shiblak. London: Al Saqi, 1986. 152p. bibliog.
Describes the modern history of the Iraqi Jews, one of the longest-established and
most fully integrated Jewish communities in the Arab world, and the impact upon it

of colonial rule, the Zionist project in Palestine, and the growth of Arab nationalism. Part one is entitled 'The Jews of Iraq'; part two 'The colonial legacy'; and part three 'Tension'.

### 498  Naji: an Iraqi country doctor.
Sami Zubaida.   In: *Struggle and survival in the modern Middle East*, edited by Edmund Burke III.   London: Tauris, 1993, p. 234-50.

A concise biography of an Jewish doctor (here given a pseudonym) born in Iraq in 1915. He worked as a doctor there until his appointment was terminated in 1955. The article describes his experiences, the poor conditions of the rural people, and the difficulties he faced in his career as a result of growing Arab nationalist hostility to Jews in post-World War II Iraq. He remained working in Iraq after the exodus of most of the Jewish community in 1950-51, but left eventually in 1970.

**Communal dialects in Baghdad.**
*See* item no. 702.

**Die arabische Dialekt der Juden von 'Aqra und Arbīl.**
*See* item no. 707.

**The Jewish Baghdadi dialect: studies and texts . . .**
*See* item no. 711.

# Christians

### 499  The Arab Christian: a history in the Middle East.
Kenneth Cragg.   Louisville, KY: Westminster/John Knox, 1991; London: Mowbray, 1992. 303p. bibliog.

A readable general history of Arab Christians from the beginnings of Christianity down to modern times. At least half of the book is devoted to the assessment of the modern impact of Arab nationalism and the creation of nation-states on the lives and self-identities of Christians in the Arab countries. Iraq is included in the general discussion throughout.

### 500  Assyrie chrétienne: contribution à l'étude de l'histoire et de la géographie ecclésiastiques et monastiques du nord de l'Iraq.
(Christian Assyria: contribution to the study of the ecclesiastical and monastic history and geography of northern Iraq.)
J. M. Fiey.   Beirut: Imprimerie Catholique, 1965-1968. 3 vols. maps.
(Recherches de l'Institut de Lettres Orientales de Beyrouth, 22-23, 42).

A sort of encyclopaedia, arranged by placename, of villages, institutions and churches of Christian communities and buildings in northern Iraq. Vol 1, Part 1 is titled 'Adiabène', Part 2 'Marga'; Vol 2, Part 3 'Bā Nūhadra'; Vol 3 'Bét Garmaï, Bét Aramāyé et Maišān Nestoriens'.

501 **Chrétiens syriaques sous les Abbasides, surtout à Baghdad (749-1258).** (Syriac Christians under the Abbasids, principally in Baghdad (749-1258).)
Jean Maurice Fiey. Louvain, Belgium: Secrétariat du CorpusSCO, 1980. 279p. (Corpus Scriptorum Christianorum Orientalium, 420: Subsidia, T. 59).

A chronological history of the Syriac-speaking Christian community in Iraq under the Abbasid Caliphs, concentrating on Baghdad.

502 **Chrétiens syriaques sous les Mongols (Il-Khans de Perse, XIIIe – XIVe siècles).** (Syriac Christians under the Mongols (Il-Khans of Iran, XIII-XIV centuries).)
J. M. Fiey. Louvain, Belgium: Secrétariat du CorpusSCO, 1975. 111p. map. bibliog. (Corpus Scriptorum Christianorum Orientalium, 362: Subsidia, 44).

Describes the experience of the Syriac-speaking Christians (Assyrians/Chaldeans/ Nestorians) who exploited their favoured position under the early Mongol conquerors (13th century) who were (or claimed to be) Nestorian Christians. Disaster followed as local Mongol rulers in Iraq and Iran adopted Islam and the Christians faced the consequent hostility of the native Muslim population as well as that of the rulers in the early 14th century.

503 **Jalons pour une histoire de l'église en Iraq.** (Approaches to a history of the Church in Iraq.)
J. M. Fiey. Louvain, Belgium: Secrétariat du CorpusSCO, 1970. 143p. (Corpus Scriptorum Christianorum Orientalium, 361: Subsidia, 36).

Fiey sketches the history of the Christian Church as an institution in Iraq up to approximately 639 CE when the country fell under Islamic control. The parts are headed: 'Evangélisation'; 'Les premiers siècles'; 'Catholicat et Patriarchat'; 'Persécutions'; 'Monachisme'; 'Le grand déchirement'.

504 **Nisibe: métropole syriaque orientale et ses suffragants des origines à nos jours.** (Nisibe: the Eastern Syriac See and its suffragan bishops from its origins to our times.)
Jean-Maurice Fiey. Louvain, Belgium: Secrétariat du CorpusSCO, 1972. 274p. maps. (Corpus Scriptorum Christianorum Orientalium, 388: Subsidia, 54).

The author describes it as the last north-west corner of the mosaic of central provinces of the Church of Persia, the great Nestorian Church implanted in the first century CE in the southern part of Ctesiphon, capital of the Parthian Empire. This is a history of the ecclesiastical school at Nisibe which was the centre of Persian Nestorianism, its monasteries and its institutional history, up to 1915 when the community was almost totally effaced from the region.

505   **Muslim–Christian relations and inter-Christian rivalries in the Middle East. The case of the Jacobites in an age of transition.**
John Joseph.   Albany, NY: State University of New York Press, 1983. 205p. bibliog.
The Introduction describes this as a modern history of the Syrian Orthodox (Jacobite) and Syrian Catholic (formerly Jacobite) Christians of the Middle East. The study concentrates on developments since the early 1800s, and is presented as a case-study of Muslim–Christian relations and inter-Christian rivalries in modern times. Much of the book concerns Syria and Iraq, where the Syrian Christians are concentrated in the Mosul area and in Baghdad.

506   **The Nestorians and their neighbours: a study of Western influence on their relations.**
John Joseph.   Princeton, NJ: Princeton University Press, 1961. 236p. maps. bibliog. (Princeton Oriental Studies, 20).
Part one covers the 19th century, and part two the 20th century. Between them they chart the political impact of Western interference on the relations of the local communities of Nestorians (also sometimes called Assyrians or Chaldeans) with the Muslim majority among whom they lived in northern Iraq. The background to the tragedy of the massacres in 1933 is explained.

**The Nestorians and their rituals . . .**
*See* item no. 42.

**The Assyrian affair of 1933.**
*See* item no. 206.

**The lost peoples of the Middle East . . . Kurds, Assyrians, and other minority races . . .**
*See* item no. 425.

**Christian Arabic of Baghdad.**
*See* item no. 699.

**Maintenance and shift in the Christian Arabic of Baghdad.**
*See* item no. 700.

**Communal dialects in Baghdad.**
*See* item no. 702.

**Mossoul chrétienne: essai sur l'histoire, l'archéologie et l'état actuel des monuments chrétiens . . .**
*See* item no. 776.

# Yazidis and others

507 **The Mandaeans of Iraq and Iran, their cults, customs, magic legends and folklore.**
E. S. Drower. Oxford: Clarendon Press, 1937, rp. Leiden, The Netherlands: Brill, 1962. 399p. bibliog.

Based on the author's own observations and fieldwork in the 1920s-1930s, this book describes the customs and beliefs of the Mandaeans of southern Iraq, whose religion the author believes to be related to ancient Iranian beliefs.

508 **The Yezidi struggle to survive.**
Amalia van Gent. *Swiss Review of World Affairs*, vol. 43, no. 6 (June 1993), p. 20-21.

The Yazidis live in a part of northern Iraq controlled by Kurds, but cling to their syncretistic religion. In recent times they have begun to fear persecution as a result of the growing influence of Islamic fundamentalism in Kurdish Iraq.

509 **Survival among the Kurds: a history of the Yezidis.**
John S. Guest. London: Kegan Paul International, 1993. rev. ed. 270p. bibliog.

Approximately half of all the Yazidis in the world live in northern Iraq. This is a history of the community, an account of the Yazidis' religious beliefs and of their relations with their mainly Kurdish neighbours, down to 1957.

# Social Conditions

## General

**510 Communities, class system and caste in Iraq.**
Abduljabbar Araim. *Bulletin of the College of Arts* (Baghdad), no. 6 (1963), p. 1-22.
The author of this general survey of the social communities and class system of Iraq discusses the tribesmen and rural society, the towns and cities, social mobility in the urban areas, and the social stratification in the country which he labels as a caste system.

**511 Social factors in Iraqi rural–urban migration.**
Fuad Baali. *American Journal of Economics and Sociology*, vol. 25, no. 4 (October 1966), p. 359-64.
Baali argues that 'the system of land ownership along with the political dissension among the peasants' was the main reason for continuous migration from the rural areas to the big cities, and especially to Baghdad.

**512 Class analysis and Iraqi society.**
Hanna Batatu. In: *Arab society: social science perspectives*, edited by Saad Eddin Ibrahim, Nicholas Hopkins. Cairo: American University in Cairo Press, 1985, rp. 1987, p. 379-92.
An article reprinted from *Peuples Méditerranéens*, 8 (1979), p. 101-16 examining class formation in Iraq during the 20th century. The structure of society has been rather unstable, but elements of class structure can be perceived.

513 **The old social classes and the revolutionary movements of Iraq: a study of Iraq's old landed classes and of its Communists, Baʿthists, and Free Officers.**
Hanna Batatu. Princeton, NJ: Princeton University Press, 1978, rp. 1989. 1230p. maps. bibliog.

A most important study of the social structure of Iraq as inherited from the days of Ottoman rule, the rise of political parties (especially the Communist Party) and movements and their impact on domestic politics. Book one 'The old social classes' contains two sections: 'Introduction' and 'The main classes and status groups'. Book two 'The Communists from the beginnings of their movement to the fifties' contains: 'Beginnings in the Arab East'; 'Beginnings in Iraq'; 'Causes'; 'Fahd and the Party (1941-1949)'; 'The Party in the years 1949-1955, or the period of the ascendancy of the Kurds in the Party'. Book three contains 'The Communists, the Baʿthists, and the Free Officers from the fifties to the present'. The Appendixes give documents, supplementary information about early Bolshevik activities, and tables of families and tribes.

514 **The photography of Kamil Chadirji 1920-1940: social life in the Middle East.**
Rifat Chadirji. Surbiton, England: LAAM, 1991. 83p.

Rifat Chadirji presents the photographs taken by Kamil Chadirji (1897-1968), who came from a well-to-do Baghdad family and founded the National Democratic Party. His photographs show many facets of the social and cultural life of Baghdad, and the majority of pictures in this collection are of Iraq. Part one contains a biographical introduction; part two photographs.

515 **Southern Mesopotamia.**
Robert A. Fernea. In: *The central Middle East: a handbook of anthropology and published research on the Nile valley, the Arab Levant, Southern Mesopotamia, the Arabian Peninsula, and Israel*, edited by Louise E. Sweet. New Haven, CT: HRAF, 1971, p. 171-93.

Reviews the anthropological literature and academic analysis of the social structure of southern Iraq. The essay is followed on p. 194-97 by 'Mesopotamia: an annotated bibliography' compiled by Louise Sweet. This is a bibliography of anthropological literature on the area.

516 **Ruling elites and the young: a comparison of Iraq and Lebanon.**
Suad Joseph. In: *Social legislation in the contemporary Middle East*, edited by Laurence O. Michalak, Jeswald W. Salacuse. Berkeley, CA: Institute of International Studies, University of California, 1986. p. 191-237. (Research Series, 64).

Joseph compares the very different relationship between the ruling élite and the state in Iraq and in Lebanon, and argues that in both cases the ruling élite have sought to gain the allegiance and control the behaviour of the young. In Iraq, where the ruling élite controls the Baʿth Party, and uses the Party to control the state, it has also exerted enormous effort to pull all social action into the state arena, including the struggle for control over the young.

517  **Tribalism and modern society: Iraq, a case study.**
Albertine Jwaideh.  In: *Introduction to Islamic civilisation*, edited by
R. M. Savory.  Cambridge: Cambridge University Press, 1976,
p. 160-67.
Provides a clear account of the importance of tribal relations in early modern Iraq,
and the manner in which these were changed by the application of the Ottoman Land
Code in the late 19th century, and later by the British administration and Agrarian
Reform Laws. The author argues that the growth of large-scale land ownership at the
expense of communal tribal lands had detrimental effects on Iraq's social structure.

518  **Impressions of sociology in Iraq.**
Ayad al-Qazzaz.  *International Social Science Journal*, vol. 27, no. 4
(1975), p. 781-86.
The author describes the nature and characteristics of sociology studies in Iraq during
the 1950s and 1960s, and the work carried out by Iraqis, both while studying abroad
and while working in Iraq.

519  **State power and economic structure: class determination and state
formation in contemporary Iraq.**
Joe Stork.  In: *Iraq: the contemporary state*, edited by Tim Niblock.
London: Croom Helm; New York: St. Martin's Press, 1982, p. 27-46.
Stork sets out to delineate modern historical aspects of class and state formation in
Iraq, and the correspondence of these structural features with the changing needs of
international capital.

520  **Land reform and development in the Middle East: a study of
Egypt, Syria and Iraq.**
Doreen Warriner.  London: Oxford University Press, for the Royal
Institute of International Affairs, 1962. 2nd ed. 229p. bibliog.
See in particular Chapter 4 'Iraq' (p. 113-83). An account of socio-economic
conditions at mid-century, and of the impact which oil revenues invested in capital
construction were beginning to have in Iraq. Since the author was unable to make
another visit to Iraq before publishing the second edition, the impact of the 1958
revolution is not described, but this study remains valuable for its description of pre-
revolutionary conditions. The author was mainly concerned with the rural poor, but
also notes the living conditions of the urban poor in the big cities.

# Rural and village life

521 **Relation of the people to the land in southern Iraq.**
Fuad Baali. Gainesville: Florida University Press, 1966. 64p. map.
(University of Florida Monographs: Social Sciences, 31).
Based on a field study carried out in 1963, this study provides a thorough description
of rural relations, land tenure, agriculture, the peasantry and rural–urban migration in
the years shortly after the Agrarian Reform in southern Iraq.

522 **The transformation of land tenure and rural social structure in
central and southern Iraq, c. 1870-1958.**
Marion Farouk-Sluglett, Peter Sluglett. *International Journal of
Middle Eastern Studies*, vol. 15, no. 4 (November 1983), p. 491-505.
Sets out to show how the economic and social structure of rural Iraq was affected by
changing world economic circumstances, and also by Ottoman and British
administrative changes in the pattern of land tenure.

523 **Der Auflösungsprozess des Beduinentums im Irak.** (The process of
dispersal among the Bedouin in Iraq.)
Ibrahim Haidari. In: *Nomadismus: ein Entwicklungsproblem?* edited
by Fred Scholz, Jörg Janzen. Berlin: Reimer, 1982, p. 139-42.
(Abhandlungen des Geographischen Instituts: Anthropogeographie,
33).
Haidari notes that the Iraqi government has consistently sought to integrate the
Bedouin into the rest of society, and that their distinctive nomadic way of life will
soon have disappeared.

524 **Araden ou le "Jardin du paradis". La terre et les hommes dans un
village chaldéen du nord de l'Irak.** (Araden or "Paradise village":
land and people in a Chaldean village of northern Iraq).
Habib Ishow. *Etudes Rurales*, no. 76 (October-December 1979),
p. 97-112.
Describes the social organization and cultural identity of the Assyrian/Chaldean/
Nestorian village of Araden 160 km. north of Mosul. The village's economic
activities, exploitation of natural resources, and systems of irrigation and collective
ownership of village lands are outlined. The author notes that political upheavals
arising from the Kurdish revolt affected the village in the 1960s and 1970s, and the
lack of government interest in the area led to the abandonment of some of the local
lands, which were left to go wild.

525    L'exode rural en Irak et ses conséquences économiques et sociales.
(The rural exodus in Iraq and its economic and social consequences.)
Habib Ishow.    L'Afrique et l'Asie Modernes, no. 136 (1st trim. 1983),
p. 27-45.
Ishow examines the evolution, causes and effects of rural–urban drift in Iraq, a
relatively recent phenomenon which has put pressure on housing, employment and
transport in the towns.

526    Obstacles to economic development in the rural sector of modern
Iraq.
Gayle McKenzie.    Jusūr, vol. 3 (1987), p. 37-59.
Describes the traditional social organization and methods of production in Iraq in the
19th century, the impact of private property laws, and the effects of British rural
development policies on land tenure and land ownership during the Mandate and
monarchy. The author concludes that it was the traditional socio-political relations
between the shaykhs and the tribesmen, and not external factors, which determined
the process of rural development, or lack of it.

527    The idea of progress in an Iraqi village.
Malcolm N. Quint.    Middle East Journal, vol. 12, no. 4 (Fall 1958),
p. 369-84. Reprinted in The modern Middle East, edited by R. H.
Nolte.    New York: Atherton Press, 1963, p. 108-23; and in Man, state
and society in the contemporary Middle East, edited by Jacob M.
Landau.    New York: Praeger, 1972, p. 390-403.
Describes peasant life and conditions in a village approximately 60 km. southeast of
Amarah in southern Iraq, where the author spent 18 months carrying out fieldwork in
1956-58.

528    Al-tabaʿiyya: power, patronage and marginal groups in northern
Iraq.
Amal Rassam.    In: Patrons and clients in Mediterranean societies,
edited by Ernest Gellner, John Waterbury.    London: Duckworth, in
association with the Center for Mediterranean Studies of the American
Universities Field Staff, 1977, p. 157-66.
Rassam explores the nature of clientelist relationships between two marginalized
social groups and powerful local landowners in the Mosul area. In one case, the
villagers belong to a small Shiʿi sect known as Shabak, and the other village is
populated by Chaldean Christians. The different effects of the land reforms of 1958
and 1970 are examined.

529    Ethnicity, cultural discontinuity and power brokers in northern
Iraq: the case of the Shabak.
Amal Vinogradov.    American Ethnologist, vol. 1, no. 1 (February
1974), p. 207-18.
An anthropological study of some aspects of the social organization of a marginal
Kurdish-speaking Shiʿi sect in northern Iraq.

**Villages et petites villes kurdes dans l'Irak actuel . . .**
*See* item no. 432.

**Die Nomadenansiedlung in der Irakischen Jezira.**
*See* item no. 455.

**L'état et la paysannerie en Irak.**
*See* item no. 660.

**Le statut foncier, la paysannerie et le pouvoir politique en Irak depuis 1921.**
*See* item no. 661.

**Räumliche Disparitäten der Lebensgrundlagen im irakischen Kurdistan: ein Beitrag zur Regionalplanung.**
*See* item no. 688.

# Women and family life

530 **Rural Iraqi women and extension centers: policies and practices.**
Sharon K. Araji. *Journal of Rural Studies*, vol. 4, no. 3 (1988), p. 263-73.
Araji discusses the activities of the agricultural extension centres in relation to rural women's needs.

531 **Knowledge and use of contraception in rural and urban Iraq.**
Mohamed el-Attar. *Arab Journal of the Social Sciences*, vol. 3, no. 2 (October 1988), p. 294-308.
The author investigates the variation in birth control knowledge and practice in Iraq as reported in the 1974 National Fertility Sample Survey.

532 **The position of women in public enterprises in Iraq.**
Mohammed H. Bakhir. *Public Enterprise*, vol. 13, nos. 3-4 (1993), p. 182-87.
Data are presented showing that the public sector is the principal employer of women in Iraq, accounting for over 60 per cent of economically active women. Women make up 33 per cent of the workforce in this sector. They are generally younger than the men, but have higher educational qualifications. The data were collected in 1991, and the statistics relate to 1987-90.

533    **Liberation or repression? Pan-Arab nationalism and the women's movement in Iraq.**
Marion Farouk-Sluglett.    In: *Iraq: power and society*, edited by Derek Hopwood, Habib Ishow, Thomas Koszinowski.    Oxford: Ithaca, for St. Antony's College, 1993, p. 51-73.
Considers the Baʿth Party's methods and ideology in taking over and controlling the women's movement and turning it into an instrument of state power.

534    **Women in Iraq.**
Jennifer Freedman.    *American-Arab Affairs*, no. 29 (Summer 1989), p. 42-46.
A study of the positive changes in women's status and employment resulting from manpower shortages during the Iran–Iraq war.

535    **The awakened: women in Iraq.**
Doreen Ingrams.    London: Third World Centre, 1983. 155p. map. bibliog.
Briefly describes the position of women in Iraq and some of the changes which occurred in women's opportunities since the 1940s in terms of professional training and employment.

536    **The emancipation of Iraqi women: women and their influence on Iraqi life and poetry.**
Yousif Izzidien.    *Bulletin of the College of Arts* (Baghdad), no. 1 (1959), p. 33-41.
The author examines the attitudes of modern Iraqi writers to women's condition and role in modern Iraqi life, as presented in their poetry, and in public discussions of the issue of emancipation.

537    **Elite strategies for state-building: women, family, religion and state in Iraq and Lebanon.**
Suad Joseph.    In: *Women, Islam and the state*, edited by Deniz Kandiyoti.    Basingstoke, England: Macmillan, 1991, p. 176-200.
Case-studies are presented for Iraq and Lebanon, contrasting the different approaches of the élite in each case to state-building projects, and focusing in particular on the their impact on women and families.

538    **The mobilization of Iraqi women into the wage labor force.**
Suad Joseph.    *Studies in Third World Societies*, vol. 16 (June 1981), p. 69-90.
Argues that the Baʿth Party has engaged women in the campaign to consolidate its power by undermining the political opposition and expanding the economy. Women have gained job opportunities, education, rights and services, but only at some expense. As the Party has no real commitment to equality, they may lose many of their gains because of economic decline and political expediency in the future.

539  **Honour and shame: women in modern Iraq.**
Sana al-Khayyat.   London: Saqi, 1990. 223p. bibliog.
A study of the process of the socialization of women in Iraq, female roles, the way in which women perceive themselves in relation to men and to others in the family, marital relationships and the way women are controlled by society. The author is an Iraqi sociologist who bases her conclusions on interviews with housewives and professional women in Baghdad.

540  **Iraqi rural women's participation in domestic decision-making.**
Qais N. al-Nouri.   *Journal of Comparative Family Studies*, vol. 24, no. 1 (1993), p. 81-97.
Argues that rural Iraqi women are becoming increasingly involved in work outside the home and taking a greater share in domestic decision-making as a result of greater opportunities for education and employment. The article is based on responses to a questionnaire from most regions of Iraq.

541  **The meaning of marriage and status in exile: the experience of Iraqi women.**
Madawi al-Rasheed.   *Journal of Refugee Studies*, vol. 6, no. 2 (1993), p. 89-104.
Examines the experience of Iraqi women living in exile in London as a result of their husbands' decisions or political involvement in opposition movements. The author argues that, faced with the difficulties of life in exile, women reconstruct images of marriage which they associate with status and security – the two aspects which their marriages lack when they become refugees.

542  **Political ideology and women in Iraq: legislation and cultural constraints.**
Amal Rassam.   In: *Women and development in the Middle East and North Africa*, edited by Joseph G. Jabbra, Nancy W. Jabbra.   Leiden, The Netherlands: Brill, 1992, p. 82-95. (International Studies in Sociology & Social Anthropology, 59).
Rassam argues that the Baʿth Party is committed to national development and the liberation of women, but that Iraq's people are concerned to maintain their traditional heritage and their ideas of the appropriate role for women. A a result, Iraq's leaders have separated women's status into two parts: the private/family and the public/economic, and confine their efforts at change mainly to the latter.

543  **Revolution within the revolution? Women and the state in Iraq.**
Amal Rassam.   In: *Iraq: the contemporary state*, edited by Tim Niblock.   London: Croom Helm; New York: St. Martin's Press, 1982, p. 88-99.
Here, Rassam argues that the Baʿth Party's ideology of emancipation and equality for women is at odds with traditional Iraqi society and that there is a contradiction between the regime's commitment to ideas of female equality and its desire to preserve a national identity in the face of the Western cultural onslaught. As women are perceived as symbols of cultural purity and authenticity, full liberation poses a dilemma.

544    **The emancipation of Iraqi women.**
Amal al-Sharqi.    In: *Iraq: the contemporary state*, edited by Tim
Niblock.    London: Croom Helm; New York: St. Martin's Press, 1982,
p. 74-87.
Describes the changes in women's condition over the last few decades, the growth of
women's participation in education and work, and changes in legislation which have
affected women.

545    **Migration and the selectivity of change: Egyptian peasant women
in Iraq.**
Camilia Fawzi el-Solh.    *Peuples Méditerranéens*, vol. 31-32
(April-September 1985), p. 243-58.
In 1975 the governments of Egypt and Iraq signed an agreement under which
Egyptian peasant families would resettle permanently in Iraq with financial support
from the Iraqi goverment. This article examines the impact on Egyptian women from
100 of these settlers and their families some 35 miles north of Baghdad.

546    **Physical education and sport in the life of Iraqi women.**
Akram M. Soubhi.    *International Review of Sport Sociology*, vol. 12,
no. 2 (1977), p. 107-09.
Soubhi notes that the participation of women in sports and physical education is
beginning to be encouraged by schools and sports associations, whereas formerly
such activities were viewed by society generally as unsuitable for women.

**Opening the gates: a century of Arab feminist writing.**
*See* item no. 754.

# Health

547 **Effect of the Gulf War on infant and child mortality in Iraq.**
Alberto Ascherio (et al.). *New England Journal of Medicine*,
vol. 327, no. 13 (24 September 1992), p. 931-36.

Ascherio argues that the results of a house-to-house survey conducted in Iraq 'provide strong evidence that the Gulf War and trade sanctions caused a threefold increase in mortality among Iraqi children under five years of age'. The data used were for the period from January 1985 to August 1991, and the report was compiled by an international team of health experts. The survey covered the whole of Iraq.

548 **Cancer in Iraq: seven-year data from the Baghdad tumour
registry.**
A. al-Fuadi, D. M. Parkin. In: *Cancer prevention in developing
countries: proceedings of the 2nd UICC Conference on Cancer
Prevention,* edited by. M. Khogali, Y. T. Omar, A. Gjorgov,
A. S. Ismail. Oxford: Pergamon, 1986, p. 35-43.

This article analyses the relative frequency, by age, sex and site, of the data for the years 1976-82 collected at the Baghdad Cancer Registry, and notes that the pattern is similar to that of other Middle Eastern populations. Also in the volume is 'The frequency and pattern of gastrointestinal tract cancer in Iraq' by H. M. al-Zahawi, A. al-Naiemi (p. 193-96).

549 **Socio-anthropological approach to primary health care – a case
study on health relevant attitudes and behaviour of a rural Iraqi
community.**
Achama George, Narjis Abdul Hussain Ajeel. *Arab Gulf*, vol. 14,
no. 3-4 (1982), p. 53-59.

The authors attempt to assess attitudes and practices affecting health in three villages near Basra. The study concentrated on aspects of diet, pregnancy and childbirth, childcare and home medical treatments.

550 **Psychiatric problems in a developing country: Iraq.**
Ihsan al-Issa, Birgitta al-Issa. *International Journal of Social Psychiatry*, vol. 16, no. 1 (Winter 1969/70), p. 15-22.

Describes the symptomatology and treatment of mental illness in Iraq, and both the traditional and modern approach to mental illness there. The effect of Westernization and modernization on a traditional society is noted.

551 **Primary health care in the Arab world.**
W. J. Stephen. Wells, England: Somerset House, 1992. 307p. bibliog.

A survey of primary health provision in Arab countries, based on visits for field research. Chapter 6 (p. 82-99) covers Iraq, and effectively describes the organization, structure and aims of the primary healthcare system as it was in the early 1980s. The effects of the long-drawn-out war with Iran, and the damage done in the Gulf War of 1991 are not described in this book.

# Education

552 **Technical education: new part in higher education in Iraq.**
H. M. S. Abdul-Wahab. *Orient* (Opladen), vol. 19, no. 1 (March 1978), p. 70-98.

A review of the development and expansion of higher education in Iraq in the 1970s, describing the structure of the Foundation of Technical Institutes established in 1972 and its constitutent institutions, and the nature of the training they offer. This article includes tables of statistics and gives the impression of an official presentation.

553 **L'enseignement technique en Irak: du mandat à la première décennie de la République.** (Technical education in Iraq: from the Mandate to the first decade of the Republic.)
Habib Ishow. *L'Afrique et l'Asie Modernes*, no. 108 (1st trim. 1976), p. 19-34.

Ishow argues that technical education has been largely neglected in Iraq, with few schools and inappropriate curricula and teaching methods, and that for these reasons teachers are unwilling to enter this part of the profession. An earlier article by the same author describes the provision and structure of technical education in Iraq; see 'L'enseignement technique en Irak' (*L'Afrique et l'Asie Modernes*, no. 95-96 (3rd-4th trim. 1971), p. 3-26).

554 **L'état de l'enseignement en Irak: de la fin de la présence ottomane à l'instauration du mandat britannique en 1920.** (The state of education in Iraq: from the end of the Ottoman presence to the installation of the British mandate in 1920.)
Habib Ishow.   In: *BriSMES: British Society for Middle Eastern Studies (in association with AFEMAM): Proceedings of the 1989 International Conference on Europe and the Middle East . . . Durham . . . 1989.*   Oxford: British Society for Middle Eastern Studies, 1989, p. 245-54.
Ishow reviews the state of the education system in Iraq from the end of the Ottoman period until the British took control in 1920.

555 **Youth education in Iraq and Egypt, 1920-1980: a contribution to comparative education within the Arab region.**
M. al-Kasey.   Leuven, Belgium: Helicon, [*ca.* 1983]. 638p.
Part one: 'Formal and non-formal youth education in Iraq' on p. 1-279 describes the Iraqi education system, and various official youth organizations, such as the General Federation of Iraqi Youth. Part two describes the Egyptian system. Part three (p. 465-586) discusses the similarities and differences between the two countries in their societies, formal education systems, and youth work.

556 **Direction and planning of sport for children and young people.**
Abdul Wahab M. Mahmood.   *International Review of Sport Sociology*, vol. 16, no. 2 (1981), p. 115-25.
Reports the results of a study to improve the effectiveness of the Ministry for Youth Affairs in Iraq, and outlines the activities of some official departments concerned with the development of sport and provision of facilities.

557 **Education in Arab countries of the Near East: Egypt, Iraq, Palestine, Transjordan, Syria, Lebanon.**
Roderic D. Matthews, Matta Akrawi.   Washington, DC: American Council on Education, 1949. 576p.
Part two, 'Iraq' (p. 121-213), gives a detailed description of the education system as it was in 1945. The organization and administration of the educational system is described, and its various constituent sectors: public education (from primary to higher), the missionary schools, and private and foreign schools.

558 **Higher education, culture and modernity: perspectives on Iraq.**
Qais N. al-Nouri.   *Higher Education Policy*, vol. 3, no. 1 (1990), p. 15-19.
The author assesses the impact of higher education on the modernization of individuals and society in Iraq, and notes problems confronting Iraqi universities and academic institutions in a largely traditional society.

559 **The higher learning in Iraq.**
Andrew G. O'Connor. *Muslim World*, vol. 48, no. 2 (April 1958),
p. 136-47.
A survey of the state of higher education in Iraq in the late 1950s, and of the state of
the teaching profession. This work is useful for its historical value.

560 **Arab education 1956-1978: a bibliography.**
Veronica S. Pantelidis. London: Mansell, 1982. 480p.
An annotated bibliography of education in all its aspects, organized by country: Iraq
is on p. 166-95, subdivided by subject, and with about 350 entries.

561 **Sociology in underdeveloped countries – a case study of Iraq.**
Ayad al-Qazzaz. *Sociological Review*, vol. 20, no 1 (February 1972),
p. 93-103.
A concise account of the state of sociology in Iraq, the history of its emergence as a
separate discipline in the universities, and the state of research as manifested in the
writings of Iraqi sociologists.

562 **The educational system of Iraq.**
Delwin A. Roy. *Middle Eastern Studies*, vol. 29, no. 2 (April 1993),
p. 167-98.
A survey of the educational system under Baʿth rule since 1974, during which time
the government's policy and efforts were directed to increasing the availability of
education in the country and the quality of schooling and of higher education. The
author argues that Iraq made considerable strides in this field, especially in combating
illiteracy and in education provision.

563 **Education in the Middle East.**
Edited by Leslie C. Schmida. Washington, DC: AMIDEAST, 1983.
136p. bibliog.
Written as a guide to interpreting the education background of students from Arab
countries, this book provides brief information on enrolment statistics, primary and
secondary education curricula, the vocational, technical and higher education offered,
the various institutions, and their programmes. Iraq is described on p. 33-37.

564 **The teaching of history in Iraq before the Rashid Ali coup of 1941.**
Reeva S. Simon. *Middle Eastern Studies*, vol. 22, no. 1 (January
1986), p. 37-51.
A study of the Arab nationalist content of the Iraqi school history curriculum from
1920 to 1941 when it was under the control of Iraqi authorities, until the British took
over and re-wrote it to place more emphasis on ancient and local Iraqi history with
the aim of reducing hostility to the West and to themselves in particular.

565 **On education in Iraq.**
Lionel Smith, introduction by E. C. Hodgkin. *Middle Eastern Studies*, vol. 19, no. 2 (April 1983), p. 253-60.
Reproduces a 'Note on the present state of education in Iraq' written in 1930 by Lionel Smith the departing Adviser to the Ministry of Education in 1931.

566 **The eradication of illiteracy in Iraq.**
Alya Sousa. In: *Iraq: the contemporary state*, edited by Tim Niblock. London: Croom Helm; New York: St. Martin's Press, 1982, p. 100-08.
Sousa describes the efforts and achievements of Iraq's literacy campaign of the 1970s.

567 **Child education in an Islamic perspective: with special reference to Iraq.**
K. F. M. al-Zubaidy. *Muslim Education Quarterly*, vol. 5, no. 4 (Summer 1988), p. 56-62.
Describes the education system in Iraq and the teaching of Islamic religion within it under the avowedly secularist Ba'th Party. The author discusses some of the problems of modernizing education in the Arab and Muslim world.

**The theological colleges of Najaf.**
*See* item no. 470.

# Labour and Employment

568  **A macroeconomic simulation model of high-level manpower requirements in Iraq.**
George T. Abed, Atif A. Kubursi.  In: *Manpower planning in the oil countries*, edited by Naiem A. Sherbiny.  Greenwich, CT: Jai Press, 1981, p. 145-71. (Research in Human Capital and Development: A Research Annual, Supp. 1).

The authors use Iraq as a case-study of the problems of estimating high-level manpower requirements by sector. Iraq is one of the oil-rich Arab countries with abundant capital and a shortage of labour. This article provides a survey of the Iraqi economy between the years 1953 and 1975, and presents a mathematical model calculated by the authors.

569  **Iraqi managers' beliefs about work.**
Abbas Ali, Dietrich Schaupp.  *Journal of Social Psychology*, vol. 125, no. 2 (April 1985), p. 253-59.

Presents results of a sample survey of 203 Iraqi managers, and notes that attitudes varied with income, sex, educational level, and social background. A 'Marxist-oriented belief system' was found to be a significant factor among Iraqi managers at the time.

570  **The challenge of human resources development in Iraq.**
J. S. Birks, C. Sinclair.  In: *Iraq: the contemporary state*, edited by Tim Niblock.  London: Croom Helm; New York: St. Martin's Press, 1982, p. 241-55.

Birks and Sinclair analyse Iraq's labour resources and employment distribution in the early 1980s.

571 **Complaint presented by the International Conference of Free Trade Unions against the Government of Iraq.**
*International Labour Office Official Bulletin*, Series B, vol. 66, no. 3 (1984), p. 133-39.

A report of Case no 1146 before the Committee on the Freedom of Association of the ILO concerning allegations received from the Workers' Democratic Trade Union Movement of Iraq about violations of trade union rights and freedoms, and about persecution, detention, and torture of members.

572 **État et mouvement syndical en Irak (1968-1978): deux conceptions du rôle et des tâches des syndicats.** (The state and the labour movement in Iraq (1968-78): two conceptions of the role and tasks of unions.)
Jacques Couland. *Sou'al*, vol. 8 (1988), p. 131-71.

Couland argues that the Ba'th Party formed a sort of temporary alliance with the union movement, but at the same time took measures to assert control over society through its Party structure. On the other hand, the union movement was dominated by the Communist Party of Iraq which was trying to construct a different network of influence. The temporary alliance was unable to mask their differences and the Ba'th Party eventually moved to isolate the Communist Party, whose only stronghold was in the union movement.

573 **Labor and national liberation: the trade union movement in Iraq, 1920-1958.**
Marion Farouk-Sluglett, Peter Sluglett. *Arab Studies Quarterly*, vol. 5, no. 2 (Spring 1983), p. 139-54.

Reviews the importance of the labour movement in Iraq's struggle for independence and describes the political involvement of the trade unions.

574 **Economic development and the labour market in Iraq.**
Abbas Salih Mehdi, Olive Robinson. *International Journal of Manpower*, vol. 4, no. 2 (1983). 40p.

A whole issue of the periodical dealing with the state of Iraq's labour market, labour force planning, labour market legislation, and labour needs for national economic development.

575 **Migrations de main-d'oeuvre et unité arabe: les enjeux unitaires du modèle irakien.** (Manpower migration and Arab unity: the challenges of the Iraqi model).
Alain Roussillon. *Tiers Monde*, vol. 26 / no. 103 (July-September 1985), p. 637-64.

Roussillon considers the limitations of Iraq's non-discriminatory policy towards Arab migrant labour, which derives from its political ideology of Arab unity and its interest in attracting manpower. This has not prevented Arab migrants from working in Iraq only to save money as quickly as possible and return home, so that sectors of the Iraqi economy dependent on migrant labour have suffered from instability in the workforce which in turn has limited the benefits to Iraq.

576    **Egyptian migrant labour in Iraq: economic expediency and socio-political reality.**
Camillia Fawzi el-Solh.    In: *Iraq: power and society*, edited by Derek Hopwood, Habib Ishow, Thomas Koszinowski.    Oxford: Ithaca, for St. Antony's College, 1993, p. 257-82.

From the 1970s onwards a considerable number of Egyptian migrant labourers worked in various sectors of the Iraqi economy, with variable economic fortune and impact on the host society. Most of these migrants fled during the crisis following the invasion of Kuwait in 1990.

577    **Mass flight in the Middle East: involuntary migration and the Gulf conflict, 1990-1991.**
Nicholas Van Hear.    In: *Geography and refugees: patterns and processes of change*, edited by Richard Black, Vaughan Robinson.
London: Belhaven Press; New York: Halstead Press, 1993, p. 64-83.

The author discusses the pattern and consequences the massive flight of millions of workers and resident aliens from Kuwait, Iraq and Saudi Arabia as a result of Iraq's invasion of Kuwait in 1990 and the ensuing Gulf War. This was followed after the war by the temporary flight of large segments of the Iraqi population from Kurdistan and southern Iraq after the failure of the uprisings in Iraq.

578    **Labor laws in the Middle East: tradition in transit.**
David Ziskind.    Los Angeles: Litlaw Foundation, 1990. 364p.

Iraq is included in the discussion throughout. Part 1 consists of the Introduction (historical antecedents; the modern milieu). Part 2 covers the gamut of labour law provisions, special classes of labour; remuneration; hours of work and leisure; occupational safety and health; employment; unionization; collective bargaining; strikes; settlement techniques and agencies; social security; labour's interest in human rights; the sum of things said. Part 3 comprises observations and evaluations.

**The position of women in public enterprises in Iraq.**
*See* item no. 532.

**The mobilization of Iraqi women into the wage labor force.**
*See* item no. 538.

# Economy

579  **The distribution of national income in Iraq, with particular reference to the development of policies applied by the state.**
Aziz Alkazaz.   In: *Iraq: power and society*, edited by Derek Hopwood, Habib Ishow, Thomas Koszinowski.   Oxford: Ithaca, for St. Antony's College, 1993, p. 193-256.
Alkazaz shows the distorted nature of the Iraqi economy, the nature of agriculture and industrialization policies and structural development from the 1950s to the 1980s. Iraq suffered a considerable rural/urban divide and regional disparities, and the Iran–Iraq war and Gulf War of 1991 added to the burdens on the economy.

580  **Financing economic development in Iraq: the role of oil in a Middle Eastern economy.**
Abbas Alnasrawi.   New York: Praeger, 1967. 171p. bibliog. (Praeger Special Studies in International Economics and Development).
A study of the impact of oil revenues on the Iraqi economy, capital requirements and other sources of finance for the years 1952-65.

581  **Iraq: economic consequences of the 1991 Gulf War and future outlook.**
Abbas Alnasrawi.   *Third World Quarterly*, vol. 13, no. 2 (1992), p. 335-52.
An assessment of the economic costs of the Iran–Iraq war, the state of the Iraqi economy in early 1990, the invasion of Kuwait as a solution to the economic crisis, the human and economic consequences of the invasion, and the estimated economic cost to Iraq of the sanctions and war from 1990 onwards.

582    **Irak et Syrie, 1960-1980: du projet national à la transnationalisation.** (Iraq and Syria, 1960-80: from national project to transnationalization.)
Samir Amin.    Paris: Editions de Minuit, 1982. 148p. bibliog.

Amin examines the economic development of Iraq and Syria during the two decades 1960-80 and their national agricultural and industrial strategies, and concludes that the world economic system has a significant impact on national industries.

583    **Economic liberalization in oil-exporting countries: Iraq and Saudi Arabia.**
Kiren Aziz Chaudhry.    In: *Privatization and liberalization in the Middle East*, edited by Iliya Harik, Denis J. Sullivan.    Bloomington: Indiana University Press, 1992, p. 145-66.

Contrasts the experience of Saudi Arabia and Iraq in restructuring their economies during the recession period of the 1980s.

584    **On the way to the market. Economic liberalization and Iraq's invasion of Kuwait.**
Kiren Aziz Chaudhry.    *Middle East Report*, no. 170 / vol. 21, no. 3 (May-June 1991), p. 14-23.

In this article, Chaudhry argues that Iraq's domestic crisis flowed directly from the economic liberalization programme of 1989 and 1990. As the crisis deepened, the regime's sources of foreign exchange shrank. He also describes how the economic liberalization had been carried out.

585    **Irak – eine sozio-ökonomische Betrachtung.** (Iraq – a socio-economic view.)
Horst Didden.    Opladen, Germany: Leske, 1969. 274p. map. bibliog.

Part one describes the population, culture and social structure; part two the various economic sectors – agriculture, industry, oil, traffic circulation, money and credit, commerce, and development planning.

586    **The meaning of *Infitah* in Iraq.**
Marion Farouk-Sluglett.    *Review of Middle East Studies*, 6 (1993), p. 35-49.

An article on the nature of the 'opening up' of the Iraqi economy in the 1980s, and its consequences. Although it was drafted before the invasion of Kuwait in 1990, it was revised in 1991.

587    **The Iraq Development Board and British policy, 1945-50.**
Gerwin Gerke.    *Middle Eastern Studies*, vol. 27, no. 2 (April 1991), p. 231-55.

Gerke discusses Britain's diplomatic manoeuvres preceding the foundation of the Iraq Development Board in 1950, when Britain's concern was to keep the United States out of the country, while the USA was criticizing British interference in Iraq and the paucity of efforts to develop the country.

588 **L'Irak: développement et contradictions.** (Iraq: development and contradictions.)
Alain Guerreau, Anita Guerreau-Jalabert.   Paris: Sycomore, 1978.
285p. map. bibliog.
A description of the geographical, historical, social and political scene of modern Iraq, followed by an analysis of each sector of the economy: agriculture, oil and industry, commerce and transport. The authors conclude that substantial oil revenues have led to uneven development.

589 **The Iraq Development Board: administration and program.**
Stanley John Habermann.   *Middle East Journal*, vol. 9, no. 2 (Spring 1955), p. 179-86.
Habermann describes the Development Board, which was set up under the monarchy to improve rural conditions, its administrative organization, and the projects which were in train in the early 1950s.

590 **The national income of Iraq 1953-1961.**
K. Haseeb.   London: Oxford University Press, 1964. 184p.
An attempt to estimate the national income of Iraq from the production side for the years 1953-61, and to give a picture of the structure of the Iraqi economy showing the importance of each sector.

591 **The national income of Iraq 1962 and 1963.**
K. Haseeb.   *Egypte Contemporaine*, vol. 55, no. 317 (July 1964), p. 19-66.
Haseeb presents estimates of the national product of Iraq for the years 1962 and 1963, analyses the performance of the economy by sector over the period, and describes the structure of the Iraqi economy.

592 **Capital formation in Iraq 1957-1970.**
Jawad Hashim.   Surbiton, England: LAAM, 1990. 256p. bibliog.
A detailed economic analysis of sectors of the Iraqi economy and estimates of capital formation during the period 1957-70. Many tables of time-series data are included.

593 **The distribution of income in Iraq, 1971.**
Shakir M. Issa.   In: *The integration of modern Iraq*, edited by Abbas Kelidar.   London: Croom Helm, 1979, p. 123-34.
Sets out to present and analyse personal income distribution in Iraq in 1971, and the differential between urban and rural areas.

594 **Iraq, 1800-1991: a study in aborted development.**
Charles Issawi.   *Princeton Papers in Near Eastern Studies*, no. 1 (1992), p. 73-84.
A survey of Iraq's economic history and development over the last two centuries, divided into three distinct periods: 1800-1914; 1914-58; and 1958-91.

595 **Divergent modes of economic liberalization in Syria and Iraq.**
Fred H. Lawson. In: *Privatization and liberalization in the Middle East*, edited by Iliya Harik, Denis J. Sullivan. Bloomington: Indiana University Press, 1992, p. 123-44.
Lawson contrasts the steps taken to liberalize the economy in Syria and Iraq. The governments of the two countries have pursued different strategies to achieve the same goal.

596 **Aspects of efficiency in a socialist developing country: Iraq.**
Victor C. Levy. New York: Garland, 1984. 73p. bibliog.
Originally submitted as a PhD dissertation to Chicago University in 1978, this study consists of three essays dealing with the theory and management of factor productivity and aspects of efficiency. Levy uses Iraq as a case-study.

597 **Economic development in Iraq. Factors underlying the relative deterioration of human capital formation.**
Robert E. Looney. *Journal of Economic Issues*, vol. 26, no. 2 (June 1992), p. 515-622.
Notes that Iraq's war with Iran (1980-88), the Gulf War of 1991, the international oil glut and sanctions imposed on Iraq have all adversely affected Iraq's economy. Iraq has consequently suffered a drastic decline in human (and related health) development during the 1980s and since.

598 **L'économie pétrolière pour l'économie de guerre permanente: l'étude socio-économique des problèmes du développement en Irak.** (Oil economy for an economy of permanent war: socio-economic study of development problems in Iraq.)
Ibrahim Maroun. Beirut: Librairie Orientale, 1986. 371p. bibliog. (Publications de l'Université Libanaise, Section des Études Économiques, 6).
A survey of Iraq's economic development under the 'socialist' military regime 1958-68 and the later efforts at development planning from 1970 to 1980, with attention to the structural problems of Iraqi society and economy and the effect of oil revenues. The latter part of the book considers the impact of the Iran–Iraq war on Iraq's society and economy. The Annexes give data on the 20 ethnic and/or religious communities in Iraq and the text of the Agrarian Reform Law of 1970.

599 **Middle East Economic Digest.**
London, 8 March 1957- . weekly.
This journal contains a regular section of short news items about the Iraqi economy, and is also a good source of up-to-date news about political events. Commonly cited as MEED.

600   **The economic consequences of the Gulf War.**
Kamran Mofid.   London: Routledge, 1990. 161p. bibliog.
Mofid analyses the effects on the economies of Iraq and Iran of the long-drawn-out
war between 1980 and 1988. The costs of the earlier militarization of the two
countries bewteen 1973 and 1978 is also considered.

601   **Gulf War reparations: Iraq, OPEC, and the transfer problem.**
Rodney J. Morrison.   *American Journal of Economics and Sociology*,
vol. 51, no. 4 (1993), p. 385-99.
On 27 February 1991 the government of Iraq accepted United Nations Security
Council Resolution 674 which requires it to pay reparations to victims of its
aggression in the Gulf War of 1990-91. This article discusses the economic problems
of such payments and the consequences that may result from Iraq carrying it out.
Germany's experience after the First World War is noted by way of comparison.

602   **Structural transformations in Iraq: empirical testing and model
building for development.**
Adil Mouhammed.   *Scandinavian Journal of Development
Alternatives*, vol. 8, no. 3 (1989), p. 139-53.
Discusses the period 1951-80 during which Iraq underwent substantial structural
transformation in most economic sectors. The author argues that Iraq was able to
follow a strategy of economic development based on the manufacturing sector, in
spite of temporary negative effects on the agricultural sector, because income from oil
exports enabled it to import food.

603   **Economy and politics in the Arab world: a comparative analysis of
the development of Egypt, Iraq and Saudi Arabia since the 1950s.**
Gorm Rye Olsen.   Aarhus, Denmark: Institute of Political Science,
University of Aarhus, 1986. 66p.
Olsen compares and contrasts the economic and social basis of the three countries,
their economic policies, and the forms of politico-ideological functioning of the state
in each.

604   **The Middle East in the world economy 1800-1914.**
Roger Owen.   London: Methuen, 1981, rp. 1987. 345p. bibliog.
A general account of the late Ottoman Middle East by an economic historian. The
first three chapters discuss the area as a whole: 'Introduction: the Middle East
economy in the period of so-called "decline", 1500-1800'; 'The Middle East economy
in 1800'; 'The economic consequences of the age of reforms, 1800-1850' (which
includes a section on the Iraqi provinces). The rest of the book discusses
developments in the various regions; see Chapter 7 'The Iraqi provinces 1850-1880'
(p. 180-88) and Chapter 11 'The Iraqi provinces, 1880-1914' (p. 273-86). Chapter 12
is headed 'A century of economic growth and transformation: conclusions'.

605 **An analysis of the error between forecast and actual expenditure in the budgetary system of Iraq, 1961-1980.**
Nicholas Perdikis, Hassan Saluom. *International Journal of Middle East Studies*, vol. 19, no. 2 (May 1987), p. 131-54.
An examination of the way in which the Iraqi government prepared its expenditure estimates and how and why they differed from actual outturn figures.

606 **The reconstruction of Iraq: 1950-1957.**
Fahim I. Qubain. London: Atlantic Books, 1958. 264p. maps.
Qubain provides a picture of Iraq's economic situation on the eve of the 1958 Revolution. The sections cover the background, the development of agriculture, industry and human resources, and conclusions.

607 **Structural change and Iraq's structure of production.**
Amer al-Roubaie. *Arab Studies Quarterly*, vol. 12, no. 3/4 (Summer/Fall 1990), p. 83-101.
Using tables for the years 1960 and 1974, the author sets out to measure the rate of structural change in Iraq's economy and to show how output in different sectors reacted to change in final demand.

608 **Economic policy in Iraq 1932-1950.**
Joseph Sassoon. London: Cass, 1987. 273p. map. bibliog.
This account considers the period after Iraq became officially independent, but was still under strong British influence and before oil revenues had a significant impact on the economy. The chapters of this study cover: 'British interests in Iraq'; 'Iraqi government policy'; 'Finance'; 'Agriculture'; 'Foreign trade'; 'Industry, oil and labour'; 'Conclusion'.

609 **The economies of the Arab world: development since 1945.**
Yusif A. Sayigh. London: Croom Helm, 1978. 717p.
This useful survey of the Iraqi economy up to 1975 describes the evolution of the economy after the Second World War. See Chapter 2 'Iraq' on p. 17-79 for a succinct survey of the development of Iraq including sectoral developments.

610 **Problems of rural development in an oil-rich economy: Iraq 1958-1975.**
Robin Theobald, Sa'ad Jawad. In: *Iraq: the contemporary state*, edited by Tim Niblock. London: Croom Helm; New York: St. Martin's Press, 1982, p. 191-218.
Analyses the problems faced by Iraq in attempting to modernize its rural economy in spite of being relatively well endowed with resources.

611 **Transfer and development of technology in Iraq. Report of an UNCTAD mission.**
Geneva: United Nations, 1978. 69p.
The report of a mission by the United Nations Conference on Trade and Development on a visit to Iraq to advise on industry and technology transfer.

612 **The economies of the Middle East.**
Rodney Wilson.   London: Macmillan, 1979. 202p.
Chapter 7 'Iraq and Syria: revolution without renaissance' (p. 101-18) notes the similarities in political style and economic policy in the two countries. Both Iraq and Syria have authoritarian regimes tending to favour urban centres over the rural areas in which the majority of the population live.

**Iraq's people and resources.**
*See* item no. 1.

**Hunger and poverty in Iraq, 1991.**
*See* item no. 291.

**From food security to food insecurity: the case of Iraq, 1990-91.**
*See* item no. 292.

**Oil revenues and accelerated growth: absorptive capacity in Iraq.**
*See* item no. 627.

**Oil and development: a case study of Iraq.**
*See* item no. 629.

**Middle East Economic Survey.**
*See* item no. 631.

**Die Entwicklungspolitik im Irak nach 1968 und ihre bisherigen Ergebnisse.**
*See* item no. 687.

# Banking, Finance and Trade

### 613  The changing pattern of Iraq's foreign trade.
Abbas Alnasrawi.  *Middle East Journal*, vol. 25, no. 4 (Autumn 1971), p. 481-90.

The author examines Iraq's foreign trade in the decade since the 1958 Revolution in terms of volume and composition, and the pattern of imports. He includes several tables of statistics.

### 614  Annual report.
Baghdad: Central Bank of Iraq, 1956- . annual.

Published in an English version as well as an Arabic version from 1956 onwards, the annual report of the Central Bank contains surveys of the economy and data on monetary and financial matters. In recent years these reports have been withheld for security reasons.

### 615  Central Bank of Iraq: laws, regulations and ordinances.
Baghdad: Government Press, 1965. 121p.

The text of the law of 1956 establishing the Central Bank of Iraq, with subsequent amendments, and regulations governing administration and service in the Bank.

### 616  The role of foreign trade in the economic development of Iraq, 1864-1964: a study in the growth of a dependent economy.
Mohammad Salman Hasan.  In: *Studies in the economic history of the Middle East from the rise of Islam to the present day*, edited by M. A. Cook.  London: Oxford University Press, 1970, p. 346-72.

An account of the growth of the export trade in Iraq from the late 19th century onwards and the transformation of Iraq from a subsistence economy to an export economy which has led to increasing economic dependence on the outside world.

617   **A report on monetary policy in Iraq.**
Carl Iversen, assisted by Poul Winding and Poul Nørregaard
Rasmussen.   Copenhagen: Munksgaard, for the National Bank of
Iraq, 1954. 331p.
A detailed report, prepared in 1952-53, on Iraq's monetary policy and the problems
confronting the country.

618   **The relative impact of monetary and fiscal policies on an oil**
**producing economy: an econometric study of the Iraqi economy.**
Saleh M. Nsouli.   *Revue Internationale de l'Histoire de la Banque*,
no. 22-23 (1981), p. 90-112.
Attempts to develop a simple macroeconometric model for the Iraqi economy and to
determine the relative impact of monetary versus fiscal policy upon key macroeconomic variables.

619   **A profile of the banking system and other financial institutions in**
**Iraq.**
*Journal of Economic Cooperation among Islamic Countries*, vol. 8,
no. 3 (July 1987), p. 27-41.
Describes the two types of financial institutions in Iraq: the main one is the banking
system; the other consists of specialized banks such as the Industrial Bank,
Agricultural Cooperative Bank, Real Estate Bank, and Life Insurance Company.

620   **Development of agricultural land taxation in modern Iraq.**
Guzine A. K. Rasheed.   *Bulletin of the School of Oriental and*
*African Studies*, vol. 25, no. 2 (1962), p. 262-74.
Describes changes in the taxation of land since Ottoman times, under British
legislation enacted in the 1920s and 1930s, and under the new law of 1961.

621   **Anglo-Japanese competition in the textile trade in the inter-war**
**period: a case study of Iraq, 1932-1941.**
Hiroshi Shimizu.   *Middle Eastern Studies*, vol. 20, no. 3 (July 1984),
p. 259-89.
A detailed study of the piece-goods imports into Iraq from Britain and from Japan
during the inter-war years after Britain abandoned free trade and began to try to
protect cotton exports from Lancashire in the face of Japanese competition for the
Iraqi market.

622  **Stellenwert und Bedeutung des Aussenhandels für die
Industrialisierungsstrategie des Irak.** (The status and importance of
foreign trade for Iraq's industrialization strategy.)
Barik Shouber.   *Orient* (Opladen), vol. 21, no. 4 (December 1980),
p. 529-48.

Shouber reviews the structure and development of foreign trade in Iraq since 1968.
The Ba'th Party tried to create a diversified industrial base, to obtain an adequate
supply of durables to satisfy Iraq's consumers, to meet development targets and to
promote Iraq's exports. While state subsidies and bureaucratic control led to some
problems, there were a number of successes. There is an English summary on
p. 611-12.

# Oil and Energy

**623 A comparison study of wind and solar energy in two selected sites at Baghdad.**
Iman T. al-Alawy. In: *Energy and the environment into the 1990s.*
*Proceedings of the 1st World Renewable Energy Congress, Reading
. . . 1990*, edited by A. M. Sayigh. Oxford: Pergamon, 1990, Vol. 3,
p. 1686-91.
The author of this paper analyses the potential of two alternative energy sources.

**624 The nationalization of the Iraq Petroleum Company.**
Michael E. Brown. *International Journal of Middle East Studies*,
vol. 10, no. 1 (February 1979), p. 107-24.
Reviews the impact of the Iraq Petroleum Company (IPC) on Iraq, the Iraqis'
capability for nationalizing it, and the demands made by the Iraqi government in an
attempt to achieve better terms from IPC, starting from 1970 and continuing right up
to the nationalization of the company on 1 June 1972.

**625 Iraq and its oil: sixty-five years of ambition and frustration.**
Michel Chatelus. In: *Iraq: power and society*, edited by Derek
Hopwood, Habib Ishow, Thomas Koszinowski. Oxford: Ithaca, for
St. Antony's College, 1993, p. 141-69.
Chatelus surveys the history of Iraq's oil industry, its present situation and the
outlook for the future (with statistics on production and reserves).

**626 Effects of leadership style on oil policy: Syria and Iraq.**
John F. Devlin. *Energy Policy*, vol. 20, no. 11 (November 1992),
p. 1048-54.
Contrasts the different state policies concerning oil resources and exports of Syria and
Iraq since 1980. Whereas Syria has virtually eliminated the country's reliance on oil

imports, Saddam Husayn has made a series of decisions which have had disastrous consequences for Iraq's oil industry – notably the war with Iran, the seizure of Kuwait, and the rejection of the United Nations' terms for the resumption of oil exports.

### 627 Oil revenues and accelerated growth: absorptive capacity in Iraq.
Kadhim A. al-Eyd. New York: Praeger, 1979. 179p. bibliog.

Revised from a PhD thesis, this is a detailed examination of the performance of the Iraqi economy from the 1930s to the 1970s, and of the effect of oil revenues.

### 628 Iraq: the eternal fire: 1972 Iraqi oil nationalization in perspective.
Adil Hussein, translated by A. W. Lúlúa. London: Third World Centre for Research & Publishing, 1981. 256p.

An Arab account of the Iraqi government's struggle to gain control of its oil industry from the international oil companies, and the negotiations involved.

### 629 Oil and development: a case study of Iraq.
Noman Kanafani. Lund, Sweden: University of Lund, Department of Economics, 1982. 211p. map. bibliog. (Lund Economic Studies, 26).

An economic study of Iraq as an oil-exporting country. The book considers the structure of the economy, national development planning over the years 1950-74, Iraq's absorptive capacity and the determinants of its economic development.

### 630 Oil in the Middle East: its discovery and development.
Stephen Hemsley Longrigg. Oxford: Oxford University Press, 1968. 3rd ed. 363p.

The third edition takes the story of the discovery and exploitation of Middle Eastern oil from its beginnings up to 1966. Iraq is included, but much of the book concerns Iran and the Gulf states. A good general introduction to the subject.

### 631 Middle East Economic Survey.
Nicosia: Middle East Petroleum & Economic Publications, no. 1, 1957- . weekly.

This weekly publication contains much information about economic and financial affairs, and also includes a short survey of the political scene in every issue. It takes a particular interest in the oil industry and its associated financial affairs.

### 632 Selected documents of the international petroleum industry: Iraq and Kuwait, pre-1966.
Vienna: OPEC Information Department, 1974. 269p.

This volume reproduces the documents on oil law and legislation relevant to the two countries for the years before 1966. Those for Iraq are on pages 1-114. For later years, see the volumes produced by the Organisation of Petroleum-Exporting Countries entitled *Selected documents of the international petroleum industry 1966-74*, etc.

633  **Petroleum Press Service.**
London: Petroleum Press Bureau, 1934- . monthly. (From 1 January
1974 renamed *Petroleum Economist*).
A specialist magazine reporting on developments in the world's oil industry.

634  **Solar heating and storage system for domestic uses in Iraq.**
Wafiq Shakir Ridha.  *Arab Gulf*, vol. 16, no. 2 (1984), p. 29-38.
Reports on experiments with solar collectors to heat domestic water which would
provide a continuous supply of hot water.

635  **Le progrès remis à plus tard: la politique pétrolière irakienne:
passé, présent, avenir.** (Progress postponed: Iraqi oil policy: past,
present and future.)
Peter Sluglett, translated by Alban Albini.  *Peuples Méditerranéens*,
no. 64-65 (July-December 1993), p. 181-210.
Reviews the development of Iraq's oil policy since 1958, and the course of Iraqi
politics since the end of the Iran–Iraq war in 1988. Written in late 1992, this article
offers a useful survey of recent developments in Iraq's oil production and export
pattern. There is an English abstract on p. 328.

636  **Iraqi oil policy: 1961-1976.**
Paul Stevens.  In: *Iraq: the contemporary state*, edited by Tim
Niblock.  London: Croom Helm; New York: St. Martin's Press, 1982,
p. 168-90.
Stevens argues that Iraqi oil policy in the 1960s and early 1970s failed by the criteria
which the government itself had set, but that these failures were minimized by the rise
in oil prices and revenues.

637  **Oil and the penetration of capitalism in Iraq.**
Joe Stork.  In: *Oil and the class struggle*, edited by Petter Nore,
Terisa Turner.  London: Zed, 1980, p. 172-98.
Stork argues that oil has been the most important single determinant of the political
economy of modern Iraq. After 1918, oil provided the motivation for British rule,
which shaped Iraqi society and constructed the state apparatus; between 1950 and
1958, oil revenues solved the financial problems of the regime, but undermined its
political base; after the 1958 Revolution, the nationalization of the oil industry
brought in revenues that allowed the Baʕth Party to consolidate its rule.

**Imperial quest for oil: Iraq 1910-1928.**
*See* item no. 183.

**Financing economic development in Iraq: the role of oil in a Middle
Eastern economy.**
*See* item no. 580.

# Industry

638 **Der private Industriesektor im Irak: staatliche Förderung, Organisation und bisherige Entwicklung.** (Private sector industry in Iraq: state aid – organization – historical development.)
Aziz Alkazaz. *Orient* (Opladen), vol. 23, no. 4 (December 1982), p. 570-99.

Since the 1970s, Iraq has attempted to implement a new private-ownership industrialization strategy and three different industrial sectors have emerged: socialist, private, and mixed. This article looks at government policies toward the private and mixed sectors and the manner of their development from 1970 to 1982. There is an English summary on p. 683-84.

639 **Development and structural change in the Iraqi economy and manufacturing industry: 1960-1970.**
Zeki Fattah. *World Development*, vol. 7, no. 8-9 (August-September 1979), p. 813-23.

An analysis of development and structural changes in the manufacturing sector financed largely from oil revenues between 1960 and 1970.

640 **The role of government in the industrialization of Iraq 1950-1965.**
Ferhang Jalal. London: Cass, 1972. 134p. bibliog.

A study of Iraq's economic and industrial development during the early years of petroleum revenues. Jalal was the Director-General of the Industrial Bank of Iraq.

641 **State incubation of Iraqi capitalism.**
ʿIsam al-Khafaji. *Middle East Report*, vol. 16, no. 5/142 (September-October 1986), p. 4-9.

Reviews the evolution of state-controlled industrial development in Iraq and the severe impact it suffered during the war with Iran (1980-88). This article is followed on p. 10-12 by 'State and capitalism in Iraq: a comment' by Hanna Batatu.

642 **The industrialization of Iraq.**
Kathleen M. Langley.    Cambridge, MA: Harvard University Press,
1961. 313p. (Harvard Middle Eastern Monographs, 5).
A detailed study of the growth of industry in Iraq and government efforts to promote
it before the Revolution in 1958.

643 **Total factor productivity, non-neutral technical change and
economic growth.**
Victor Levy.    *Journal of Development Economics*, vol. 8, no. 1
(February 1981), p. 93-109.
A technical study analysing the productivity of the industrial sector in Iraq.

644 **Industrial policy and performance in Iraq.**
Edith Penrose.    In: *The integration of modern Iraq*, edited by Abbas
Kelidar.    London: Croom Helm, 1979, p. 150-70.
Penrose reviews the development of industry in Iraq from the 1960s to the late 1970s.

645 **Le développement industriel de l'Irak.** (The industrial development
of Iraq.)
Makram Sader.    Beirut: CERMOC, 1983. 135p. bibliog.
Describes the industrial development of Iraq before the Revolution of 1958, efforts
and achievements in industrialization and planning in Iraq from 1958 to 1980, and the
evolution of the manufacturing industry from 1958 to 1978.

646 **Arab military industry: capability, performance and impact.**
Yezid Sayigh.    London: Brassey's, in association with the Centre for
Arab Unity Studies (Beirut, Cairo, London), 1992. 260p. bibliog.
Mostly prepared before the Gulf War of 1991, but revised and updated to take its
consequences into account. See chapter five: 'Iraq: emergent arms producer and
regional power' (p. 103-30). This study gives technical data on the types of arms and
military equipment manufactured in Iraq, a country which became a significant
producer in the late 1980s.

647 **Industrial development and the decision-making process.**
John Townsend.    In: *Iraq: the contemporary state*, edited by Tim
Niblock.    London: Croom Helm; New York: St. Martin's Press, 1982,
p. 256-77.
A contribution on the problems of management in Iraqi industry which is dominated
by the public sector.

# Agriculture and Water

648　**Sozialistische Agrargestaltung im Irak unter der Herrschaft der Baʿth-Partei.** (Socialist agricultural policy under Baʿth Party leadership.)
Tarik Abdullatif.　*Orient* (Opladen), vol. 19, no. 3 (September 1978), p. 21-43.

A short summary in English follows the article on p. 43. The Baʿth Party implemented an agricultural reform programme in 1970 intended to improve cultivation as well as to carry out further land reform and redistribution begun under the 1958 reform. This article reviews the impact on social organization and the mobilization of the rural sector which was entrusted to mass organizations and People's Councils, and resulted in some successes.

649　**Lessons from agrarian reform in Iraq.**
Martin E. Adams.　*Land Reform, Land Settlement & Cooperatives*, 1972, no. 1, p. 56-64.

A detailed survey of agricultural practice in an irrigated area of Diyalah Province which identifies limitations placed on the potential of the land reform by physical factors (land, salinity, etc), by the organization of agriculture in land distributed under the Reform Law, and by the problems attending intensification of agriculture.

650　**Land reform in Iraq: an economic evaluation of the Al-Wahda irrigation project.**
Mohammed M. A. Ahmed (et al.).　*Land Reform, Land Settlement & Cooperatives*, 1970, no. 1, p. 62-77.

Describes and evaluates the performance of the Wahda irrigation project some 30 km. from Baghdad in which farm units were distributed in 1964 to landless farmers under the provisions of the 1958 Agrarian Reform Law.

651 **The role of supervised credit in land settlement: case studies of Mikdadiya and Kanaan, Iraq.**
Mohammed M. A. Ahmed, J. M. al-Ezzy. *Land Reform, Land Settlement & Cooperatives*, 1971, no. 2, p. 21-28.

The 1958 Agrarian Reform Law distributed land expropriated from large landowners to landless farmers. This study was carried out because most of the farmers who participated in the Supervised Credit Programme in Diyalah Province for one year deserted it the next. It identifies six reasons why farmers disliked the scheme or found problems with it.

652 **Agrarian systems and development in Iraq.**
Abdul Sahib Alwan. *Land Reform, Land Settlement, and Cooperatives*, 1986, no. 1-2, p. 19-29.

Describes the evolution of the land tenure system in Iraq, the consequences of the Agrarian Reform Laws of 1958 and 1970, and the 'socialisation' of agriculture in the form of cooperative societies, collective farms, and state farms. The concluding remarks note that the dominant pattern of landholding is now small to medium-size farms and state farms.

653 **Water resources in Iraq.**
Nadhir A. al-Ansari, Hedeff I. Essaid, Yousif N. Salim. *Journal of the Geological Society of Iraq*, 14 (1981), p. 35-42.

The authors provide data on water resources available in Iraq in the form of surface water and ground water.

654 **Agrarian reform in Iraq: some socio-economic aspects.**
Fuad Baali. *American Journal of Economics and Sociology*, vol. 28, no. 1 (1969), p. 61-76.

Describes the character of the recent agrarian reform carried out in Iraq, and examines the uses and limitation of the Agrarian Reform Law of 1958. Some statistics are included.

655 **Water resources in Iraq.**
M. M. Badry, M. S. Mehdi, J. M. Khawar. In: *Irrigation and agricultural development*, edited by S. S. Johl. New York: Pergamon Press for the United Nations, 1980, p. 315-26.

The papers in this volume were originally given as part of an International Expert Consultation, Baghdad, 1979. This paper provides a country case-study of the state of Iraq's water resources at that time. Also on Iraq in this volume: 'Studies on crop consumptive use of water in Iraq' by N. S. Kharrufa, G. M. al-Kawaz, H. N. Ismail, (p. 245-56) and 'A review of some aspects of soil reclamation in Iraq' by J. S. Dougrameji, K. I. Musleh, A. B. Hana (p. 293-303).

656 **Iraq: environmental, resource and development issues.**
Peter Beaumont. In: *Iraq: power and society*, edited by Derek
Hopwood, Habib Ishow, Thomas Koszinowski. Oxford: Ithaca, for
St. Antony's College, 1993, p. 117-40.
Surveys agriculture and water resources and the impact of oil revenue over the last 50
years. The various constraints on economic development over and above the impact
of the Gulf War of 1991 are outlined. Statistics are provided.

657 **Machinery selection and crop planning on a state farm in Iraq.**
Abdulla Danok, Bruce McCarl, T. Kelly White. *American Journal of
Agricultural Economics*, vol. 60 (1978), p. 544-49.
Discusses the problems of state farms in choosing and managing machinery, selecting
crops, managing labour and making profits, based on a case-study of one of the state
farms in central Iraq established as a demonstration unit for the introduction of new
technology.

658 **Communism and agrarian reform in Iraq.**
Rony Gabbay. London: Croom Helm, 1978. 222p. map. bibliog.
Discusses the attitude of the Iraqi Communist Party towards the agrarian problems of
Iraq from its foundation in 1934 up to the 1970s. Part one deals with pre-
Revolutionary Iraq (1932-58); part two post-Revolutionary Iraq from 1958 onwards.

659 **The development of agrarian policies since 1958.**
Habib Ishow. In: *Iraq: power and society*, edited by Derek
Hopwood, Habib Ishow, Thomas Koszinowski. Oxford: Ithaca, for
St. Antony's College, 1993, p. 171-92.
Describes the impact of the Agrarian Reform Laws after the Revolution in 1958 and
the changes in agrarian policies. Agriculture has also suffered from constraints
imposed by the years of war with Iran, government interference and the state's
dependence on oil revenue.

660 **L'état et la paysannerie en Irak.** (The state and the peasantry in
Iraq.)
Habib Ishow. *Revue de l'Occident Musulman et de la Méditerranée*,
no. 45 (1987), p. 113-25.
Considers the effects of state intervention in the agricultural sector on rural life, and
argues that central government has been the main cause of the disequilibrium in
agrarian structures, of the disintegration of rural communities, and decline of
agricultural production. Includes statistical tables for the period since 1958.

156

661 **Le statut foncier, la paysannerie et le pouvoir politique en Irak depuis 1921.** (The land regime, the peasantry and political power in Iraq since 1921.)
Habib Ishow. *Revue de l'Occident Musulman et de la Méditerranée*, vol. 34 (2e trimestre 1982), p. 105-18.
Ishow reviews the state of land tenure in Iraq in 1921 when the modern state was created, and the evolution of the land regime up to 1958.

662 **Lower Tigris basin: mismanagement of surface water resources.**
Jassim al Khalaf. *Iraqi Geographical Journal*, vol. 2 (1964), p. 1-20.
Describes the pattern of water and soil use in the lower Tigris basin between the Kut barrage and the city of Qurnah, examines the economic consequences of current use, and suggests improvements in management of resources.

663 **Co-operative societies in Iraq.**
A. K. S. Lambton. *Yearbook of Agricultural Co-operation*, 1972, p. 37-57.
Provides a detailed description of the cooperative societies formed after the enactment of the Agrarian Reform Laws of 1958 and 1970, their activities, successes and failures.

664 **Iraq: problems of regional development.**
Keith McLachlan. In: *The integration of modern Iraq*, edited by Abbas Kelidar. London: Croom Helm, 1979, p. 135-49.
The author discusses the constraints on agricultural development in Iraq and present state of exploitation.

665 **The agricultural development of Iraq.**
Herbert W. Ockerman, Shimoon G. Samano. In: *Agricultural development in the Middle East*, edited by Peter Beaumont, Keith McLachlan. Chichester, England: Wiley, 1985, p. 189-207.
Describes the state of agriculture, soils, irrigation, livestock-rearing and crop production in Iraq. There are also comments on marine resources. Much statistical information is included.

666 **Farm studies in Iraq: an agro-economic study of the agriculture in the Hilla-Diwaniya area in Iraq.**
A. P. G. Poyck. Wageningen, The Netherlands: Veenman, 1962. 99p. (Mededelingen van de Landbouwhogeschool te Wageningen, Nederland, 62).
Originally prepared as a university thesis, this study provides a detailed and valuable account of the rural economy of central Iraq at the time of the Revolution.

667 **Agricultural production and development in Iraq.**
Mohsin Shaik Radhi, Mohammad Douglah. *Agriculture and Development*, no. 6 (November 1983), p. 19-43.

A survey of the situation of agriculture in Iraq and of recent efforts undertaken to improve production.

668 **Baathism in practice: agriculture, politics and political culture in Syria and Iraq.**
Robert Springborg. *Middle Eastern Studies*, vol. 17, no. 2 (April 1981), p. 191-209.

Springborg describes the problems of agriculture, especially in Iraq where it has been starved of funds in favour of industry, and compares the strategies for agricultural development employed by the Baʿth regimes in Syria and in Iraq. His article provides a reasonably detailed account of the state of agriculture in Iraq and the effects of government policies.

669 **Infitah, agrarian transformation, and elite consolidation in contemporary Iraq.**
Robert Springborg. *Middle East Journal*, vol. 40, no. 1 (Winter 1986), p. 33-52.

Discusses changes in land tenure enforced by the land reforms from 1958 to the mid-1970s, and argues that government policy since 1979 has significantly affected credit supply and prices by allowing private operators a very prominent role in agriculture, while the state sector has been relatively disadvantaged.

670 **Ecology and utilization of desert shrub rangelands in Iraq.**
D. C. P. Thalen. The Hague: Junk, 1979. 407p. maps. bibliog.

A study of the ecological state and utilization of rangelands carried out in 1970-73. Thalen considered the types of vegetation and the impact of grazing, cutting for fuel, ploughing and cultivation, and the effect of exclosures and protection measures.

**The role of agricultural planning in the development of Iraq.**
*See* item no. 691.

# Transport

671  **Das Eisenbahnsystem im Irak und die Probleme des Gütertransports. Gegenwärtige Situation und Entwicklungprojekte.** (The railway system in Iraq and the problem of goods transport. Current situation and development project.)
Aziz Alkazaz.  *Orient* (Opladen), vol. 17, no. 2 (June 1976), p. 44-64.
Since 1974, the inadequacy of the Iraqi railway system has become clear and efforts have been made to upgrade the system. This article provides a summary of the network, the capacity of the rolling-stock, and improvements in hand. An English summary appears on p. 63-64, along with a map.

672  **Native river boats in 'Irāq.**
Touvia Ashkenazi.  *Ethnos* (Stockholm), vol. 22 (1957), p. 50-56.
Ashkenazi describes the shape and characteristics of the six types of traditional river boats used in various parts of Iraq.

673  **Middle East railways.**
Hugh Hughes.  Kenton, England: Continental Railway Circle, 1981. 128p. maps.
Mainly intended for the railway and steam enthusiast, but including a brief historical sketch of the development of railway transport. See chapter 7 'Mesopotamia and Iraq' on p. 86-99.

674  **Studies on the development of inland navigation systems in Iraq.**
S. Seetharaman, Hamed S. Saeedy.  *Arab Gulf*, vol. 13, no. 3 (1981), p. 9-25.
Discusses the state of inland water transport and the navigation characteristics and potential of Iraqi rivers.

# Urban Studies and Housing

### 675 Morphology of Baghdad.
Ghouse Mounir Ahmed. *Iraqi Geographical Journal*, vol. 5 (1969), p. 1-26.

The author considers the physical factors which have influenced the shape of modern Baghdad in the form of transport and industry.

### 676 A neighbourhood cluster of Baghdad: its evolution and urban pattern.
Ghouse Mounir Ahmed. *Iraqi Geographical Journal*, vol. 4 (1967), p. 1-33.

Analyses the growth and structure of a modern neighbourhood of Baghdad called Raghida Khatun, which has grown up on the north-eastern edge of the city.

### 677 The retail structure and function of Baghdad.
Ghouse Mounir Ahmed. *Iraqi Geographical Journal*, vol. 3 (1965), p. 1-23.

Examines the structure and distribution of retail marketing in the central business district of Baghdad, which includes both traditional and Western styles of store.

### 678 The rebuilding of Fao city, Iraq: a case of central government post-war reconstruction.
Sultan Barakat. In: *Disasters and the small dwelling: perspectives for the UN IDNDR*, edited by Yasemin Aysan, Ian Davis. London: James & James, 1992, p. 194-206.

A case-study of the exceptional effort made by the Iraqi government to rebuild the cities of Basra and Fao after the devastation caused by the war with Iran. This article looks at the efficacy of the reconstruction policy for Fao which was rebuilt in 114 days between December 1988 and June 1989. The UN IDNDR is the United Nations International Decade for Natural Disasters Reduction.

679   **Der Suq (Bazar) von Bagdad: eine wirtschafts- und
socialgeographische Untersuchung.** (The Baghdad suq: an
examination in economic and social geography.)
Hashim K. N. al-Genabi. Erlangen, Germany: Selbstverlag der
Fränkische Geographische Gesellschaft, in Kommision bei Palm &
Enke, 1976. 142p. maps. bibliog. (Erlanger Geographischer
Arbeiten, 36).

A detailed geographical study of the traditional market of Baghdad and the social and
economic environment in which it operates.

680   **Baghdad: portrait of a city in physical and cultural change.**
John Gulick. *Journal of the American Institute of Planners*, vol. 33,
no. 4 (July 1967), p. 246-55.

Gulick describes the changes taking place in the city, its population, built structures
and lifestyle, and relates these to its growth as a national capital.

681   **Revitalizing a historical citadel.**
Diana Ladas. *Ekistics*, vol. 43, no. 256 (March 1977), p. 140-44.

Based on a conservation study prepared for the municipality of Kirkuk, this article
describes the problems faced by the overcrowded historic centre of the town, and
plans to renovate it.

682   **Housing and social segregation in Iraq.**
L. A. N. Raouf. *International Journal of Urban & Regional
Research*, vol. 9, no. 3 (September 1985), p. 368-82.

Shows that before the Second World War segregation was by ethnic origin, religious
affiliation and occupation and trade, and that rich and poor of each group lived side-
by-side in the same city quarters. Since the incorporation of Iraq into the capitalist
world market, economic power, market relations and social class have instead become
the ultimate factors determining urban housing forms. The rich have moved out to the
modern suburbs, leaving the poor in decaying traditional centres, while rural migrants
have squatted in bad conditions on marginal land.

683   **Housing in postrevolutionary Iraq.**
L. A. N. Raouf. *International Journal of Urban & Regional
Research*, vol. 8, no. 3 (September 1984), p. 332-53.

The author discusses the role of two major housing institutions in post-revolutionary
Iraq in providing access to housing for various social groups, and in shaping a
particular urban physical form. The Housing Cooperative Societies and the Real
Estate Bank are the main source of housing finance.

684  **Réforme agraire, pétrole et urbanisation en Irak.** (Agrarian reform, oil and urbanization in Iraq.)
Hafedh Sethom.   *Annales de Géographie*, vol. 92, no. 513 (September-October 1983), p. 548-73.

Reviews Iraq's recent economic history and notes that large-scale rural–urban migration arising from large feudal-style landholdings, together with the impact of oil revenues, led to increased urbanization from 1947 to 1977 and the decline of agriculture. An English abstract appears on p. 573.

685  **Social and economic conditions of Shaikch-Omar community.**
Shahzenan Shakerchi.   *Bulletin of the College of Arts* (Baghdad), no. 8 (1965), p. 31-37.

Report on surveys of 447 families in the housing scheme for low-income workers and government employees in a poor area of Baghdad, some 30 years after it was established for migrants from other parts of Iraq.

**Passive solar design: traditional courtyard houses, Baghdad.**
*See* item no. 773.

**Baghdad resurgent.**
*See* item no. 774.

# Planning

686 **Investment allocations and plan implementation: Iraq's absorptive capacity, 1951-1980.**
Abdul Wahab al-Ameen. *Journal of Energy and Development*, vol. 6, no. 2 (Spring 1981), p. 263-80.
Examines planning machinery, development programmes and plan implementation between 1951 and 1980 when Iraq's oil revenues brought in plenty of capital, but the economy's absorptive capacity remained limited.

687 **Die Entwicklungspolitik im Irak nach 1968 und ihre bisherigen Ergebnisse.** (Iraq's policy for economic development after 1968 and its achievements.)
Reinhardt Bolz. *Orient* (Opladen), vol. 20, no. 1 (March 1979), p. 68-89.
Bolz describes the Ba'th Party's economic development plan and the extent to which it was put into practice, and argued that Iraq was well on the way to achieving the goals set out in the plan before the Iran–Iraq war. An English summary appears on p. 116-17.

688 **Räumliche Disparitäten der Lebensgrundlagen im irakischen Kurdistan: ein Beitrag zur Regionalplanung.** (Spatial disparities in living conditions in Iraqi Kurdistan: a contribution to regional planning.)
Abdul-Cader Cader. Berlin: Universitätsbibliothek der Technischen Universität, Abteilung Publizistik, 1978. 446p. maps. bibliog. (Arbeitshefte des Instituts für Stadt- und Regionalplanung der Technischen Universität Berlin, 7).
Originally presented as a thesis, this study provides an account of rural economic conditions in Kurdistan in the 1970s and proposals for improvement.

689 **Critical evaluation of development planning in Iraq: 1951-1980.**
Adil H. Mouhammed. *Scandinavian Journal of Development Alternatives*, vol. 7, no. 2-3 (1988), p. 297-306.
Iraqi development planning suffered from poor formulation (in terms of feasibility and consistency) and poor implementation, and in addition the economy was battered by external political and economic shocks partly as a result of oil price rises. The author concludes that in some cases development plans actually hampered the potential growth of the economy by causing bottlenecks.

690 **An econometric identification of development strategies in Iraq: 1951-1980.**
Adil Mouhammed. *Canadian Journal of Development Studies / Revue Canadienne d'Etudes du Développement*, vol. 11, no. 2 (1990), p. 99-118.
A technical econometric analysis of Iraq's development plans from 1951 to 1980 which concludes that the economy will remain backward if the structure of the economy and dependence on oil revenues remain unaltered.

691 **The role of agricultural planning in the development of Iraq.**
Mahdi al-Najjar, R. Swarup. *Adab al-Rafidain*, vol. 2 (1971), p. 55-64.
The authors review the history of agricultural planning which became systematic only after 1953, with the establishment of the Iraq Development Board (later part of the Ministry of Planning).

692 **Western, Soviet and Egyptian influences on Iraq's development planning.**
Rodney Wilson. In: *Iraq: the contemporary state*, edited by Tim Niblock. London: Croom Helm; New York: St. Martin's Press, 1982, p. 219-40.
Wilson traces the development of national planning in Iraq since the Second World War, and examines the major outside influences upon it.

# Statistics

693 **Annual abstract of statistics / Al-Majmūʿah al-iḥṣāʾīyah al-sanawīyah.**
Baghdad: Central Statistical Organization. annual.
A statistical abstract published in Arabic and English covering climate, agriculture, trade, banking, industry, population and finance, etc. Since 1979, few issues have been published, because Iraq has been at war, and little real information has been released in those that have appeared. Previously, Iraqi statistics were published regularly from 1929 onwards.

694 **Demographic yearbook.**
New York: United Nations, 1948- . annual.
Gives demographic statistics for all countries. Data for Iraq are based on the results of the 1957 and 1977 population censuses, but other statistics for Iraq are estimates or provisional figures since 1980.

695 **The Arab world: an international statistical directory.**
Rodney Wilson. Brighton, England: Wheatsheaf, 1984. [191]p.
Iraqi official publications have published few statistical data since the beginning of the war with Iran in 1980, largely for security reasons. In this book, Tables 54-57 give the following statistical data for Iraq for the 1970s: Investment expenditure in Iraq; national budget; non-oil exports and imports; balance of payments.

696 **Al-Kitāb al-sanawī lil-iḥṣāʾāt al-zirāʿīyah al-mujallad raqm 8 / Yearbook of agricultural statistics Volume 8. (December 1988).**
League of Arab States Arab Organisation for Agricultural Development, Khartoum, 1988. 400p.
This volume contains statistical data for 1984, 1985 and 1986, together with a three-year average for the period 1973-75, and a three-year average for the food gap and commodity trade balance. Data for Iraq are included in many, but not all, the tables

for land use, population, labour force, agricultural land and rainfall, agricultural inputs, crop and animal production, and prices, imports and exports of agricultural commodities, and the 'food gap' section for 1984-86. The text is in Arabic and English.

697 **Statistical yearbook (Arab member states) / Annuaire statistique (états membres arabes) / Al-ḥawlīyah al-iḥṣā'īyah (al-duwal al-ʿarabīyah al-aʿḍā').**
UNESCO. Paris: UNESCO, 1982- . annual.
The work includes tables (in three languages) as follows: reference tables; education; educational expenditure; science & technology; libraries; museums & related institutions; theatre & other dramatic arts; book production; newspapers & other periodicals; cultural life; film & cinema; radio broadcasting; television. Data for Iraq are often scanty or missing, but these volumes provide some information.

698 **UN statistical yearbook.**
New York: United Nations, 1948- . annual.
Contains economic statistics from member countries, including some from Iraq showing data on production, energy, trade (internal and external), transport and communications, and on total and per capita consumption of agricultural products, fertilizers, etc. Summary statistics are included on financial matters, social phenomena, health, housing, education, science and technology, and culture. Data on Iraq for recent years are estimates or provisional figures.

**The population of Ottoman Syria and Iraq, 1878-1914.**
*See* item no. 162.

# Language

## Arabic

**699 Christian Arabic of Baghdad.**
Farida Abu-Haidar. Wiesbaden, Germany: Harrassowitz, 1991.
200p. bibliog. (Semitica Viva, 7).
A linguistic study, with an introduction setting the context and briefly describing the present-day Christian community in Baghdad, and noting the location and size of other Christian communities in Iraq. The author is herself from a Christian Baghdadi background and collected the data in 1987. The book is divided into three sections dealing with phonology, morphology, and syntax. Chapter 4 provides a brief socio-linguistic survey of Christian Baghdadi Arabic, and chapter 5 gives texts with translations and notes.

**700 Maintenance and shift in the Christian Arabic of Baghdad.**
Farida Abu-Haidar. *Zeitschrift für Arabische Linguistik*, vol. 21 (1990), p. 47-62.
Considers the adjustments made by speakers of a minority dialect – Christian Arabic – towards the majority Muslim dialect and discusses the extent to which this accommodation is short or long term.

**701 The problem of diglossia in Arabic. A comparative study of classical and Iraqi Arabic.**
Salih J. Altoma. Cambridge, MA: Harvard University Press, 1969.
167p. (Harvard Middle East Monographs, 21).
A study of linguistic divergences between classical Arabic and modern colloquial usage, based on the spoken Arabic of Baghdad and lower Iraq.

702 **Communal dialects in Baghdad.**
Haim Blanc. Cambridge, MA: Harvard University Press, 1964. 204p.
map. (Harvard Middle East Monographs, 10).
The author carried out his research among Iraqi emigrants in Israel and the United States of America, and concluded that the three non-regional dialect groups of Arabic speakers present in Baghdad corresponded with Muslim, Jewish and Christian backgrounds. The book describes phonology, morphology, syntactic and lexical features of Baghdad Arabic.

703 **Die Verbalsyntax des neuarabischen Dialektes von Kwayriš (Irak), mit einer einleitenden allgemeinen Tempus- und Aspektlehre.** (The verb syntax of the modern Arabic dialect of Kuwayrish (Iraq).)
Adolf Denz. Wiesbaden, Germany: Deutsche Morgenländische Gesellschaft, Kommissionsverlag Franz Steiner, 1971. 141p. bibliog.
A linguistic study of verbs in the Arabic dialect of Kuwayrish.

704 **A basic course in Iraqi Arabic.**
Wallace M. Erwin. Washington, DC: Georgetown University Press, 1969. 389p. (Richard Slade Harrell Arabic Series, 11).
A course book in the spoken Arabic of Baghdad, for use with a teacher.

705 **A short reference grammar of Iraqi Arabic.**
Wallace M. Erwin. Washington, DC: Georgetown University Press, 1963. 392p. (Arabic Series, 4).
A grammar of the spoken Arabic of Baghdad.

706 **Word order in Iraqi Arabic.**
Henryk Jankowski. *Lingua Posnaniensis*, vol. 32-33 (1989-90), p. 109-12.
Examines word order as a syntactic structural characteristic in the Iraqi-spoken Arabic of Baghdad.

707 **Der arabische Dialekt der Juden von ʿAqra und Arbīl.** (The Arabic dialect of the Jews from ʿAqra and Arbil.)
Otto Jastrow. Wiesbaden, Germany: Harrassowitz, 1990. 438p. map. (Semitica Viva, 5).
A linguistic study of the Arabic dialect spoken by the Jews in two towns in the Iraqi part of Kurdistan. It contains an analysis of the grammar, sample texts from each of the towns, glossary and appendix of Hebrew loan-words. Material was collected from informants now in Israel.

708 **Remarks on the Iraqi-Arabic lexicon: problems and characteristics.**
George Krotkoff. In: *Semitic studies in honor of Wolf Leslau on the occasion of his eighty-fifth birthday Novermber 14th 1991*, edited by A. S. Kaye. Wiesbaden, Germany: Harrassowitz, 1991, Vol. I, p. 886-89.

On the particularities of Iraqi Arabic as compared with modern standard Arabic of other Eastern Arab countries. Also in this *Festschrift*, see 'Language and sex: the case of expatriate Iraqis' by Farida Abu-Haidar, p. 28-38, which discusses differences in vocabulary and grammar, and the extent to which speakers incorporate English words, among Iraqi men and women living in Britain.

709 **Spoken Arabic of Baghdad.**
R. J. McCarthy, Faraj Raffouli. Beirut: Librarie Orientale, 1964-65. 2 vols. (Publications of the Oriental Institute of Al-Hikma, Linguistic Series, 1-2).

Volume one contains grammar and exercises, volume two contains texts of Iraqi colloquial Arabic as spoken in Baghdad.

710 **Grundzüge der Grammatik des Arabischen Dialektes von Bagdad.**
(Fundamentals of the grammar of the Arabic dialect of Baghdad.)
Nisar Malaika. Wiesbaden, Germany: Harrassowitz, 1963. 85p. bibliog.

Malaika discusses orthography, phonology, accidence and syntax of the Arabic dialect of Baghdad.

711 **The Jewish Baghdadi dialect: studies and texts in the Judaeo-Arabic dialect of Baghdad.**
Jacob Mansour. Or-Yehuda, Israel: Babylonian Jewry Heritage Center, Institute for Research on Iraqi Jewry, 1991. 329p. (Studies in the History and Culture of Iraqi Jewry, 7).

A systematic description of the dialect of Arabic spoken by the Jewish community in Baghdad, with a discussion of its characteristic and distinctive forms, studies in its phonology and morphology, and the presentation of sample texts. Materials were collected from informants now in Israel. There is a Hebrew summary.

712 **A sociolinguistic study of apology in Iraqi Arabic.**
Ibrahim Khidhir Sallo, Iman Adil Alias. *Adab al-Rafidayn*, vol. 20 (1989), p. 53-84.

The authors consider the social contexts of apologizing, and the chosen manner of so doing in colloquial Iraqi Arabic.

713   **On the Arabic dialect spoken in Širqāṭ (Assur).**
Erkki Salonen.   Helsinki: Suomalainen Tiedeakatemia, 1980. 131p.
bibliog. (Suomalaisen Tiedeakatemian Toimituksia Annales
Academiae Scientiarum Fennicae, Sarja-Ser. B Nide Tom, 212).
A linguistic study of the dialect of Shirqat approximately 100 miles south of Mosul. It
contains texts collected in the area presented together with extensive grammatical
analysis of phonology, pronouns, verbs, particles, the article, possessives and
negation.

714   **The spoken Arabic of Iraq.**
John van Ess.   Oxford: Oxford University Press, 1938, rp. 1975.
2nd ed. with revised and additional vocabulary. 280p.
First published in 1917 under the title 'Spoken Arabic of Mesopotamia', this book
was written to teach the spoken dialect of southern Iraq. It uses Arabic script with
transliteration to represent pronunciation, and gives keys to the exercises.

715   **A dictionary of Iraqi Arabic: Arabic–English.**
Edited by D. R. Woodhead, Wayne Beene under the technical
direction of Karl Stowasser.   Washington, DC: Georgetown
University Press, 1967. 509p. (Richard Slade Harrell Arabic Series,
10).
A dictionary of spoken Iraqi Arabic, entirely transliterated in modified Roman script,
arranged under triliteral roots, rather than alphabetically. A companion English–
Arabic dictionary was published in 1964, edited by B. E. Clarity, K. Stowasser and
R. G. Wolfe.

**A linguistic analysis of Kurdish–Arabic code-switching.**
*See* item no. 723.

**A sociolinguistic study of language choice among Kurdish students at
Mosul University.**
*See* item no. 724.

# Kurdish

716   **Kurdish basic course. Dialect of Sulaimania, Iraq.**
Jamal Jalal Abdulla, Ernest N. McCarus.   Ann Arbor: University of
Michigan Press, 1967. 482p.
A text-book designed for class-room use, not a self-teaching course. The same two
authors also produced *Kurdish readers I-III* (Ann Arbor, 1967) which give Kurdish
texts in original script with transcriptions. Volume one contains 'Newspaper'
Kurdish, volume two Kurdish essays, and volume three Kurdish short stories.

717  **The phonemic system of modern standard Kurdish.**
Abdul-Majeed Rashid Ahmad.    Dissertation, University of Michigan,
1986. 169p. (UMI order No. DA 8612458).
Modern Standard Kurdish is a written form of Kurdish adopted by Iraqi Kurds to
establish a standard written language which substitutes for the various Kurdish
dialects spoken in Iraqi Kurdistan. It is based on the Sulaymaniyah dialect, and
written documents are the main sources for this linguistic study.

718  **Manuel de kurde (dialecte Sorani): grammaire, textes de lecture,
vocabulaire kurde–français et français–kurde.** (Manual of Kurdish
(Sorani dialect): grammar, reading exercises, Kurdish–French and
French–Kurdish vocabulary.)
Joyce Blau.    Paris: Klincksieck, 1980. 287p.
Contains material of the language course given at the Institut des Langues et
Civilisations Orientales in Paris for the Sorani dialect of Kurdish used in Iraqi
Kurdistan. Kurdish text is written in the Arabic script with French transliterations.

719  **Nationalism and language in Kurdistan, 1918-1985.**
Amir Hassanpour.    San Francisco: Mellen Research University Press,
1992. 520p. bibliog.
Hassanpour focuses on Iraq, and discusses how the Sorani dialect became
standardized in the period after 1918 when the Kurds acquired limited official status
in the newly created state of Iraq.

720  **A Kurdish grammar: descriptive analysis of the Kurdish of
Sulaimaniya, Iraq.**
Ernest N. McCarus.    New York: American Council of Learned
Societies, 1958. 138p. map. (American Council of Learned Societies
Program in Oriental Languages, Publications Series B – Aids, 10).
A grammatical study of the language of Iraqi Kurdistan covering phonology,
morphology and syntax.

721  **Kurdish dialect studies I-II.**
D. N. MacKenzie.    London: Oxford University Press, 1961-62.
(Vol. 2 rp. London: School of Oriental & African Studies, 1990.)
2 vols. maps. bibliog. (London Oriental Series, 10).
Based on material gathered in Iraqi Kurdistan in 1954-55. Volume 1 contains an
analysis of the phonology of two groups of dialects, while Volume 2 contains texts in
transcription in individual dialects of northern Iraq with translations.

722 **Kurdish–English English–Kurdish (Kurmancî) dictionary.**
Baran Rizgar. London: M. F. Onen, 1993. 400p.
A dictionary of Kurdish in the Turkish romanized alphabet which includes words from all Kurdish dialects, but is based on Kurmanji which is spoken by some Iraqi Kurds. A survey of grammar is included, and also a table of correspondences for Arabic and Cyrillic scripts.

723 **A linguistic analysis of Kurdish–Arabic code-switching.**
Ibrahim Khidhir Sallo. *Adab al-Rafidayn*, vol. 17 (1988), p. 139-54.
The author analyses the choice of language among bilingual Kurdish and Arabic speakers from a linguistic viewpoint.

724 **A sociolinguistic study of language choice among Kurdish students at Mosul University.**
Ibrahim Khidhir Sallo. *Adab al-Rafidayn*, vol. 16 (1986), p. 108-17.
Sallo studies the use of language among bilingual Kurdish and Arabic speakers at the University, and concludes that social or psychological factors rather than linguistic ones systematically determine the speaker's choice.

725 **A Kurdish–English dictionary.**
Taufiq Wahby, C. J. Edmonds. Oxford: Clarendon Press, 1966. 179p.
A dictionary of standard Kurdish used for belles-lettres, journalism and formal speech, based on the southern Kurmanji dialect of Sulaymaniyah in Iraq. The Kurdish words are given in romanized forms, with a table of transliteration for Arabic script.

# Other

726 **The sound system of modern Assyrian (Neo-Aramaic).**
Edward Y. Odisho. Wiesbaden, Germany: Harrassowitz, 1988. 130p. bibliog.
A description of the phonetics and phonology of a dialect of Neo-Aramaic spoken in northern Iraq by a native speaker who conducted his research between 1973 and 1986. Chapter one provides an ethnolinguistic history of the Assyrian (Chaldean/Nestorian) Christians of northern Iraq which discusses the 'controversial issue of the historical origin of the speakers of this dialect'.

# Literature

## Arabic poetry

727 **When the words burn: an anthology of modern Arabic poetry:**
**1945-1987.**
Translated and edited by John Mikhail Asfour. Dunvegan, Ontario:
Cormorant Books, 1988. 226p. bibliog.
Translations of poems, with an extensive introduction describing the development of
modern Arabic poetry. The book is arranged in sections reflecting the different styles
and trends. Eight Iraqi poets are represented: Nazik al-Mala'ikah, Buland al-Haydari,
ʿAbd al-Wahhab al-Bayyati, Shadhil Taqah, Saʿdi Yusuf, Khalid al-Khazraji, Badr
Shakir al-Sayyab, and Sadiq al-Sa'igh. Additionally some poems by Jabra Ibrahim
Jabra, a Palestinian who lived in Iraq from 1948 to 1994, are included.

728 **From "Al-Hallāj", a poem by ʿAbd al-Wahhāb al-Bayātī.**
[ʿAbd al-Wahhab al-Bayyati], translated by Khalil I. Semaan.
*Journal of Arabic Literature*, vol. 10 (1979), p. 65-69.
A translation of a long extract from the poem on the Sufi mystic crucified in Baghdad
in 922 CE for declaring that he was God.

729 **Love, death and exile: poems.**
Abdul Wahab al-Bayati, translated by Bassam Frangieh.
Washington, DC: Georgetown University Press, 1990. 307p.
An introduction gives information about the poet, a leader of the Free Verse
movement in Arabic poetry which began in Iraq in 1948. The poems translated are
taken from the following collections: 'The eyes of the dead dogs' (1969) – 3 poems;
'Writing on clay' (1970) – 4 poems; 'Love poems at the seven gates of the world'
(1971) – 4 poems; 'The book of the sea' (1973) – 4 poems; 'Autobiography of the
thief of fire' (1974) – 4 poems; 'Shiraz's moon' (1975) – 8 poems; 'The kingdom of

grain' (1979) – 4 poems; 'Aisha's orchard' (1989) – 23 poems. The poems are presented in parallel Arabic script texts and English translations.

## 730  Modern Arab poets 1950-1975.
Translated and edited with an introduction and biographical notes by Issa J. Boullata.  Washington, DC: Three Continents Press, 1976. 168p.

The section on Iraq (p. 3-28) contains 'A city without rain' and 'The song of rain' by Badr Shakir al-Sayyab; 'Five songs to pain' by Nazik al-Mala'ikah; 'The village market', 'The sorrows of violets', and 'Apology for a short speech' by ʿAbd al-Wahhab al-Bayyati; and six poems by Buland al-Haydari. Also in this book are four poems by Jabra Ibrahim Jabra, a Palestinian resident in Iraq from 1948 to 1994. Brief biographical notes about each author are given at the end of the book.

## 731  The poetic technique of Badr Shākir al-Sayyāb (1926-1964).
Issa J. Boullata.  *Journal of Arabic Literature*, vol. 2 (1971), p. 104-15.

Boullata discusses Badr Shakir al-Sayyab's use of technique and imagery in his poetry and the recurrence of mythical themes in his work.

## 732  Women of the Fertile Crescent: an anthology of modern poetry by Arab women.
Edited with translations by Kamal Boullata.  Washington, DC: Three Continents Press, 1981. 253p.

The section on Iraq (p. 13-22) contains English translations of five poems by Nazik al-Mala'ikah: 'I am', 'Insignificant woman', 'My silence', 'Washing off disgrace', 'Jamila'. Brief biographical notes are provided.

## 733  A new reading of Badr Shākir al-Sayyāb's 'Hymn of the rain'.
Terry Deyoung.  *Journal of Arabic Literature*, vol. 24, no. 1 (March 1993), p. 39-61.

Deyoung discusses the symbolism used in Badr Shakir al-Sayyab's poem which was originally published in Arabic in 1954 and includes a translation of it into English.

## 734  The lode, the word. Poems and collages.
Salah Faiq, translated by the poet's friends with Paul Hammond. London: Melmoth, 1985. 71p.

Thirty-one poems by Salah Fa'iq, a Kurd from Iraq, translated into English with only a very brief introduction. An earlier collection, *Another fire befitting a city (poems)*, was published by the same house in 1979.

## 735  Modern Iraqi poetry.
Edited and introduced by Yaseen Taha Hafiz, translated by Abdul-Wahid Lu'lu'a.  Baghdad: Dar al-Ma'mun, 1989. 165p.

Poems by 32 Iraqi poets translated into English with a short introduction about the development and vicissitudes of cultural life in modern Iraq. The poets included are:

Badr Shakir al-Sayyab; Nazik al-Mala'ikah; ʿAbd al-Wahhab al-Bayyati; Buland al-Haydari; ʿAbd al-Razzaq ʿAbd al-Wahid; Shadhil Taqah; Lamiʿah ʿAbbas ʿImarah; Husayn Mardam; Muhammad Jamil Shalash; Rashid Yasin; Ali al-Hilli; Akram al-Witri; Saʿdi Yusuf; Yusuf al-Sayigh; Rushdi al-ʿAmil; Hasab al-Shaykh Jaʿfar; Sami Mahdi; Yasin Taha Hafiz; Hamid Saʿid; Khalid ʿAli Mustafa; ʿAbd al-Amir Muʿallah; Malik al-Muttalibi; ʿAli Jaʿfar al-ʿAllaq; Maʿd al-Juburi; May Muzaffar; Amjad Muhammad Saʿid; Faruq Sallum; Zahir Al-Jizani; Khazʿal al-Majidi; Faruq Yusuf; Adnan al-Sayigh; and Sajidah al-Musawi.

736 **Songs of the tired guard.**
Buland al-Haidari, translated by Abdullah al-Udhari.   London:
TR Press, 1977. 46p.
Fifteen poems translated into English, by an Iraqi poet generally associated with the Free Verse movement in modern Arabic poetry. No notes accompany the text. This collection of poems was first published in Arabic in 1971 in Beirut.

737 **Three poems by Buland al-Haydari.**
Buland al-Haydari, translated by Mohammad Bakir Alwan.   *Journal of Arabic Literature*, vol. 9 (1978), p. 150-51.
Translations, without notes or annotations, of 'The journey of yellow letters', 'Dreaming of snow', and 'Abandoned gate'.

738 **Death in the early poetry of Nāzik al-Malā'ika.**
Ronak Hussein, Yasir Suleiman.   *British Journal of Middle Eastern Studies*, vol. 20, no. 2 (1993), p. 214-25.
Explores the attitude to death manifested in the early poetry of Nazik al-Mala'ikah, a leading poet of Iraq's Free Verse movement, as represented in the three collections.

739 **The social problems in ʿIraq, and their influence on the poetry, 1900-1950.**
Yousif Izzidien.   *Bulletin of the College of Arts and Sciences* (Baghdad), vol. 3 (1958), p. 73-80; *Bulletin of the College of Arts* (Baghdad), no. 5 (1962), p. 1-22.
Discusses themes such as rural poverty, and other social problems appearing in modern Iraqi poetry, and concludes that authors from poor backgrounds sympathized with the difficulties faced by their own people and wished to raise awareness of social problems. On a similar theme, Dr Izzidien published *Poetry and Iraqi society 1900-1945* in Baghdad in 1962.

740 **Modern Arabic poetry: an anthology.**
Edited by Salma Khadra Jayyusi.   New York: Columbia University
Press, 1987. 498p.
Translations into English of modern Arabic poetry, with an introduction describing its development over the last hundred years. The selection includes works by 24 poets from Iraq, the largest number from any single nation. They are: Muhammad Mahdi al-Jawahiri (2 poems); Ahmad al-Safi al-Najafi (4); Maʿruf al-Rasafi (2); Jamil Sidqi al-Zahawi (1); ʿAbd al-Razzaq ʿAbd al-Wahid (3); ʿAli Jaʿfar al-ʿAllaq (2); ʿAbd al-

Wahhab al-Bayyati (4); Sargun Bulus (4); Mahmud al-Buraykan (2); Zuhur Dixon (4); Salah Fa'iq (1); Yasin Taha Hafiz (4); Buland al-Haydari (4); Hasab al-Shaykh Ja'far (2); Shafiq al-Kamali (3); 'Abd al-Karim Kassid (3); Sami Mahdi (5); Nazik al-Mala'ikah (4); Salah Niyazi (2); Kamal Sabti (1); Hamid Sa'id (2); Yusuf al-Sa'igh (7); Badr Shakir al-Sayyab (5); and Sa'di Yusuf (7).

## 741 Trends and movements in modern poetry.
Salma Khadra Jayyusi. Leiden, The Netherlands: Brill, 1977. 2 vols. 831p. bibliog. (Supplement to the *Journal of Arabic Literature*, 6).

Volume 1 (Parts 1-3) describes the cultural roots of modern Arabic poetry and developments in the first half of the 20th century. Iraq is specifically discussed on p. 26-33. On p. 175-203 five Iraqi poets are considered: 'Abd al-Muhsin al-Kazimi, Muhammad Rida al-Shabibi, Jamil Sidqi al-Zahawi, Ma'ruf al-Rasafi, al-Safi, and Muhammad Mahdi al-Jawahiri. Volume 2 (Parts 4-8) and the conclusion discuss the various differing trends that have emerged more recently. Iraqi poets are particularly mentioned in the course of the discussion of romanticism (p. 472-74), and the Free Verse movement which was led by Iraqi poets after the war.

## 742 'Abdul Majid Lutfi's 'Rejuvenation of words'.
'Abd al-Majid Lutfi, translated by Safa Khulusi. *Journal of Arabic Literature*, vol. 11 (1980), p. 65-67.

A translation of six stanzas from a 152-stanza poem entitled 'Rejuvenation of words'. An introductory paragraph notes that 'Abd al-Majid Lutfi was one of the outstanding poets and thinkers of Iraq and an early pioneer of the Free Verse movement in Arabic poetry.

## 743 The visitor who did not come.
Nazik al-Mala'ika, translated by Shafiq Megally. *Journal of Arabic Literature*, vol. 7 (1976), p. 85-87.

The first poem in the section entitled 'Modern Arabic poems' is a translation, without notes, of 'The visitor who did not come' by Nazik al-Mala'ikah.

## 744 Literatura Iraquí contemporánea. (Contemporary Iraqi literature.)
Prólogo y nota preliminar de Pedro Martínez Montávez. Madrid: Instituto Hispano-Árabe de Cultura, 1973. 432p. (Serie Antologías Nacionales, 1).

A comprehensive collection of translations into Spanish of poetry, prose fiction and essays by modern Iraqi writers. The literature is divided into three periods of writing: 1920-45; 1945-58; and 1958-72.

## 745 Zahâwi's philosophy and his views on Islam.
Sadok Masliyah. *Middle Eastern Studies*, vol. 12, no. 2 (May 1976), p. 177-87.

Masliyah discusses the philosophical outlook of the Iraqi poet Jamil al-Zahawi (1863-1936) who came from an orthodox Muslim background but who was influenced by Western scientific ideas and ancient and modern philosophers.

746 **Modern Arabic poetry 1800-1970: the development of its forms and themes under the influence of Western literature.**
S. Moreh. Leiden, The Netherlands: Brill, 1976. 325p. bibliog.
(Supplement to the *Journal of Arabic Literature*, 5).
This study is divided into three parts: Strophic verse; Blank verse; and Free verse. Iraqi poets are particularly discussed in Part three, chapter 6 'The Iraqi school of *al-shiʿr al-ḥurr* and its followers since 1947' (p. 196-215), which describes the Free Verse school led by Nazik al-Mala'ikah and Badr Shakir al-Sayyab.

747 **An ancient song; Hymn to rain.**
Badr Shakir al-Sayyab, translated by Adel Salama. *Journal of Arabic Literature*, vol. 3 (1972), p. 118-26.
The first two poems in a selection entitled 'Modern Arabic poetry' are translations of 'An ancient song' and 'Hymn to rain'. There are no notes and no introduction to the translations.

748 **Selected poems.**
Badr Shaker As Sayab, translated with an introduction by Badia Bishai. London: Third World Centre for Research & Publishing; Beirut: Arab Institute for Research & Publishing, 1986. 54 + 42p.
This volume contains the Arabic texts with English translation of ten poems by Badr Shakir al-Sayyab, with an introduction setting the poet's work in the context of modern Arabic literature and Sayyab's own development as a poet.

749 **Modern poets of Iraq, 1948-79: cockroach or martyr in the inn by the Persian Gulf.**
Pieter Smoor. *Oriente Moderno*, N.S. 9 (70), nos. 1-6 (January-June 1990), p. 7-38.
Examines the political engagement of Iraqi poets after the Second World War, and the choice of political themes and social criticism.

750 **Badr Šākir as-Sayyāb: Untersuchungen zum poetischen Konzept in den Diwanen azhār wa-asāṭīr und unšūdat al-maṭar.** (Badr Shākir as-Sayyāb: investigations of the poetic scheme in the Diwans Azhār wa-asāṭīr and Unshudat al-maṭar.)
Leslie Tramontini. Wiesbaden, Germany: Harrassowitz, 1991. 184p.
A study of the poet Badr Shakir al-Sayyab, his early poetry and his efforts at literary criticism. The final chapter is an analysis of the poetry collection called *Unshūdat al-maṭar*.

751 **Modern poetry of the Arab world.**
Translated and edited by Abdullah al-Udhari. Harmondsworth, England: Penguin Books, 1986. 142p.
English translations, with minimal notes, of recently composed poetry, and including a short introduction to the principal schools and trends. Seven Iraqi poets are

represented in this collection: Badr Shakir al-Sayyab, Nazik al-Mala'ikah, ʿAbd al-Wahhab al-Bayyati, Buland al-Haydari, Salah Niazi, Sami Mahdi, and Saʿdi Yusuf.

**The poetic content of the Iraqi *Maqām*.**
*See* item no. 782.

**Le martyre de Ḥusayn dans le poésie populaire d'Iraq.**
*See* item no. 799.

# Arabic prose

752  **The cat, the maid, and the wife.**
Daisy al-Amir.   In: *An Arabian mosaic: short stories by Arab women writers*, collected and translated by Dalya Cohen-Mor.   Potomac, MD: Sheba Press, 1993, p. 115-20.
A short story about women among the smart set of modern Baghdad.

753  **The future.**
Daisy al-Amir.   In: *An Arabian mosaic: short stories by Arab women writers*, collected and translated by Dalya Cohen-Mor.   Potomac, MD: Sheba Press, 1993, p. 41-48.
A short story by an Iraqi writer long resident in Beirut and set in Lebanon during the Lebanese war.

754  **Opening the gates: a century of Arab feminist writing.**
Edited by Margot Badran, Miriam Cooke.   London: Virago Press, 1990. 407p.
A substantial Introduction explains the choice and arrangement of the anthology, and sets the chosen texts, which include fiction and documentary material, within a historical and social framework. The anthology is divided into three sections: Awareness, Rejection, and Activism. Two Iraqi short stories are included: 'The eyes in the mirror (1981)' by Daisy al-Amir on p. 115-18 in the first section, on the experiences of a professional woman on her own in a hotel restaurant; and 'Personal papers (1973)' by May Muzaffar on p. 180-85 in the second section – a story about a young woman defying the rules of society in spite of the likely price she would pay.

755  **Die Schwarze Abaya: irakische Erzählungen.** (The black abayah: Iraqi stories.)
Edited by Ikbal Hasson.   Berlin: Express Edition, 1985. 119p.
(Express Internationale Frauenliteratur).
A collection of short stories by Iraqi women writers translated into German. The contents are as follows: 'Die schwarze abaya' by K. H. (p. 11-23); 'Warten' (p. 25-26), 'Erwartung' (p. 27-29) and 'Tod eines Mädchens' (p. 31-33) by Salema

Saleh; 'Ein Mann und eine Frau' (p. 35-43) and 'Tod eines Hundes' (p. 45-49) by Buthaina al-Nasseriy; 'Er heiss Dari (p. 51-63) and 'Aus dem Leben einer Steppdecke' (p. 65-80) by Suheila Dawud Salman; 'Suche nach einer Verschwundenen' by K. H. (p. 81-92); 'Ein Frauenbildnis' by Ikbal Hasson (p. 93-94); 'Die Verabredung' by Raja Ahmad (p. 95-101); 'Nachwort' by Nadia al-Baghdadi (p. 102-18).

### 756 **Hunters in a narrow street.**
Jabra I. Jabra, with an introductory essay by Roger Allen.
Washington, DC: Three Continents Press, 1990. 232p.

Written in English and first published in London in 1960, this novel about a Palestinian arriving in Baghdad to take up a teaching post is an allegory on the state of the Arab world after 1948. The author claimed that the novel was not autobiographical although he himself came from Bethlehem and taught in Iraq since arriving there as a refugee in 1948. Jabra Ibrahim Jabra died in Baghdad in December 1994.

### 757 **The ship.**
Jabra I. Jabra, translated and introduced by Adnan Haydar, Roger Allen. Washington, DC: Three Continents Press, 1985. 200p.

A novel set on board a week's cruise in the Mediterranean, which symbolically describes the post-1948 Arab world. The Introduction states that Jabra, born in Palestine, but living and working in Iraq since 1948, was among the most versatile writers in the Middle East. The novel was originally published in 1970.

### 758 **Arabic short stories.**
Translated by Denys Johnson-Davies. London: Quartet, 1983. 173p.

A collection of 25 short stories which includes two by modern Iraqi writers: 'Clocks like horses' by Muhammad Khudayyir (Khudayr) (p. 27-39); and 'Voices from near and far' by ʿAbd al-Ilah ʿAbd al-Razzaq (p. 111-15).

### 759 **La princesse et le démon: nouvelles sur la guerre Irak–Iran.**
(The princess and the demon: new stories on the Iran–Iraq war.)
Dhia Khudayr, translated from the Iraqi by Driss Jabeur. Paris: L'Harmattan, 1989. 80p.

Six short stories inspired by the war with Iran, entitled: 'Retrouvailles'; 'Le regard'; 'La colombe de Dieu'; 'Le testament'; 'La cité imaginaire'; 'Parmi les monts enneigés'.

### 760 **When I found myself.**
Dia' Khudair, translated by Sharif S. Elmusa. *MERIP Middle East Report*, no. 148 / vol. 17, no. 5 (1987), p. 27-31.

A short story based on the Iran–Iraq war, where the writer himself served at the front. At the time of publication, he was living in Paris.

761 **Modern Arab stories.**
London: Ur Magazine, 1980. 132p.

Contains translations into English of twelve modern Arabic short stories, of which
seven are by Iraqi authors: 'The billy-goat and the menfolk' by Samira al-Mana;
'Tomorrow' by Daisy al-Amir; 'From behind the veil' by Dhu 'l-Nun Ayyub;
'Arnoun' by Saʿd al-Bazzaz; 'The marsh god' by Muhammad Khudayr (Khudayyir);
'When the clouds were on the point of tears' by ʿAbd Allah Niyazi; 'Fatouma' by
ʿAbd al-Malik Nuri.

762 **Short stories by Jewish writers from Iraq, 1924-1978.**
Edited and with an introduction by Shmuel Moreh. Jerusalem:
Hebrew University of Jerusalem, 1981. 299 + 25 + 39p.

The stories are in Arabic, but the Introduction discussing the writers and the cultural,
social and political context of Iraqi Jewish literature is also in Hebrew and in English.

763 **The long days.**
Abdul-Ameer Mu'alla, translated by Mohieddin Ismail, A. W. Lu'lu'a.
London: Alam Press; Baghdad: Dar al-Ma'mum, 1979-82. 3 parts.

An historical novel by an Iraqi poet, critic and writer about Iraq in the days after the
Revolution of 1958.

764 **Von Sozialkritik bis Mystik. Der Islam in Spiegel irakischen
Erzählliteratur.** (From social criticism to mysticism: Islam in the
mirror of Iraqi narrative literature.)
Wiebke Walther. *Die Welt des Islams*, no. 23-24 (1984), p. 222-44.

Walther discusses the choice of themes in Iraqi prose from the early 20th century up
to the 1970s and the trend away from early social criticism towards a more mystical
and spiritual style.

765 **Zur Entwicklung der Kurzprosa im Irak.** (On the development of
short-story writing in Iraq.)
Wiebke Walther. *Wissenschaftliche Zeitschrift der Martin-Luther-
Universität Halle-Wittenberg: Gesellschafts- und
Sprachwissenschaftliche Reihe*, vol. 33, no. 6 (1984), p. 3-16.

A survey of the development of the short story in Iraq, and of the various literary
production of writers of short stories in Iraq up to the Revolution in 1958.

766 **Arabic literature in Iraq during the Ottoman period.**
Ali A. al-Zubeidi. *Prilozi za Orijentalnu Filologiju*, vol. 30 (1980),
p. 495-99.

Reviews the sources and argues that the period of Ottoman rule was not a sort of Dark
Ages, but that the literature of the period was essentially a continuation of the Arabic
literature of earlier times, although it showed more concern with highly ornamented
modes of expression and figures of speech.

**Three plays by Yousif al-Ani.**
*See* item no. 789.


# Kurdish

767 **Mémoire du Kurdistan.** (Memoire of Kurdistan.)
Joyce Blau.   Paris: Findakly, 1984. 215p.
Subtitled on the cover 'Recueil de la tradition littéraire orale et écrite établi' par
Joyce Blau, this book contains translations into French of popular tales, poems,
songs, etc. collected from Iraq, Iran, Turkey, Syria, Lebanon and the Soviet Union.
The second part presents a selection of Kurdish literature from the 18th and 19th
centuries and a larger collection of literary works from the modern period.

# Arts

## General

768 **Culture in the service of** *wataniyya*: **the treatment of Mesopotamian-inspired art in Ba'thi Iraq.**
Amatzia Baram. In: *Studies in Islamic society: contributions in memory of Gabriel Baer*, edited by Gabriel R. Warburg, Gad G. Gilbar. Haifa: Haifa University Press, 1984, p. 265-313.
Baram discusses the extensive use of ancient Mesopotamian themes in modern Iraqi culture – in literature (especially poetry and drama), but more widely in pictorial art – and argues that such themes were encouraged by the Ba'th Party as part of a campaign to develop a local Iraqi nationalism and identity by linking the people with their ancient, pre-Islamic, past.

769 **Aspects of Iraqi cultural policy.**
Abdel-Gawad Daoud El-Basri. Paris: UNESCO, 1980. 38p.
One of a series of booklets intended to show how cultural policies are planned and implemented in member-states. Although this is effectively an official report, it does contain some basic information about institutions, museums, music, cinema, theatre, the arts and book production.

770 **Gilgamesh.**
Baghdad: Ministry of Information & Culture, 1987- .
This describes itself as a journal of modern Iraqi arts.

771 **The monument: art, vulgarity and responsibility in Iraq.**
Samir Khalil (Kanan Makiya). London: Deutsch, 1991. 146p.
Written under a pseudonym, this book explores the symbolism of the enormous and vulgar monument built by Saddam Husayn in Baghdad in 1989. The political and

ideological messages contained in the techniques, style and materials chosen for this
structure and what it says about Saddam himself and his regime are considered in
some detail.

772   **Ur.**
     London: Iraqi Cultural Centre, 1978- . irregular.
A periodical about modern arts in the Arab world, with particular emphasis on Iraq.
Articles on cinema, music, theatre, modern art, calligraphy etc. are included.

# Architecture

773   **Passive solar design: traditional courtyard houses, Baghdad.**
     Subhi al-Azzawi.   In: *Energy and the environment into the 1990s.*
     *Proceedings of the 1st World Renewable Energy Congress, Reading*
     *. . . 1990*, edited by A. M. Sayigh.   Oxford: Pergamon, 1990, Vol. 4,
     p. 2179-97.
Discusses the design advantages of the traditional courtyard-style house of Baghdad
and its adaptation to the hot-dry subtropical climate of the city, and identifies ways in
which energy efficiency could be enhanced.

774   **Baghdad resurgent.**
     Sherban Cantacuzino.   *Mimar*, vol. 6 (1982), p. 56-71.
On the architecture of the development sites of two areas of Baghdad: Bab al-Shaykh
(an office and shopping area), and Kadhimiya (the site of the Shiʿi shrine).

775   **Concepts and influences: towards a regionalized international**
     **architecture, 1952-1978.**
     Rifat Chadirji.   London: KPI, 1986. 189p.
The Preface states that this is an 'original kind of graphic *catalogue raisonné* of his
own buildings and projects . . . of . . . architectural practise in Iraq and elsewhere in
the Middle East'. Most of the book consists of phototgraphs of buildings by Chadirji,
preceded by an essay describing the cultural and architectural crisis which the author
perceives in Iraq and elsewhere in the developing world where new technology
competes with traditional forms.

776 **Mossoul chrétienne: essai sur l'histoire, l'archéologie et l'état actuel des monuments chrétiens de la ville de Mossoul.** (Christian Mosul: essay on history, archaeology and current state of the Christian monuments of Mosul.)
J. M. Fiey. Beirut: Imprimerie Catholique, [1959]. 154p. maps. bibliog. (Recherches Publiées sous la Direction de l'Institut de Lettres Orientales de Beyrouth, XII).

An outline history of the Christian monuments in Mosul, which describes the regulations governing the construction of ancient churches (Chaldeo-Nestorian and Syro-Jacobite), and the churches themselves. The text covers the period approximately from 570 CE to the 19th century CE and concentrates on the churches and the architectural evidence.

777 **Studies in mediaeval Iraqi architecture.**
Tariq Jawad Janabi. Baghdad: State Organization of Antiquities & Heritage, 1982. 269p. bibliog.

Originally a doctoral thesis submitted at Edinburgh University, this describes in detail the standing monuments of Iraq built between the 12th and 14th centuries, and remaining specimens of architectural decoration from the same period. Many plates are included at the end of the book.

778 **Contemporary Arab architecture: the architects of Iraq.**
Udo Kultermann. *Mimar*, vol. 5 (1982), p. 54-61.

Kultermann briefly describes the work of three Iraqi architects: Mohammed Saleh Makiya (born 1917), Hisham A. Munir (b. 1930), and Rifat Chadirji (b. 1926).

779 **Post-Islamic classicism: a visual essay on the architecture of Mohamed Makiya.**
Kanan Makiya. London: Saqi, 1990. 159p.

Kanan Makiya has written this essay on the work of his father, Mohamed Makiya, an Iraqi architect who was widely regarded as 'Islamic', but who was not consciously an 'Islamic architect'. Some case-studies of his designs for prestigious city mosques are given, with many drawings and illustrations.

780 **The Islamic architecture of Baghdad: the results of a joint Italian–Iraqi survey.**
Vincenzo Strika, Jābir Khalīl. Naples: Istituto Universitario Orientale, 1987. 79p + plans and plates. (Supplemento agli *Annali*, 52).

These are the results of an archaeological survey of the remaining Islamic monuments in Baghdad, including mosques, shrines, tombs and secular architecture. The work was begun in 1971 and the book completed in 1980.

781 **Traditional houses in Baghdad.**
John Warren, Ihsan Fethi. Horsham, England: Coach Publishing,
1982. 207p. bibliog.
Contains a short history of the city of Baghdad, the origins and evolution of the
colonnaded house and its form, and describes the social and climatic factors that have
determined building in Baghdad. The text then deals with the details of building
materials, the design of structures and decorative patterns, the house as a home, and
matters of conservation in present times. Many illustrations and drawings are
included.

# Music

782 **The poetic content of the Iraqi *Maqām*.**
Farida Abu-Haidar. *Journal of Arabic Literature*, vol. 19 (1988),
p. 128-41.
On the poetic element of the *Maqām*, urban Iraqi music in the form of orally
transmitted song cycles, which were popular until the mid-20th century.

783 **La musique en Irak: éclats et éclipses.** (Music in Iraq: ups and
downs.)
J-C. Chabrier. *Etudes Orientales. Dirāsāt Sharqīya*, vol. 11/12
(December 1991), p. 104-15.
A concise history of classical Arab music in Iraq, its revival since the 1970s, and
government efforts to stimulate musical life through the creation of the National
Symphony Orchestra and the National School of Music and Dance.

784 **Problèmes contemporains du musicien et de la musique dans le
monde arabe oriental, selon l'Ecole de Bagdad (Cherif Muhieddin,
Jamil Bachir, Munir Bachir).** (Contemporary problems of musicians
and music in the eastern Arab world, according to the Baghdad School
(Sharif Muhyi 'l-Din, Jamil Bashir, Munir Bashir).)
Jean-Claude Chabrier. *Ethno-Psychologie*, vol. 32, no. 1 (March
1977), p. 37-67.
Considers the social status of the player of traditional music in contemporary times,
the training of professional musicians and attempts to reform it, and music-making in
general. The musicians discussed are contemporary practitioners of solo per-
formances in traditional style on the oriental lute (ʿud).

785 **Die Entwicklung und der gegenwärtige Stand der Musikforschung im Irak.** (The development and present state of music research in Iraq.) Schéhérazade Qassim Hassan, translated by Wolfgang Suppan. *Acta Musicologica*, vol. 54, no. 1-2 (January-December 1982), p. 148-62.

Hassan describes the history of classical music in Iraq, and present-day efforts to research the classical music tradition and to study and collect traditional popular songs and folk music.

786 **Les instruments du musique en Irak et leur rôle dans la société traditionnelle.** (Musical instruments in Iraq and their role in traditional society). Schéhérazade Qassim Hassan. Paris: Mouton, 1980. 241p. maps. bibliog. (Ecole des Hautes Etudes en Sciences Sociales, Cahiers de l'Homme, Ethnologie – Géographie – Linguistique Nouvelle Série, XXI).

Describes the traditional musical instruments which are still to be found today, and considers their function in the communities where they are used. Part one deals with the instruments themselves; part two discusses musicians; part three describes the social functions in which music plays a role (life-cycle rituals and magical practices) in Islamic ceremonies, among the Yazidis, and in Oriental churches.

787 **The long necked lute in Iraq.** Schéhérazade Qassim Hassan. *Asian Music*, vol. 13, no. 2 (1982), p. 1-18.

Describes the long-necked lute which is today known in only three areas of northern Iraq and used by Kurds and Turkmens. The local names for the instrument are given, and a number of drawings show its form and variants.

788 **Kurdish music and dance.** Nezan Kendal. *World of Music*, vol. 21, no. 1 (1979), p. 19-32.

Describes the instruments, folk music, folk songs and styles of dance of Kurdistan (including Iraqi Kurdistan).

**The Choobi songs of the Upper Euphrates in Iraq.**
*See* item no. 797.

# Theatre and cinema

789 **Three plays by Yousif al-Ani: translation and introduction.** Waleed Shamil Hussain. Dissertation, University of California at Los Angeles, 1989. 263p. (No. AAC8907549).

Examines the works of Yusuf al-Ani, one of the major figures of modern Iraqi theatre, and discusses the place of his work in the Iraqi theatre. Three of his plays 'Welcome,

Life', 'A new picture', and 'The past repeats itself' which represent three distinct periods of his writing, are included in translation.

790   **La traduction du théâtre français en Irak.** (The translation of
      French theatre to Iraq.)
      Dhia Kudayir.   *Etudes Orientales. Dirāsāt Sharqīya*, vol. 3 (Spring
      1988), p. 19-27.
Since the end of the last century foreign theatrical pieces, translated or adapted, have had a large place in Iraqi theatre. Iraqis discovered European theatre through Christian theatre which developed in churches and religious schools, especially in the Mosul area. This article looks at French plays which were performed in Iraq and the manner in which they were translated and/or altered by the Iraqis who recreated them.

791   **Social consciousness in the Iraq drama.**
      Matti Moosa.   *Muslim World*, vol. 71, no. 3-4 (July-October 1981),
      p. 228-46.
Moosa reviews the content of Iraqi plays since the 1920s and the extent to which they deal with contemporary issues of modernization and social change.

792   **A la recherche du cinéma irakien: histoire, infrastructure,**
      **filmographie (1945-1985).** (In search of the Iraqi cinema: history,
      infrastructure, filmography (1945-1985).)
      Shakir Nouri.   Paris: L'Harmattan, 1986. 229p. bibliog.
Describes film production in Iraq in both the private and public sector, the structure and characteristics of production and distribution, the nature of the film-going public, and cinema critics. Nouri also discusses the government's ideological control over content, and the themes favoured by Iraqi directors. A list of films, and notes on principal film-makers are given at the end.

**Zur Soziologie des schiitischen Chiliasmus: ein Beitrag zur Erforschung**
**des irakischen Passionsspiels.**
*See* item no. 469.

# Folklore and Customs

**793 Some Iraqi proverbs and proverbial phrases.**
Arthur B. Allen. *Journal of the American Oriental Society*, vol. 75 (1955), p. 122-25.
A collection of 30 Arabic proverbs from Baghdad, with translations and comments, and notes on comparison with Syrian proverbs.

**794 Kurdische Märchen. (Kurdish tales).**
Gesammelt und aufgeschrieben von Ordichane und Celile Celil. Frankfurt am Main, Germany: Insel-Verlag, 1993. 364p.
A collection of folktales and stories made in all the Kurdish-inhabited areas from the Soviet states in 1954 to Kurdistan in Turkey, Syria and Iraq in 1982. Over 125 stories are translated into German.

**795 An introduction to Kurdish rugs and other weavings.**
William Eagleton. New York: Interlink, 1988. 140p. maps.
Part one describes the people and their history, part two Kurdish tribes – see chapter 4 'Kurdish tribes of Iraq' (p. 26-30). Part three deals with the rugs and other types of weavings – see chapter 8 'Kurdish rugs of Iraq' (p. 75-97) which includes 31 coloured plates illustrating styles and types.

**796 Proverbes baghdadiens. (Baghdadi proverbs.)**
Geneviève Ghanima. *Orient* (Paris), vol. 13, nos. 51-52 (3rd and 4th quarter 1969), p. 43-69.
Ghanima reviews the various types of Arabic proverbs used in Baghdad, their availability in written sources (manuscript and printed), and provides 56 examples of current proverbs more-or-less specific to Baghdad.

797    **The Choobi songs of the Upper Euphrates in Iraq.**
Saʿdi al-Hadīthi.    Doha, Qatar: Arab Gulf States Folklore Centre,
1990. 248p. map.
A literary and folkloric treatment of the folksongs which accompany popular dances
performed on festive occasions in the Arab-inhabited areas along the Tigris and
Euphrates within northern Iraq. The texts which are transcribed and analysed were
mainly collected in Hadithah town and its environs. The changing lifestyle in the
area, especially with mechanization, means that there are no more caravans or
collective agricultural work which formerly provided the setting or occasion for the
performance of these songs. The study is in three parts: the framework, the songs, the
analysis.

798    **Folktales from the city of the golden domes.**
Sarah Powell Jamali, illustrated by Jeanne Shelsher.    Beirut: Khayats,
1965. 110p.
This book of folk stories, mostly collected from her Iraqi mother-in-law, was put
together by an Englishwoman living in Baghdad in the 1940s and 1950s. An earlier
collection was published by E. S. Stevens in 1931: *Folk-tales of ʿIrāq set down and
translated from the vernacular* (London: Oxford University Press).

799    **Le martyre de Ḥusayn dans la poésie populaire d'Iraq. Thèse.**
(Husayn's martyrdom in Iraq's popular poetry. Thesis.)
Anatoly Kovalenko.    Geneva: Edition de l'auteur, 1979. 297p.
bibliog.
A study of the poetry concerned with the martyrdom of Husayn at Karbala, an event
much commemorated by the Shiʿi Muslims. The historical introduction is followed by
the discussion of the socio-cultural, philological and linguistic background. The texts
are presented in Arabic script, transliterated and translated.

800    **Tattooing among the Arabs of Iraq.**
Winifred Smeaton.    *American Anthropologist*, vol. 39, no. 1
(January-March 1937), p. 53-61.
Smeaton describes the practice of tattooing of both men and women which she
observed during her residence in Iraq in 1933-35. The various patterns are noted, and
the reasons for tattooing – ornamental, curative, and magical (as talismans) – are
outlined.

801    **The influence of environment on Iraqi folktale.**
Omar M. al-Talib.    In: *Folk culture, Vol. 5: Folk culture and the
great tradition.*    Cuttack, India: Institute of Oriental and Orissan
Studies, [1983?], p. 1-28.
The author identifies some themes and recurring motifs in Iraqi folktales.

**Mémoire du Kurdistan.**
*See* item no. 767.

# Cookery

802 **Traditional Arabic cooking.**
Miriam al-Hashimi. Reading, England: Garnet, 1993. 194p.
This is a book of recipes, with coloured photographs, and hints for cooking dishes
from all over the Arab world. The menu planner includes a 'typical Iraqi meal'.

803 **Middle Eastern cookery.**
Robin Howe, illustrated by Tony Streek. London: Eyre Methuen,
1978. 183p.
A cookery book which includes among its recipes a number of specifically Iraqi
dishes.

804 **The Baghdad kitchen.**
Nina Jamil-Garbutt. London: Kingswood Press, 1985. 91p.
A cookery book specifically for Iraqi food, with illustrations.

805 **The new book of Middle Eastern food.**
Claudia Roden. London: Viking, 1985. Harmondsworth, England:
Penguin, 1986, new and enlarged ed. 525p. bibliog.
Earlier published as 'A Book of Middle Eastern Food' by Nelson in 1968, this is
much more than just a cookery book. Claudia Roden was born and raised in Egypt,
and her book is full of information about habits and customs of the Middle East,
folklore, traditions, and history – in fact everything to do with food and the social
aspects of eating, serving and sharing meals. The recipes are practical and easy to
follow, and include dishes associated with Iraq.

# Libraries, Publishing and Mass Media

806 **Iraq's first printed book.**
Michael W. Albin. *Libri*, vol. 31, no. 2 (August 1981), p. 167-74.
Albin briefly describes the early history of printing in Ottoman Iraq and concludes that the first book printed was an Arabic text *Dawḥat al-wuzarā'* by Rasul Hawi published in 1830-31.

807 **Radio and television in Iraq: the electronic media in a transitionary Arab world country.**
Douglas A. Boyd. *Middle Eastern Studies*, vol. 18, no. 4 (October 1982), p. 400-10.
Describes the history of radio and television in Iraq, the languages in which they broadcast, the general content of programmes, and the degree of government involvement and direction.

808 **Bibliographie zur Geschichte der Presse im Irak.** (Bibliography of the history of the press in Iraq.)
Werner Ende. *Orient* (Opladen), vol. 15, no. 2 (June 1974), p. 84-86.
Also published in *Dokumentationsdienst Moderner Orient Mitteilungen*, vol. 3, no. 1 (1974), p. 23-30, this bibliography contains examples and comments on 50 publications which have appeared on the history of the press in Iraq.

809 **Iraq and its national library.**
Syed Ali Hashmi. *Libri*, vol. 33, no. 3 (September 1983), p. 236-43; *National libraries 2: 1977-1985*, edited by Maurice B. Line, Joyce Line. London: Aslib, 1987, p. 220-26. (Aslib Reader Series, 6).
Gives the history of the modern national library established in Baghdad in 1961, its growth, organization and activities.

810 **Computerizing information services in Iraq.**
Péter Jacsó, Faik Abdul S. Razzaq. *Information Development*, vol. 2,
no 2 (April 1986), p. 85-92.

The authors describe the large-scale computerization project set up in Iraq to
automate library and information work for research which was jointly implemented
by the Iraqi Scientific Documentation Centre and the Hungarian Computer
Applications and Service Company under the auspices of UNESCO.

811 **Iraq.**
Amer Ibrahim Kindilchie. In: *ALA world encyclopedia of library and
information services*, edited by Robert Wedgeworth. Chicago, IL:
American Library Association, 1986, 2nd ed., p. 387-89.

Kindilchie sketches the history of libraries in Iraq, the founding of the modern
National Library, and a brief note about academic, public, special and school libraries
in the country.

812 **Academic libraries in Iraq.**
Suhail Manzoor. *International Library Review*, vol. 17 (1985),
p. 283-91.

Describes recent developments in Iraqi academic libraries, and library systems and
services.

813 **The Arab world: libraries and librarianship 1960-1976: a
bibliography.**
Veronica Pantelidis. London: Mansell, 1979. 94p.

This bibliography is arranged by country. The Iraq section (p. 35-41, nos. 376-445) is
divided under the sub-headings: general, bibliography and documentation, libraries,
archives, library education, library and related associations, librarians. Many items in
the 'Arab world' section are also relevant.

**Aspects of Iraqi cultural policy.**
*See* item no. 769.

# Bibliographies

817    **A bibliography of Iraq: a classified list of printed materials on the land, people, history, economics, and culture published in Western languages.**
Abdul Jabbar Abdulrahman.    Baghdad: Al-Irshad Press, 1977. 304p.

An unannotated listing of items in Western languages on all aspects of Iraq from ancient to modern times including a large number of theses. The material is arranged under subject headings, with author and title indexes. The same author compiled the first edition of the bibliography of Iraq in the Clio Press World Bibliographical Series published in 1984.

818    **Middle East and Islam: a bibliographical introduction. Supplement 1977-1983.**
Edited by Paul Auchterlonie.    Zug, Switzerland: IDC for Middle East Libraries Committee, 1986. 223p. (Bibliotheca Asiatica, 20).

A supplement to D. Grimwood-Jones' *Middle East and Islam: a bibliographical introduction*, revised ed. (Zug: IDC for Middle East Libraries' Committee, 1979). A good, wide-ranging basic bibliography, arranged by subject, and by area. A regional bibliography for Iraq is given on p. 155-58.

819    **Ausgewählte neuere Literatur / A selected bibliography of recent literature.**
Hamburg: Deutsches Übersee-Institut, 1970- . quarterly.

A bibliography of articles from periodicals and collective volumes, and of books on the modern Middle East. Items included are mainly in English, German, French or Arabic. Many are annotated, and some annotations are in English. The work includes much information on current economic and political affairs.

195

820 **Documentation survey.**

C. H. Bleaney. *Arab Gulf Journal*, 1981-86.

A regular feature of the quarterly journal published from 1981 to 1986 which provided a short annotated bibliography of non-book materials (principally reports and documents produced by international organizations) and statistics. A section for Iraq was always included.

821 **Arab agricultural bibliography derived from AGRIS 1975-1982.**

FAO. Rome: FAO Regional Office for the Near East, [1984]. 518p.

A bibliography extracted from the FAO's International Information System for the Agricultural Sciences and Technology. It is arranged by subject with the following headings: agriculture; geography and history; education, extension and advisory work; administration and legislation; economics, development, and rural sociology; plant production; protection of plants and stored products; forestry; animal production; aquatic sciences and fisheries; machinery and buildings; natural resources; food science; home economics, industries and crafts; human nutrition; pollution; auxiliary disciplines. There are approximately 1100 entries for Iraq under the geographical index on pages 416-35.

822 **Mid-East File.**

Oxford: Learned Information. 1982-88. quarterly.

A source of abstracts and citations of articles, documents, books and book reviews, reports, broadcasts, and official statements. This periodical, which was arranged by country, contained material in European languages (principally English), Arabic and Hebrew, and was very strong on current affairs.

823 **The Middle East: abstracts and index.**

Pittsburgh, PA: Library and Information Research Service, 1978- . annual.

Gives abstracts of periodical articles, doctoral dissertations, books and listings of editorials, interviews, statistical reports, book reviews etc., including many weekly magazines and newspapers. This bibliography is restricted almost entirely to English-language material, and is arranged by country. Recent issues for 1990-93 are dominated by items on the invasion of Kuwait and Gulf War of 1991 and reports of US government involvement.

824 **Index Islamicus, 1906-1955: a catalogue of articles on Islamic subjects in periodicals and other collective publications.**

Compiled by J. D. Pearson (et al.). Cambridge: Heffer, 1958, rp. London, 1972. 807pp.

An unannotated bibliography of articles from a very wide range of periodicals, and the major bibliography of Western-language works. It is organized by country and subject. Supplements have been published as follows: *Supplement, 1956-1960* (Cambridge, 1962, rp. London, 1973); *Second supplement, 1961-1965* (Cambridge, 1967, rp. London, 1974); *Third supplement, 1966-1970* (London, 1972); *Fourth supplement, 1971-1975* (London, 1977); *Index Islamicus 1976-1980* (London, 1983); *Index Islamicus 1981-1985* (London, 1991). The volumes for 1976-1980 and 1981-1985 also include books published during the respective periods. For the period 1986-

1993, see *The Quarterly Index Islamicus*. From 1994, *Index Islamicus* will be published as annual volumes for the years 1993- , with three interim fascicules a year listing new books and articles, compiled by G. J. Roper and C. H. Bleaney, and published by Bowker-Saur.

825    **Articles on the Middle East 1947-1971: a cumulation of the bibliographies from *The Middle East Journal*.**
       Edited by Peter M. Rossi, Wayne E. White, Arthur E. Goldschmidt, foreword by William Sands.    Ann Arbor, MI: Pierian Press, 1980.
       4 vols. 1646p.

A reproduction of the extensive, but not exhaustive, bibliographies of periodical literature on the Middle East published in every issue of *The Middle East Journal* for the years 1947-71. For more recent years, see the Bibliography of Periodical Literature in *The Middle East Journal*, published quarterly by the Middle East Institute in Washington, DC. This journal frequently contains scholarly articles about Iraq and every issue has a chronology of events and book reviews.

826    **American doctoral dissertations on the Arab World, 1883-1974.**
       George Dmitri Selim.    Washington, DC: Library of Congress, 1976.
       2nd ed. 129p.

A supplement for the years 1975-81 was published in 1983; and for 1981-87 in 1989. This work is an unannotated bibliography of US doctoral theses arranged alphabetically by author; see Iraq in the index, with subheadings.

827    **Theses on Islam, the Middle East and North-West Africa, 1880-1978, accepted by Universities in the United Kingdom and Ireland.**
       Compiled by Peter Sluglett.    London; the Bronx, NY: Mansell, 1983. 124p.

The bibliography gives title, date of submission and library location for each entry. It is arranged by subject (Islamic studies, Arabic studies, and Christianity in the Middle East); then by country. The section on Iraq (p. 75-82) contains nos. 1836-2022 divided by major subject-headings, and the addenda for 1978 on p. 121 contain further references under nos. 2966-2986.

# Index

The index is a single alphabetical sequence of authors (personal and corporate), titles of publications and subjects. Index entries refer both to the main items and to other works mentioned in the notes to each item. Title entries are in italics. Numeration refers to the items as numbered.

217

227

237

# Map of Iraq

This map shows the more important towns, physical features and archaeological sites.

## ALSO FROM CLIO PRESS

## INTERNATIONAL ORGANIZATIONS SERIES

Each volume in the International Organizations Series is either devoted to one specific organization, or to a number of different organizations operating in a particular region, or engaged in a specific field of activity. The scope of the series is wide-ranging and includes intergovernmental organizations, international non-governmental organizations, and national bodies dealing with international issues. The series is aimed mainly at the English-speaker and each volume provides a selective, annotated, critical bibliography of the organization, or organizations, concerned. The bibliographies cover books, articles, pamphlets, directories, databases and theses and, wherever possible, attention is focused on material about the organizations rather than on the organizations' own publications. Notwithstanding this, the most important official publications, and guides to those publications, will be included. The views expressed in individual volumes, however, are not necessarily those of the publishers.

## VOLUMES IN THE SERIES

1 *European Communities*,
  John Paxton
2 *Arab Regional Organizations*,
  Frank A. Clements
3 *Comecon: The Rise and Fall of an
  International Socialist
  Organization*, Jenny Brine
4 *International Monetary Fund*,
  Anne C. M. Salda
5 *The Commonwealth*, Patricia M.
  Larby and Harry Hannam

6 *The French Secret Services*, Martyn
  Cornick and Peter Morris
7 *Organization of African Unity*,
  Gordon Harris
8 *North Atlantic Treaty Organization*,
  Phil Williams
9 *World Bank*, Anne C. M. Salda
10 *United Nations System*, Joseph P.
  Baratta

## TITLES IN PREPARATION

*British Secret Services*, Philip H. J.
  Davies
*Israeli Secret Services*, Frank A.
  Clements

*Organization of American States*, David
  Sheinin